WITH *Four* PRIME MINISTERS

ALSO BY THE SAME AUTHOR

1. *My Tryst with Manipur: A Memoir*, Konark Publishers, New Delhi, 2018

2. *Manipur University: Restoring Normalcy*, Konark Publishers, New Delhi, 2022

3. *Project Appraisal, Risk Analysis and Risk Management Techniques,* (co-authored with Dr D.N.S. Dhakal), Konark Publishers, New Delhi, 2022

WITH *Four* PRIME MINISTERS

My PMO Journey

Jarnail Singh

KONARK
Konark Publishers Pvt Ltd
New Delhi

Konark Publishers Pvt Ltd
206, First Floor,
Peacock Lane, Shahpur Jat,
New Delhi - 110 049
Tel : +91-11-4105 5065
e-mail : india@konarkpublishers.com; us@konarkpublishers.com
website : www.konarkpublishers.com

First Impression 2023

Cataloging in Publication Data--DK
Courtesy: D.K. Agencies (P) Ltd. <docinfo@dkagencies.com>

Jarnail Singh (Civil servant), **author.**
With four prime ministers : my PMO journey / Jarnail Singh.
pages cm
Includes index.
ISBN 9788194201830

1. Jarnail Singh (Civil servant). 2. Civil service--India--Biography. 3. India. Prime Minister--Officials and employees--Biography. 4. Prime ministers--India. 5. India--Politics and government--1947- I. Title.

LCC JQ247.J37 2020 | DDC 352.63092 23

Jacket by Misha Oberoi
Jacket sketch by Meinam Irikhomba Meetei
Printed and bound at Saurabh Printers Pvt. Ltd.

Fondly dedicated to
my late parents Sardar Dalip Singh and Sardarni Surjit Kaur,
my wife Smt. Seraphina Singh
and my sons Paramjit Singh and Vikramjit Singh

CONTENTS

Preface *ix*
Acknowledgements *xi*
Acronyms *xiii*
Introduction *xvii*

PRIME MINISTER H.D. DEVE GOWDA
(August 1996 – April 1997)

1. A Call from the Prime Minister's Office 3
2. Joining Prime Minister's Office 9
3. Initial Days at the PMO 16
4. Learning the Ropes: People, Personalities and Perspectives 24
5. Getting to know the North-East 32
6. New Initiatives for North Eastern Region 44

PRIME MINISTER I.K. GUJRAL
(April 1997 – March 1998)

7. PM Gujral: The Kind-Hearted Democrat 55
8. Visits to J&K and the North-East 65

PRIME MINISTER ATAL BIHARI VAJPAYEE - I
(March 1998 – October 1999)

9. Atal Bihari Vajpayee takes over as Prime Minister 73
10. Big Development Push for North-East 84

PRIME MINISTER ATAL BIHARI VAJPAYEE - II
(October 1999 – May 2004)

11. A Single-Vote Defeat but BJP Storms Back to Power 93
12. Surface Transport Systems 99
13. Strategic Issues of Petroleum Sector 108
14. Petroleum and Natural Gas: Challenges and Solutions 118
15. Power Sector: Old Legacies, New Paths 125
16. Challenges to Power Initiatives 135
17. Focus on North-East 145
18. A Push for Big Projects 154
19. Ministry of Development of North Eastern Region 160
20. Anomalies and Some Strange Cases 166
21. Coal Challenges 171
22. A Matter of Security 176
23. Working with Governors 186
24. Jammu and Kashmir: Development and Security Issues 193
25. More Emphasis on Jammu and Kashmir 204
26. It's all about Rules 209
27. People and Personalities 216
28. Dealing with Complexities 224
29. Resolving Challenges: A New Approach 234
30. Vajpayee Years: Two Commendable Contributions 245
31. India Shining and An Election Lost 249
32. Unfinished Initiatives 254

PRIME MINISTER DR MANMOHAN SINGH
(May 2004 – August 2004)

33. Dr Manmohan Singh takes over as Prime Minister 263
34. Dr Manmohan Singh: A Man of Details 268

35. My Reflections of Working in the PMO 275
Index 281

PREFACE

In the Indian government system, the Prime Minister's Office (PMO) is the most important office. It is the seat of power of the Government of India from where the Prime Minister's approval is conveyed to the Cabinet Secretariat, the ministries, departments and agencies of the government. People speak of the PMO with respect and awe, though most do not know its structure, functioning and the sway it has on all government machinery.

It is the dream of every bureaucrat to work in the PMO. The vacancies here are not filled by the Civil Services Board as it happens for other government posts. It is mostly the personal knowledge of the PM or senior officers working in the PMO who play a major role in the selection and posting of officers. Thus, those who get a posting are considered lucky. Those who work here are also perceived powerful as compared to their counterparts in other ministries and departments.

I was lucky to get a chance to work as Joint Secretary to Prime Minister for eight years (August 1996 to August 2004), and work with four Prime Ministers—H. D. Deve Gowda, I. K. Gujral, A. B. Vajpayee and Dr Manmohan Singh. It was also an opportunity to work with three different governments—United Front, National Democratic Alliance and United Progressive Alliance. I handled a diverse range of responsibilities at the PMO with great satisfaction in those eight years.

After my tenure at the PMO, I wanted to document my experience at the PMO. While doing so, I have not mentioned any matter or issue which violates the Official Secrets Act or hurts the national security in any way. I have avoided all such matters. I have mentioned those matters and issues, which project the positive traits of personalities as well as their contribution to governance.

This book provides an insight into the functioning of the PMO, its working environment, the process of taking initiatives and translating them into actions, and the rules and regulations which make the PMO the nerve centre of the government. I have illustrated the working relationships among different functionaries in the PMO, the personalities of different prime ministers and individuals who played an important role in speeding up the tempo of economic development.

An important take-away is that a bureaucrat can be politically neutral and yet, work with ease in different governments. The main qualifications a bureaucrat should have are that he should be professionally competent, dedicated to work and maintain a low profile. The PMO works the same way under different governments. I clearly remember what PM Vajpayee said of the PMO the first time he met us after assuming office. Speaking in Hindi, he said, 'I thought the PMO functioned more like a political office, but I see that it works like any other government office without political influences. I want this PMO to continue working that way and I am happy. When I was outside the PMO, I had a different perception of its functioning. Congratulation to all of you and keep on working this way.' His words reflect broadly the political neutrality of the PMO functioning; the credit for which goes to all PMs and senior officers.

Lastly, but equally important, is that the officers in PMO work according to rules and procedures that are clearly laid down. Technically, a PMO under any government should wield the same power. Yet, the power of the PMO also depends on the personality of the PM and the dependency of a government on its coalition partners for survival. If the ruling party commands a majority in Parliament, the PM can take decisions (even unpleasant ones) with the least amount of consultations and force its decisions and writ easily. In a way, the power of the PMO is directly proportionate to the majority of the ruling political party.

I hope this book would be useful to readers and throw light on how the PMO functioned in the years August 1996 to August 2004.

ACKNOWLEDGEMENTS

At the outset I acknowledge with profound thanks B. N. Yugandhar, the then Secretary to Prime Minister H. D. Deve Gowda, who gave me the opportunity to work in the PMO.

I am grateful to Prime Ministers H. D. Deve Gowda, Inder Kumar Gujral, Atal Bihari Vajpayee and Dr Manmohan Singh with whom I worked during these eight years. I learnt a lot while working with them. I am grateful to the personal staff of all four prime ministers with whom I worked during my years in PMO.

I learnt immensely from my senior officers namely Principal Secretaries T. R. Satish Chandran, N. N. Vohra, Brajesh Mishra and T. K. A. Nair, Secretary B. N. Yugandhar, Officer on Special Duty N. K. Singh, Economic Adviser S. Narayan and Additional Secretary Ashok Saikia. They always guided, supported and encouraged me to work freely.

I received excellent cooperation from all my senior as well as junior colleagues, particularly S.S. Meenakshisundaram, Harnam Singh, C. Phunsog, Chhatar Singh, Pankaj Saran, Anup Wadhawan, Rashmi Verma, Shakti Sinha, Arun Mathur, Pushpa Subrahmanyam, Sunil Jain, Rakesh Kakkar, Ajay Bisaria, Mahendra Jain, K. V. Pratap, Prabhat Shukla, P. S. Raghawan, Jawed Usmani, Vikram Doraiswamy, Renuka Kumar, Anand Rajan, R. P. Singh, Rohit Khera, B. S. Chouhan, Ashwini Vaishnav, Bir Dutt, S.N. Sahai, Jaideep Mukerjee, V. Vidyavathi and Vikram Misri.

I thank the personal staff of all principal secretaries who helped arrange meetings and discussions at the principal secretary level. I specially thank Y.S. Parmar, principal private secretary to principal secretary, who was always courteous, polite and accommodating.

I had the opportunity to work closely with media advisors to the prime ministers as well as the officers who used to prepare speeches for the prime ministers. I specially thank H. K. Dua, Ashok Tandon, Sudheendra Kulkarni, Kanchan Gupta, Sanjay Baru and B. S. Chouhan.

I am particularly thankful to my personal staff who were punctual and efficient in their work, particularly, in taking dictations and completing their tasks on time. I must admit that their proficiency in work improved my performance.

Almost all work in PMO is time-bound and demands full attention. My wife Seraphina Singh always encouraged me to work with dedication and stood by me during my eight years of demanding work. She was always a source of strength for me during these years which required hard work, dedication and punctuality.

I am grateful to Meinam Irikhomba Meetei of the Department of Fine Arts of Manipur University, who prepared the sketch of the South Block, a part of which houses the Prime Minister's Office, for designing the cover of this book.

Last but not the least, I am grateful to K.P.R. Nair and the editorial staff at Konark Publishers for doing a wonderful job of editing and publishing this book.

ACRONYMS

7 RCR: 7 Race Course Road
AAI: Airport Authority of India
ACC: Appointments Committee of the Cabinet
AG: Accountant General
AGMUT: Arunachal Pradesh–Goa–Mizoram–Union Territories
AIADMK: All India Anna Dravida Munnetra Kazhagam
AIIMS: All India Institute of Medical Sciences
APM: Administered Price Mechanism
BJP: Bharatiya Janata Party
BMSs: Basic Minimum Services
BADP: Border Area Development Programme
BRO: Border Roads Organisation
BSNL: Bharat Sanchar Nigam Limited
BTC: Bodo Territorial Council
CAG: Comptroller and Auditor General of India
CBI: Central Bureau of Investigation
CCEA: Cabinet Committee on Economic Affairs
CEA: Central Electricity Authority
CIC: Community Information Centre
CIL: Coal India Limited
CPI (M): Communist Party of India-Marxist
CSB: Civil Services Board

CSE: Centre for Science and Environment
DEA: Department of Economic Affairs
DESU: Delhi Electricity Supply Undertaking
DGH: Directorate General of Hydrocarbons
DMK: Dravida Munnetra Kazhagam
DoPT: Department of Personnel and Training
DPRs: Detailed Project Reports
EO: Establishment Officer
EPC: Engineering Procurement and Construction
FCI: Food Corporation of India
FDI: Foreign Direct Investment
FSA: Fuel Supply Agreement
GFR: General Financial Rules
HRC: Hanumantha Rao Committee
HSCCL: Hospital Services Consultancy Corporation Limited of India
HSD: High Speed Diesel
IB: Intelligence Bureau
IFIs: International Financial Institutions
IMDT Act: Illegal Migrants (Determination by Tribunal) Act
INC (I): Indian National Congress (Indira)
IPPs: Independent Power Producers
ISPRL: Indian Strategic Petroleum Reserves Limited
IVRs: Inter Village Roads
JPC: Joint Parliamentary Committee
Kgoe: Kilogramme of oil equivalent
LoC: Line of Control
LPG: Liquefied Petroleum Gas
MEA: Ministry of External Affairs
MFI: Micro Finance Institution

MHA: Ministry of Home Affairs
MDoNER: Ministry of Development of North Eastern Region
MoS: Minister of State
MoU: Memorandum of Understanding
MOS: Memorandum of Settlement
MPC: Mangalore Power Company
MSCP: Manipur State Congress Party
MSP: Minimum Support Price
MTNL: Mahanagar Telephone Nigam Limited
MW: Mega Watt
NABARD: National Bank for Agriculture and Rural Development
NASSCOM: National Association of Software and Services Companies
NDA: National Democratic Alliance
NDFB: National Democratic Front of Bodoland
NEC: North Eastern Council
NEDFi: North Eastern Development Finance Corporation Limited
NEEPCO: North Eastern Electric Power Corporation Limited
NEIGRIHMS: North-Eastern Indira Gandhi Regional Institute of Health and Medical Sciences
NELP: New Exploration Licensing Policy
NHAI: National Highways Authority of India
NHDP: National Highways Development Programme
NHPC: National Hydroelectric Power Corporation Limited
NHRC: National Human Rights Commission
NISG: National Institute for Smart Government
NLCPR: Non-Lapsable Central Pool of Resources
NNC: Naga National Council
NPA: Non-Performing Asset
NSCN (IM): National Socialist Council of Nagaland (Isak-Muivah)

NTPC: National Thermal Power Corporation Limited
NUG: Non-Utility Generator
OIDB: Oil Industry Development Board
OIL: Oil India Limited
OMCs: Oil Marketing Companies
ONGC: Oil and Natural Gas Commission
OSD: Officer on Special Duty
OVL: ONGC Videsh Limited
PAC: Public Accounts Committee
PFC: Power Finance Corporation Limited
PIB: Public Investment Board
PIL: Public Interest Litigation
PLF: Plant Load Factor
PMGSY: Pradhan Mantri Gram Sadak Yojana
PMO: Prime Minister's Office
PoK: Pakistan Occupied Kashmir
PPAs: Power Purchase Agreements
PSUs: Public Sector Undertakings
PWD: Public Works Department
R&R: Relief and Rehabilitation
RIDF: Rural Infrastructure Development Fund
RSS: Rashtriya Swayamsevak Sangh
SAIL: Steel Authority of India Limited
SOP: Standard Operating Procedure
SPA: Special Plan Assistance
SPG: Special Protection Group
SPR: Strategic Petroleum Reserves
THDC: Tehri Hydro Development Corporation
VHP: Vishva Hindu Parishad

INTRODUCTION

I had been serving the government of Manipur from May 1986 to August 1996 and was keen for a deputation to the Central government. The tendency among officers who belong to other states but are allocated to the North-Eastern cadres of All India Services such as Indian Administrative Service, Indian Police Service and Indian Forest Service (IAS, IPS, IFS respectively), was to serve for as long as required by the cooling-off periods. They would then try for a deputation to the Central government or to their home states. Similarly, I too was keen for a Central deputation after nearly 10 years in my cadre state Manipur.

The initial attempt by the Department of Personnel and Training (DoPT) to post me as Development Commissioner for Handicrafts in the Ministry of Textiles did not succeed because of opposition from the Minister of Textiles. After some months, though appointment order was issued for me to join as Deputy Election Commissioner, it was cancelled after a few days because a lady officer serving in the Election Commission of India had become eligible for appointment as Deputy Election Commissioner. Colleagues and friends advised that lobbying helps in an early deputation in Delhi. I was serving in the Manipur-Tripura cadre, a small cadre of IAS, and with no senior officer serving in the Centre to help me with my deputation, I had begun to feel the disadvantages of a small cadre.

When all efforts, including meeting with the Establishment Officer (EO) yielded nothing, I reconciled to my fate of serving in Manipur much longer and possibly, for all remaining years of my service period. Then as luck would have it, on 9 August 1996, I got a telephone call from B. N. Yugandhar, Secretary to Prime Minister H. D. Deve Gowda. He rang up to ask if I would like to join the Prime Minister's Office (PMO) as Joint Secretary. I conveyed my willingness and joined the PMO on 16 August 1996 and was there till 6 August 2004, a record period of about eight years. During these eight years I worked with four prime ministers—H. D. Deve Gowda, Inder Kumar Gujral, Atal Bihari Vajpayee and Dr Manmohan Singh.

This book unravels my journey of working in the PMO of those eight years. These years stand out for the economic development and opening up of the many sectors of the Indian economy. In this span of time, I handled ministries of Power, Petroleum and Natural Gas, Coal, Mines, Home Affairs, Renewable Energy Sources, matters relating to north-eastern states, Jammu and Kashmir and southern states. Later, Ministries of Railways, Road Transport and Highways, Telecommunications and Information Technology, Chemicals and Fertilizers, Textiles, Disinvestment, etc. were also added. I contributed whatever I could and worked with sincerity and dedication. For many, a few years working in the PMO was a path to foreign postings. However, a few colleagues and I did not opt for foreign postings and continued working in the PMO.

The PMO was an unparalleled experience of learning. It gave me deep insights into a diverse range of subjects and methods of working in a government. I worked with equal zeal and ease in all governments whether it was the United Front, the NDA or the UPA. I enjoyed my work and gave my best in all of them. Working in the PMO is like working in any other office of the government except that one cannot afford to make mistakes in quoting or using facts, data or numbers. All files go to the PM who could use these for any speech or reference. The authenticity of numbers and data thus given by any officer must be hundred per cent correct as any mistake would be noticed by the media and become a source of embarrassment for the government.

There are some mistaken notions about the PMO which I highlight here. Most people do not know that under the Government of India (Allocation of Business) Rules, which specify the work handled by each ministry and each department of the government, there is no specific topic regarding business of the government allotted to the PMO, and there are no special powers vested in it. As per these Rules, the PMO has been established to provide secretarial assistance to the Prime Minister. That is all. I also found that while working as a Joint Secretary in the PMO, one can be completely politically neutral. Of course, there could be people working in the PMO with some leaning or affiliation to the party in power. This perhaps leads to the general perception that those working in the PMO must be influential and powerful. I never felt that way. I feel that power lies in laws and the rules and not in the individuals. I was as powerful or powerless as I was when working in the PMO as I was outside.

Similarly, it is important to know how and what rules endow the PM with powers. When the PM is in charge of any ministry, his power is only that of a Cabinet minister and nothing more. Under Rule 12 of the Government of India (Transaction of Business) Rules, in case of any urgent situation, the PM can approve any proposal that requires approval of the Cabinet, which could be obtained post facto. Since the PM is chairman of the Appointments Committee of the Cabinet (ACC), chairs Cabinet meetings and appoints persons to constitutional positions such as governors, he is all powerful in the present system of government.

My tenures with Prime Ministers H. D. Deve Gowda, I. K. Gujral and Dr Manmohan Singh were short—with the first two PMs about nine months each and with Dr Singh about three months. I worked with Prime Minister Atal Bihari Vajpayee for six years.

H. D. Deve Gowda, who was sworn in as Prime Minister of United Front government on 1 June 1996, took several important initiatives for the welfare of rural people and farmers. He initiated a set of new programmes called Basic Minimum Services (BMSs) for the rural areas, which included provision of drinking water, sanitation, electricity, nutrition, education and housing. He was the only PM who visited the north-eastern states for six days at a stretch. His 'New Initiatives for North-Eastern Region', which later became a mantra for development of North-East not only increased the fund flow to these states, but also led to the setting up of a Non-Lapsable Central Pool of Resources

(NLCPR) and a separate Ministry of Development of North Eastern Region during the tenure of PM Atal Bihari Vajpayee.

Many of the projects and schemes initiated by PM Deve Gowda are now benefitting the people of the North-East. These include North Eastern Indira Gandhi Regional Institute of Health and Medical Sciences (NEIGRIHMS), upgradation of airports, Tuirial Hydroelectric Project, Numaligarh refinery, extension of railway lines, completion of Jogigopa bridge, etc. His efforts for a development push of the region were well-supported by B.N. Yugandhar, the then Secretary to PM and G. K. Pillai, Joint Secretary (North-East) in the Ministry of Home Affairs (MHA) at that time.

I.K. Gujral became the Prime Minister of the second United Front government on 21 April 1997. He continued the projects and the programmes initiated by his predecessor. However, his focus was more on external affairs issues and improving relations with Pakistan. It was during his term that the government of India signed a ceasefire agreement with the National Socialist Council of Nagaland (Isak-Muivah) [NSCN (IM)]. The matters relating to autonomy for Central Bureau of Investigation (CBI) arising out of Vineet Narain case in the Supreme Court were also handled and resolved during this period. The Jain Commission Report on the assassination of the former Prime Minister Rajiv Gandhi and its leaked findings affected the government functioning and led to the downfall of the Gujral government.

Prime Minister A. B. Vajpayee's tenure was for about six years. He was politically strong, liberal and a quick decision taker. His tenure as Prime Minister could be termed as the period when major economic decisions were taken, and many important sectors of the Indian economy were opened. Important initiatives taken during the Vajpayee period included construction of national highways, east-west and north-south expressways, Pradhan Mantri Gram Sadak Yojna, opening of telecommunications sector and corporatization of Department of Telecommunications into Bharat Sanchar Nigam Limited (BSNL) and Mahanagar Telephone Nigam Limited (MTNL), construction of new private airports in Hyderabad and Bangalore, the new Electricity Act

2003 and allowing private sector in power transmission, privatisation of electricity supply in Delhi, entry of private airlines in India, safety fund for railways, railway line to Baramulla with tunnel at Qazigund, construction of Mega Thermal Power Stations, restarting Dulhasti Power Project, Delhi Metro, race to Moon with the start of Chandrayaan-I, setting up of NLCPR and Ministry of Development of North Eastern Region.

The Petroleum and Natural Gas sector saw major initiatives for providing energy security to the country. The Administered Price Mechanism (APM) was dismantled and the New Exploration Licensing Policy was announced to provide a levelled platform both for public and private players in oil and gas exploration. It would not be wrong to term the Vajpayee period from March 1998 to May 2004 as a 'Golden Era' for infrastructure development in the history of India. Major initiatives were taken in all sectors of the economy, particularly in the infrastructure sectors. The Vajpayee period was also an era of quick decision-making, which is the soul of public administration. This was primarily possible because the PM was politically the centre of decision-making in the Bharatiya Janata Party (BJP) and National Democratic Alliance (NDA).

I worked under Dr Manmohan Singh for about three months from May to August 2004. Dr Singh was very simple and polite and a man of details. He would take a writing pad and note down the points during meetings and briefings. He always went into details of issues brought before him for discussion or any decision. Dr Singh laid special emphasis on rural development and employment generation. During his tenure, maximum funds were provided to the north-eastern states. A special scheme called 'Reconstruction Plan', later called Special Plan Assistance (SPA) was started to build infrastructure and complete ongoing infrastructure projects in the region. Priority was given to the completion of ongoing irrigation projects. I had excellent working relations with him.

This book is about the PMO and its working under four remarkable prime ministers. It is a personal narrative brought alive through several cases, incidents, illustrations, projects and programmes that the PMO of the day and I witnessed and handled. It is important to state that I have not mentioned any sensitive or secret matter, which either attracts Official Secrets Act or could hurt Indian interests in any way. I have illustrated the incidents in a manner as these appeared to me, even though another person, working in my place, looking at the same incident could act, react or write in a different way.

Two things surprised me the most in the PMO. The first one was the lack of knowledge among the senior officers of the government about the *Government of India (Allocation of Business) Rules* and the *Government of India (Transaction of Business) Rules*. I found many senior officers had not read these at all. It seemed they had conducted and managed the affairs of the government by the support and knowledge of juniors or by common sense. This was a rude shock to me. How could the government officers, particularly the senior functionaries, be ignorant about the *Rules*, I wondered. Without this understanding, senior officers could not possibly suggest modifications or changes in the *Rules* to improve government functioning.

The second thing was that if an officer working in the PMO took an initiative—be it related to any project, programme, or any other issue—it immediately materialised. I took some initiatives which were successful. Almost nobody from any ministry or department raised objections to these as it was perceived to have the blessings of the prime minister. Any objection to an initiative from the PMO could be seen as being on the wrong side of the power. I realised that such initiatives get implemented very fast. Many new ideas, schemes and programmes initiated during my tenure in the PMO were implemented quickly.

My extended term in PMO was coming to an end on 15 August 2004. At that time, my cadre state Manipur was facing serious law and order problems after the 'alleged' murder of Th. Manorama Devi by security forces. In the first week of August 2004, a high-level meeting was called by Prime Minister Dr Manmohan Singh. It was attended by Home Minister Shivraj Patil, Defence Minister A.K. Antony, senior officials of the PMO, Ministry of Home Affairs and Mrs Sonia Gandhi. In that meeting, it was decided to replace senior government functionaries, including the state Governor, immediately.

S. S. Sidhu IAS (Retd) was appointed the new Governor of Manipur. The incumbent Chief Secretary was posted on deputation to the Central government and I was asked to go back to Manipur immediately. As soon as I reached Manipur, I was appointed as Chief Secretary to the state government.

I enjoyed my work in the PMO even though it was sometimes quite strenuous. All work and files in PMO require time-bound disposal. To the best of my knowledge, before me no officer had worked at Joint Secretary level for eight years. More important than the years is that I was a part of major initiatives for economic and infrastructure development in the country. Personally, I kept low profile and worked quietly, and this proved useful for me.

Two ministries of the government which remained largely untouched by reforms and continued as before during this period were Railways and Coal. These sectors had strong inbuilt resistance to any reform and change. Despite the best efforts of the government, these sectors did not see worthwhile reforms as other sectors did. Perhaps, the bureaucracy in these two ministries was resistant to change and the senior officers were not bold enough to initiate changes and reforms.

PRIME MINISTER
H. D. DEVE GOWDA

(AUGUST 1996 – APRIL 1997)

Author's Take

"H.D. Deve Gowda was the Chief Minister of Karnataka before becoming the Prime Minister of India. His pro rural development initiatives comprised a number of schemes for farmers. The Basic Minimum Services (BMSs) for the rural areas—one of the important schemes initiated by him—consisted of provision of electricity, water supply, marketing facilities, education, etc., in the rural areas. The only Prime Minister to have toured all seven states of the North-East at a stretch, the initiatives taken by him during this tour led to the creation of the Non-Lapsable Central Pool of Resources (NLCPR), and the completion of a large number of infrastructure projects in the North-East. PM Deve Gowda's economic and infrastructure development push for the North-East was the first big initiative which was later supplemented by his successors. He was known to be a quick decision taker."

1

A CALL FROM THE PRIME MINISTER'S OFFICE

After a four-and-a-half-year deputation in the Department of Power, Ministry of Energy in the Central government, I reverted to my cadre state Manipur in June 1986. From then on I worked in various capacities in the state. While working here, I had the opportunity to go to John F. Kennedy School of Government, Harvard University for the Master in Public Administration (Public Policy and Management) under the Edward S. Mason Program. In 1994, after I was empanelled as Joint Secretary, I applied for a deputation to the Central government.

During 1994-95, I came to know that my name was being circulated, on and off, by the EO in DoPT to different ministries and departments but it was not being picked up anywhere. Some of my colleagues in the IAS advised me that I should go to Delhi and meet some senior officers who were working in the government and also lobby if I wanted my deputation to come through. Otherwise, I was advised, it would be very difficult as there were fewer posts available than the persons who were aspiring for deputation at this level. I waited patiently till December 1995, but nothing materialised. It was also becoming apparent to me that there was not much hope of getting it soon as I did not know any Secretary in the government who could assist in pushing my case for a deputation.

Nevertheless, I kept abreast of the progress. As a result, I came to know that the Civil Services Board (CSB) headed by the Cabinet Secretary had prepared panels for different posts, which would become available to various government departments and ministries. I also subsequently, learnt that my name was at the top of the panel prepared by the CSB for the post of Development Commissioner for Handicrafts in the Ministry of Textiles. This panel of names was forwarded to the Ministry for consideration and to select a suitable officer for the said position. Normally, the ministry would have picked up my name as I was at the top of the panel. However, they did not select anyone. Instead, they asked for a new panel with a suggestion to include a particular person's name and referred it back. The DoPT did not agree to this request and insisted that they select a person from the original panel as it had been approved by the Minister of State for Personnel and could not be reviewed again.

This tug of war between the two continued for more than six months. The resultant stalemate led to a situation where nothing materialised for me. Neither was I getting selected as Development Commissioner for Handicrafts nor was I getting rejected so that my Annual Confidential Reports (ACRs) dossiers could be released and I could be considered for other vacancies.

Feeling helpless, I met Dr E.A.S. Sarma, Additional Secretary, Ministry of Commerce at Udyog Bhawan in 1995-96. He was an old colleague who was Director in the Department of Power in 1983 when I was there first as Under Secretary and then Deputy Secretary. Dr Sarma advised me to meet Javed Chaudhary, the EO at the DoPT. He spoke to Mr Chaudhary and got an appointment for me.

I met the EO in the North Block and requested that EO office should circulate my name for future vacancies. I brought to his notice my outstanding record and informed him that having served my cadre state for the last 10 years I now deserved a deputation. When I was speaking to Mr Chaudhary, V. Lakshmi Ratan, Additional Secretary in the DoPT who was also sitting in the room said it was difficult to get deputation to the Central government as the number of posts available were lesser than the aspirants. Surprisingly, it was Lakshmi Ratan who was replying to some of my requests to the EO.

I tried to convince them that after a long service stint in a north-eastern state it was truly time for a deputation. They both informed me that the CSB was the authority to decide on preparation of panels for different posts. Moreover, the secretaries of different ministries and departments also made recommendations to the EO and CSB to include their favourite candidates in the panels pertaining to their ministries and departments. Mr Chaudhary explained his helplessness. My meeting with the EO was a total failure and I went back to Manipur disappointed. I felt that I may not get a deputation soon and would have to depend on my luck as and when it happened.

Manipur and some other small cadres of IAS and other all India services are at a disadvantage in comparison to bigger cadres such as Uttar Pradesh, Tamil Nadu, Maharashtra, etc. as far as getting deputation in the Central government is concerned. Officers from bigger cadres have experiences of working in state public sector undertakings (PSUs) and other important departments. Also many officers of these cadres work in senior positions in the Central government and are in a position to facilitate the postings of junior officers of their own cadres for deputation. On the other hand, for officers from small cadres such as Manipur there are only a handful of senior officers in the Central government, who cannot help much.

Under the system of CSB headed by the Cabinet Secretary, the upcoming vacancies and eligible officers available are discussed with the EO and a panel of eligible officers for each vacancy is prepared. Yet, a lot of subjectivity comes in as the concerned secretaries of departments, where vacancies need to be filled, have personal knowledge about officers from their cadres. One way to reduce such subjectivity could be to specify points for experience in particular areas of work as well as academic qualifications of each officer and give weightage to these points at the time of preparing the panels. It is difficult to suggest a foolproof and fair system of selection of officers at the Central government. This is not to say that a lot of deserving officers from states and services cadres do not get selected for Central government posts.

A CLOSE CALL FOR CHANGE

It was 1996, when I got an order from the EO appointing me as Deputy Election Commissioner (DEC) in the Election Commission of India (ECI). I was happy to get a deputation order. Though I must say, I was a bit disappointed as I would have to work with T. N. Seshan, the then Chief Election Commissioner. He was known to have a mercurial temperament and quite often behaved very abruptly. His working style kept his juniors on tenterhooks. This was not what I wanted. However, I also knew that it was difficult to get a Central government deputation changed, more so by me sitting in Manipur. According to the guidelines issued by DoPT, a refusal of a deputation would get the member of service debarred for five years from being considered for any deputation. It was a catch twenty-two situation.

I went through all pro and cons and spoke to a colleague in DoPT as well. He informed me that Mr Seshan had specially picked me from about a dozen people. Mr Seshan had called him to ECI and asked him to read the bio data of all eligible candidates in the list. In the end, my colleague said that Mr Seshan preferred the Sikh gentleman who was serving in Manipur as chief electoral officer. That was how I was selected and got the appointment order as DEC in ECI.

I started packing my bags for the move to Delhi. I was still in the process when an unexpected call came from the office of the Chief Secretary, Manipur. The word had come from DoPT that my deputation order in ECI was under review and hence, I should not be relieved to join in Delhi. I immediately put my packing on hold. In a while, I came to know that an IAS officer serving in the ECI had become eligible for promotion as DEC and was being appointed the same.

A few days later, I got an order from EO cancelling my deputation order. While I was happy that I did not have to jeopardise my service by saying no to the DoPT deputation order, there was also the worry that it may never materialise. I could only hope that something better would come my way sooner than later.

EVENTUALLY GOOD NEWS

Every year, militants in Manipur step up their violent activities before Independence Day and Republic Day celebrations. There were a number of bomb blasts in Imphal to scare away people from participating in the Independence Day celebrations of 1996. In the first week of August, a bomb blast on the main road between the Secretariat and the Accountant General's office left a rickshaw puller injured. He lay unattended as the people fearing an unexploded bomb did not go near him. I witnessed the scene from the window of my private secretary's office on the first floor, North Block of the Manipur Secretariat.

It was mid-morning, around 11 a.m. on 9 August 1996. I was sitting in my office in the North Block of the Secretariat when, once again I heard a loud bomb blast. My personal staff informed me that the blast happened in a nearby area. A few minutes later, my Private Secretary M. A. Khalique told me there was telephone call for me from the Secretary to the PM. Thinking that the PMO might be trying to convey a message to the Chief Secretary Manipur to tighten security arrangements for the upcoming Independence day celebrations, I told Khalique to connect him to the PS to the Chief Secretary. Khalique told me that it was I that he wanted to speak to. I felt strange and took the call. The voice on the other end said that Mr B. N. Yugandhar, Secretary to the PM wanted to talk to me urgently. A few seconds later, Mr Yugandhar was on the line informing me that I had been selected for a posting as Joint Secretary to Prime Minister from the list of eligible officers. He asked me if I was willing to join and I replied in affirmative. He informed that I would get the orders of posting the very next day.

I jumped with joy. What wonderful luck, I thought! Within a day I got the order from the EO, DoPT asking me to join as Joint Secretary to PM. I quickly packed my belongings and reached Delhi. It was a dream posting for me. I had got the the most sought after posting in the Central government.

A position in the PMO was a very rare and godsent opportunity for my family and I. Normally, the PMO does not invite applications for postings in the PMO. Officers are selected based on their records or personal knowledge of senior officers about them. It seemed my record had spoken well after all. I had known Mr Yugandhar from when he was Director at Lal Bahadur Shastri National Academy of Administration (LBSNAA), Mussoorie. In June 1989, I had suggested to Mr Yugandhar the improvements in the training modules of IAS officers. I was invited to LBSNAA in September 1989, when I suggested a modified training module with a set of exercises containing quantitative techniques for informed decision-making by the officers. In a few months, I had prepared a brochure called 'Brochure on Public Policy Analysis Techniques' which contained all quantitative techniques such as project and investment appraisal methods, optimisation and linear programming, decisions analysis, queuing models, sensitivity analysis, distributive analysis, regression analysis, etc. This seemed to have worked in my favour with Mr Yugandhar who was in charge of selection of joint secretaries in the PMO.

I left Manipur two days after I got the order. On 16 August 1996, I joined the PMO where I served for eight years, a record for any Joint Secretary there. It was a privilege to work with four prime ministers in the course of these years and gain a wide array of experiences, especially in framing of policies and programmes.

2

JOINING PRIME MINISTER'S OFFICE

I reached New Delhi on 15th August. I had informed the Prime Minister's Office in advance that I wanted to join the very next day. At 10 a.m. sharp I was at the PMO reception and talked to the Joint Secretary in charge of administration there. The security officer issued me a pass to enter the PMO and I went through a surprisingly elaborate number of checks, screening machines and arrangements for security. The undersecretary at the PMO issued the order of my appointment as Joint Secretary to the PM with effect from the same day. My predecessor, K. S. Money was waiting and he handed over charge to me immediately. He was going back to his state cadre, Rajasthan. He told me that he had sought a time to meet T. R. Satish Chandran, Principal Secretary to PM, to bid goodbye, and at the same time to introduce me to him. When we met the Principal Secretary, my predecessor introduced me. I had worked with Satish Chandran when he was Secretary, Department of Power in 1982-83. He was a quiet and polite officer, very meticulous in his work but very firm in decision-making. He was busy with the organisation of a World Energy Conference which was to be conducted in Goa under the aegis of the Ministry of Petroleum and Natural Gas. He welcomed me and briefly informed me about the work I would be handling in the PMO. He also informed me that later on he would have a detailed discussion on the important issues regarding the work assigned to me.

The PMO building in South Block is small and compact with the offices of the prime minister, the principal secretary and the secretary to PM in three different corners of the first floor. In the fourth corner is the Cabinet room where Cabinet meetings are held. Apart from these there are several beautifully decorated waiting rooms with painted ceiling. I was impressed with the aura of the PMO complex. The importance of being in the PMO had not sunk in me yet, let alone understand the system of working there, which included processing of proposals, decision-making and servicing PM's meetings among other responsibilities.

PMO – A ZERO-ERROR OFFICE

In the afternoon I called on Secretary B.N. Yugandhar. His office was on the first floor in the north-eastern corner of the PMO building. As soon as I entered his office chamber, he recognised me and welcomed me. After a few pleasantries, he informed me that my work allocation order would be issued the same day. He then explained to me the working of the PMO. One thing which he told me in my first meeting has stayed with me till today. He said:

> "The PMO is a zero-error office. Whatever you write or record in office files or in office notes must be hundred per cent correct. If you get any data or figures or information from any ministry or department, you must get these only from secretary of the ministry or the department and nobody else, as other persons could give old or incorrect data or information. It becomes difficult to fix responsibility later if information is found incorrect. Whatever should be written by you as Joint Secretary could be quoted by the PM in any speech or in any meeting in any context. Therefore, there is zero scope of error in information contained in your file

notings and also in preparing brief notes for meetings of the PM."

I said, 'Yes sir, I am always careful. But keeping in view the sensitive nature of the office, I would be more careful and meticulous.'

He replied, 'If you continue to have doubts even after getting information from any ministry or department and you find some contradictions, which gives rise to the slightest doubt about some information or data, you should not quote it and should not put up to PM.' He hammered in this point again and again. Towards the end of our meeting he reiterated again that, 'This is why PMO is a zero-error office.' He mentioned a few cases as examples. I followed his advice meticulously during my tenure at the PMO. From that moment onwards it was my responsibility to ensure that no incorrect data or information should be mentioned in the notes sent to the PM from my division at the PMO.

Another point which I learnt fast in my first few days in PMO was that quick and timely decision-making is of utmost importance. In the prime minister's office all decisions are to be taken in a time-bound manner. Whether the matters are for processing cases for Cabinet meetings or appointments of PM or for any other specific purposes, all matters are time bound. It is the responsibility of the officer-in-charge to make sure that the actions are taken on time, and all persons concerned in the PMO and other ministries know about the actions they need to take. I knew that delayed decision-making could breed corruption. When decisions are delayed, the affected parties and officials in the bureaucratic hierarchy impute motives about delays. Some also get tempted to delay at their end in the hope of getting some benefits. I, for one, have always believed in quick decision-making.

THE FIRST MEETING WITH THE PM

After I joined PMO, I got an opportunity to call on the Prime Minister for the first time in the PMO. S.S. Meenakshisundaram, Joint Secretary to PM, who belonged to the Karnataka cadre introduced me. This was the first time I had either entered the prime minister's office chamber in South Block or met any prime minister personally. When I entered, Prime Minister Deve Gowda was sitting on a sofa placed on one side of the room. Mahendra Jain, Private Secretary to PM was also there. As soon as I entered, Meenakshisundaram introduced me. He mentioned my study at Harvard and my work in Manipur.

PM Deve Gowda asked me a few questions. His tone was low, and I found him very pleasant to talk with. I spoke briefly about my background and work experience, and the Prime Minister congratulated me and advised me to work hard. He also said that he was thinking of visiting all the states of the North-East soon. The meeting lasted for about five minutes and I thanked him and left. The Prime Minister, a quiet person, had been a very successful Chief Minister of Karnataka. I was very pleased to see the office chamber of the PM. Since it was the first time that I had met any prime minister, it was a great day for me.

I was allocated the work of my predecessor the same day I joined the PMO. It included the Ministries of Power, Petroleum and Natural Gas, Coal, Renewable Energy Sources, Mines and MHA. In addition, all matters relating to Arunachal Pradesh, Assam, Manipur, Mizoram, Meghalaya, Nagaland, Sikkim, Tripura, Jammu and Kashmir, Tamil Nadu, Kerala, Andhra Pradesh and Goa were to be attended by me. Later, ministries of Railways, Road Transport and Highways, Telecommunications and Information Technology, Chemicals and Fertilizers, Textiles, Disinvestment, etc. were added for some years. My predecessor briefed me about the different procedures followed for processing of files and papers received in the PMO.

As per the *Government of India (Allocation of Business) Rules*, the main work of the PMO is to provide secretarial assistance to the prime minister. There is no other work allocated to the PMO. Whenever, the prime minister is in charge of any ministry, he works as a minister of that ministry. The assistants or under secretaries in the PMO do not write notes on files as is done in other ministries and departments of the government. The files in the PMO are stored in five sections, each headed by a section officer, namely: Economic and Social-I called as

E&S–I, Economic and Social-II called as E&S-II, Political-I called Pol.-I, Political-II called as Pol. II and 'Not to Go Out' called as NGO section. As the name itself implies, the files of the NGO section have to be read and dealt with carefully. It becomes the responsibility of the officer taking out the file or paper from the NGO section to keep it back in the same section.

Whenever the files or papers are received from other ministries, it is linked with the previous files or papers in the PMO by the specific section and given to the Deputy Secretary, Director or Joint Secretary. Thereon, it is their responsibility to initiate the proposal in the shadow file of the PMO. The PMO officials concerned record their notes in the shadow file and mention the previous decisions taken on the same subject or any other related matter as well. The ministry file is used as a link file in the processing of the proposal in the PMO. After a decision on the proposal is taken on the shadow file, the relevant papers from the ministry or department file are photocopied and kept in the shadow file. Following this, the decision taken is recorded in the file received from the ministry or department and their file is sent back. In cases where the files are to go to the President of India, the prime minister's signature is required on the original files before they are sent to the Rashtrapati Bhavan.

When the prime minister has meetings with different chief ministers, ministers or other persons, the officers concerned of PMO cover these meetings. If required, the prime minister is briefed beforehand. Records of such meetings are kept in files for follow-up action or for future meetings. The work in the PMO is hectic, sensitive and with no scope for delay in recording decisions or in conveying decisions to all concerned. Before the next meeting of the prime minister on the same subject, all issues which had been flagged or decisions taken should be brought to conclusion. This routine is followed and it is the responsibility of the Joint Secretary concerned to complete the action and be ready for next meeting if needed. If decisions taken are recoded concisely/correctly and are conveyed to the concerned officers in the different ministries or departments, the decisions are implemented faster.

A HIGH-STATUS OFFICE

PMO is perceived as a hallowed place and the most powerful office in the country. People look at all those who work in the PMO as very powerful individuals. During the initial weeks, whenever I mentioned that I was working as Joint Secretary to PM, people would look at me in awe. The sense that the PMO was a powerful office in the country took some time to sink in. I slowly adjusted to the newly acquired status though I did not find any difference either in my working style, my approach to life or in my behaviour in public. I took it lightly and kept a low profile during the eight years I worked there. I enjoyed the work and was fully focused on the job. I have always believed that it is not officers or people who are powerful, but the power flows from the rules and regulations, which confer power on individuals and the system. I took it that way and carried on with my job.

ROUTINES AT THE PMO

While entering the PMO one day, I happened to meet Union Minister of Social Welfare Balwant Singh Ramoowalia. He used to represent Sangrur district Lok Sabha constituency, to which I too belonged. I had known him for many years and had met him a number of times in the past. As soon as he saw me he remarked, 'I have seen a Sikh Joint Secretary in the PMO for the first time'. He was happy to see me and said that we meet later on. Ramoowalia was wrong in saying so as there had been Sikh officers at Joint Secretary and higher positions earlier too. It appeared to me that he was referring to a period after the assassination of Prime Minister Indira Gandhi, when there was a feeling among the Sikhs that Sikh officers were not being considered for sensitive positions in the Central government. However, that period was long over.

The system of entry and exit of visitors plays an important role in the security system at the PMO. The security measures and screening of people and articles at the entry gates into PMO is thorough as it should rightly be so. All visitors to the PMO are screened first and then taken to the specific officer whom they want to meet. If the officer is not free they sit in a waiting room and are not allowed to loiter, as it happens in other government offices. After the meeting, the visitor is escorted out of the building and the entry pass is deposited back with the security personnel at the inner gate, thus, ensuring the visitor's departure is fully accounted for. Generally, officers below the Deputy Secretary level are not allowed to have visitors.

I used to bring my lunch from home. While I used to enter the PMO through the main door, my briefcase and tiffin box used to be taken by my assistant through the screening machines. A couple of times my assistant told me that the security personnel in charge of screening opened my tiffin box and stirred the dal or vegetables with a spoon or a stick. I asked the SPG personnel about this. They told me that most often they do not check the food packets of senior officers but if the tiffin box was made of steel it would not show properly on the screen, and they then had to check it manually. It is always good to follow the security drill and procedure laid down by the security personnel. Since it was not possible to avoid the screening, I requested the security personnel to use a clean spoon or wooden stick to stir and ensure that the food is opened with clean hands.

During my eight years stay in PMO, there were three cases of cancer among the employees. There was a talk that these cases were due to excessive exposure to the powerful screening machines. Some also wondered if these could be due to the excessive screening of the food the employees ate. When the whispers became loud, the administration wing asked for the opinion of the Atomic Energy Commission (AEC) on this. My colleague in the PMO who was dealing with the AEC requested the chairman to study the radiation levels and give their opinion. The AEC examined and informed that radiation levels at the PMO entrance were not excessive and not the reason for cancer among the employees, thus laying to rest all apprehensions.

3

INITIAL DAYS AT THE PMO

WORK ENVIRONMENT

The work and working environment in the state, Central government and in the PMO are vastly different. At the Central level, most of the work relates to the framing of policies for socio-economic development programmes and other areas falling within the Central government jurisdiction. Some ministries and departments also implement programmes and policies of the Central government, particularly those which are in the Central or Concurrent List of the Constitution of India, through the agencies of Central ministries/departments and the Central PSUs. The work in the state relates to implementation of the policies and programmes of the Central and state governments and less on the framing of policies. In the PMO, the work is related to framing and approving of policies and programmes of the Central government.

In PMO, the Deputy Secretaries, Directors or Joint Secretaries initiate proposals unlike other ministries and departments where assistants or section officers initiate proposals. This helps in improving the quality of proposals which are put up to PM. The support staff such as stenographers are also relatively more for each Joint Secretary as compared to other ministries or departments.

I had three assistants who efficiently organised and arranged my daily routines of meetings, papers and notes for the PM. Their good work was helpful in improving my performance. Even though officially the working hours were the same as any other department or ministry, yet these were longer at the PMO due to meetings of the PM, actions required to be taken for these meetings as well as follow up actions required on the different issues discussed in the meetings. The nature of work in PMO required punctuality, quick disposal and full dedication.

LEARNING ON THE JOB

After my initial meetings with the Principal Secretary and the Secretary, I was on my own to find my way. I learnt and worked on my own. As each file or case that comes to the PMO are different from others, I had to handle each one on my own. I did not receive any specific briefings from any superior except that in specific cases I could consult concerned persons in the PMO, or different ministries or departments and process the proposals. I was learning on the job, which after 22 years in the IAS I was used to. I got copies of the *Government of India (Allocation of Business) Rules* and the *Government of India (Transaction of Business) Rules* to understand work allocation to different departments and transaction of business, which guided and helped in processing proposals.

The work in PMO is streamlined. The channels of processing files and proposals are clearly laid out and known to all officers, and all work is time-bound.

A PROTECTED ENVIRONMENT

The officers working in the PMO, from Deputy Secretary to Secretary, remain well-protected and kept far away from the media gaze. It is the media advisor to the PM who interacts with the press as and when required. The officers in PMO are not subjected to ministerial pressures as is the case with officers in other ministries. Working in the PMO is like working in a protected environment. Since entry of outsiders in the PMO is restricted, it is difficult for anyone to know the stages of processing of files here. The prime minister is the ultimate authority in the government and decisions taken by him is agreed to by all without any dissent from any minister or ministry. As the PMO uses the shadow file system for processing proposals and taking approval of the PM, it is not possible for other ministries to know the methods adopted or arguments given for taking or not taking a decision by the PMO on different proposals. These mostly remain in the PMO files.

Since many of the matters handled are sensitive, the officers selected to join here are subjected to positive vetting by the Intelligence Bureau (IB). This process requires new officers and employees to provide complete personal information about their family members, past postings, relatives, places of residences, interests in businesses, bank accounts, etc. in an elaborate format. The IB officials then verify all these details and vet their suitability for the job in the PMO. This comprehensive verification system is good from the point of view of security as it is quite different from the normal clearances given by the IB, which is more like a no objection letter. The officers are regularly vetted and kept under watch during their tenures in the PMO.

A few days after I joined the PMO, my mother rang up from my village Balian, Sangrur district, Punjab. She told me that some police personnel had come to our village and were collecting information about all our family members and our bank accounts. The police personnel visited all my close relatives and verified the information I had detailed. I was surprised but happy that the verification system was working well.

PRINCIPAL SECRETARY SATISH CHANDRAN

I had briefly met Principal Secretary Satish Chandran on my first day when I was introduced by my predecessor K. S. Money. He belonged to the Karnataka cadre and had been Chief Secretary of Karnataka. One of the most unassuming officers I have seen in the Indian Administrative Service, he was very straight-forward and a soft-spoken man. I have never seen him raise his voice in any meeting ever. He made his points clearly and firmly. He was very punctual in attending office and was in office every morning before time and left just after office time. Often, I saw him leave office around six in the evening even though the Prime Minister was still in office. Yet, he was able to finish all his work on time and was very clear about decision-making. I have seen him make payments to the PMO administration unit for all the private calls he made from the official telephone at the PMO. I was told that he diligently did so every month.

WHO IS PM IN THE PMO?

Mr Chandran always went by the rule book. I recall getting a call from the MoS Power, informing me that the Prime Minister had approved his visit to the USA to attend a conference on energy. I had not seen any such proposal from the Ministry till this call came in. About fifteen minutes later, I received some papers from his personal staff about the energy conference. A close read showed that it was actually meant for officials and not for ministerial-level participation. Based on this proposal, the MoS had prepared a note for the PM's approval to attend the conference. The MoS did not follow the laid down procedure to get the PM's approval for his visit abroad. It was not proper on his part to place a raw proposal before the PM in some meeting and request for approval. The Prime Minister had recorded his note approving the proposal and this note was sent to me by the MoS's personal staff. He kept a photocopy of the PM's approval note and also spoke to me about it.

I examined the proposal in the light of guidelines and policy of government for participation of ministers in such conferences. As per these guidelines, if international conferences were attended by officials of different countries and not ministers, then no ministerial-level participation was required from India. Ministry of External Affairs (MEA) and our embassies abroad have also been quite emphatic about the correct level of participation in such conferences. I submitted the proposal about the minister's participation in the energy conference with my views and the government policy in such matters to the PM through the Principal Secretary. The following evening, I got the file back mentioning that the approval given by the PM for the visit had been reviewed and cancelled. I was asked to convey the same to the MoS. The MoS and his entourage had booked their tickets to board flight from Mumbai. I informed his office since the minister was on a tour of south India and was to fly directly from there to Mumbai and New York.

The minister was very angry and rang me up. He asked me, 'Who is the Prime Minister in the PMO? I have a photocopy of his approval with me. Who has cancelled the approval given by him?' I quietly informed him that the PM had not given his approval as the conference was not for ministerial-level participation. The Principal Secretary was very firm that a minister should not attend a conference meant for officers. So much for the firmness of Mr Chandran that a proposal approved by the Prime Minister, albeit based on incomplete information, could not escape the rule book.

Mr Chandran had a vast knowledge of the energy sector in India and abroad. Before he became Secretary (Power), he was Adviser (Energy) in the Planning Commission of India. He had also been the President of the World Energy Conferences in India and abroad. I have seen his long notes in official files on energy policy issues particularly about Iran-India Gas Pipeline in the PMO. Even though it eventually did not come through, yet, the arguments given by him completely demolished the stand of MEA against the pipeline. One of the main arguments of MEA against the Gas Pipeline was the security of the gas pipeline and gas supply due to possible disruptions in Pakistan by anti-India elements.

Mr Chandran's arguments were sound, practical and made business sense. An important point he made was that the gas brought by the Iran-India Gas Pipeline would provide energy less than 10 per cent of total energy requirements of the northern India. Therefore, the disruptions of the gas pipeline now and then would hardly make any differences in India. On the contrary the gas use in both India and Pakistan would create vested economic interests for safety of the gas pipeline and be a strong deterrent against any disruption or sabotage.

Satish Chandran dictated comprehensive notes and kept records in files. It was an enlightening experience to read his notes. I remember an incident from way back in 1982 when we were at the Department of Power. The budget session of parliament was to begin in a few days and self-contained notes for the Minister (Energy) on important issues of the power sector had to be prepared for him for the budget debate. We were waiting for Mr Chandran so that we could prepare notes on different issues facing the energy sector. To our surprise, we got a terse message from his private secretary that we needn't wait and could go home. All he wanted was three or four stenographers who could take dictations and type the notes. During the course of that evening, he dictated notes on all power sector issues ranging from generation, transmission and distribution of power. The next morning copies of the comprehensive notes given to the Minister (Energy) were on our desks too.

S.S. MEENAKSHISUNDARAM

Another powerful bureaucrat in the PMO was S. S. Meenakshisundaram who was Joint Secretary to PM. He belonged to the Karnataka cadre and was considered a confidante of the Prime Minister. He was an upright rule-book bureaucrat considered as the second-most important man in the PMO. He used to get the PM's approval on important files including appointments files. At that time all appointments up to the level of Deputy Secretary needed the approval of the Appointments Committee of the Cabinet (ACC), which is headed by the PM. Any important matter which required the PM's attention or approval would require Mr Meenakshisundaram's attention too. He was a very pleasant and helpful person, and easily accessible too. Since he had worked with the Prime Minister earlier, he knew the PM's style of working. We could discuss any issue with him at any time and he was always supportive. He kept low profile and never showed off that he wielded power because of nearness to PM. Many times I saw senior bureaucrats, who were aspirants for important positions in the government, sitting in his office chamber and lobbying for better positions. But my understanding of him was that he always went by rule book only and could not be influenced by lobbying.

MAHENDRA JAIN

Mahendra Jain, Private Secretary to PM Deve Gowda, belonged to the Karnataka cadre. He was earlier District Collector of Hasan district and was known to the PM. His main work was to organise meetings and appointments of the PM. He was a quiet and soft spoken person, polite and always helpful. He was assisted by a team of junior officers which included the Additional Private Secretary.

ACC AND SPEEDIER DISPOSAL OF ACC PROPOSALS

C. Phunsog, my senior colleague in the PMO, handled the processing of all ACC proposals. These proposals used to be sent to the PMO for the PM's approval as he was chairman of the ACC. The PMO hardly made any contribution to most of these appointments of Deputy Secretaries, or Directors and it took a lot of the PM's time. The PM one day, was reported to have remarked, 'What is this ACC, BCC? Please rationalise the system and reduce the number of files coming to me'. Immediately, a proposal was prepared by Phunsog and his juniors and with the approval of the PM, the rules governing proposals which were to be placed before the ACC for approval were amended. After this, only appointments related to the Joint Secretary and above required the approval of the ACC, thus, reducing the workload in the PMO substantially.

Between 1994-96, when I was trying for my deputation, I used to discuss with my colleagues and batchmates about Central government postings and vacancies in various ministries and departments. Invariably, the delay in processing ACC proposals at the PMO would emerge in the discussions. I used to think that the PMO might be having some elaborate procedures to vet appointments before according ACC approvals. I wondered about the value addition the PMO was making in processing these proposals. I had also heard that in some ACC proposals, changes used to be made at the PMO. The general impression was that it was better to know someone in the PMO to speed up the ACC approval. I did not know then that the PMO followed a straight-forward procedure for processing proposals in almost all cases.

During PM Deve Gowda's government, ACC proposals were cleared within hours of their receipt in the PMO. This was possible because of the clarity on the part of the officers processing them and the Prime Minister's clear-headed approach. I must say that credit for this goes to the PM, for it was he who made the system of appointments to senior positions very fair and objective.

4

LEARNING THE ROPES: PEOPLE, PERSONALITIES AND PERSPECTIVES

HARKISHAN SINGH SURJEET

The general secretary of the Communist Party of India-Marxist (CPI-M), Harkishan Singh Surjeet, had played a key role in ensuring the Left parties support to PM Deve Gowda's United Front government. Though I did not see him often in the PMO, I knew that the letters written by him were attended to quickly by the Prime Minister. He seemed to have played a role in choosing important ministers in the Cabinet. He also had very good relations with senior leaders of the coalition. Some called him the 'Chanakya' of the time as he was able to hold together a coalition government of many partners with divergent interests at the state level.

Mr Surjeet wrote a letter to the PM about a case relating to the death of three people, including an NRI businessman named Paramjit Singh

Sahota, in September 1996. The triple murder case came to light when their bodies were recovered from a vehicle which had been set on fire but shown as an 'accident' by the Punjab police in their investigations. The matter was reported widely in various newspapers as the persons who were reportedly killed had been partners in a factory set up near Chandigarh to produce holograms. They were in partnership with the relatives of a senior police officer. This was a high-tech venture, which the relatives of the police officer looked to usurp. Mr Surjeet requested the Prime Minister to hand over the investigation to the CBI, as the main accused was a senior officer. He suggested that the truth would not come out if the investigation remained with the Punjab police.

It is widely known that the junior-ranking officers in the police forces cannot fairly investigate cases against their seniors. Even if they attempt, they may not get full cooperation from their colleagues in most cases. As a result, the senior officials are most likely to go scot-free.

PM Deve Gowda directed the case be handed over to the CBI. At that time, I was handling matters relating to the MHA and conveyed this to the Home Secretary and DoPT. The case was quickly handed over to the CBI.

A few days later, the police officer concerned came to my house along with his wife and one of my distant relatives from Ludhiana. They wanted my help in pressurising the CBI not to investigate the case and, if possible, be lenient with them. They already knew of Mr Surjeet's recommendation to the PM. I was taken aback at the way they projected themselves as innocent and the case to be a handiwork of some forces in Punjab to frame the officer so that he did not get the top post in Punjab police. I told them not to discuss the issue with me since I had handled it in the PMO. I gave them tea and requested them to leave my house.

The CBI was able to charge sheet the accused involved in the case quickly. Later, I learnt that the police officer and some others were convicted by the District and Sessions Judge, Patiala and sentenced to rigorous life imprisonment. A few years later, the officer was acquitted by the Punjab and Haryana High Court. In the process, an enterprising NRI lost his life and a senior police officer who could have risen to the top police post in Punjab languished in prison. Greed does make a person blind to the consequences of one's actions.

JOGINDER SINGH

After assuming charge, Prime Minister Deve Gowda appointed Joginder Singh IPS of the Karnataka cadre as the Director of the CBI. The officers who had worked in the CBI at junior levels and knew the working of the organisation had a better chance of becoming its Director. This was not the case with Joginder Singh. He had neither worked in the CBI earlier nor had a brilliant investigation record in his favour. Whatever may be the reasons for the appointment of Joginder Singh, he brought the CBI into daily media headlines. Every day, I read in the news about the progress of different cases being investigated by the CBI. He enjoyed every bit of publicity he was getting.

DICK CHENEY MEETS PM

Dick Cheney came to meet Prime Minister Deve Gowda in 1996-97. He was the Chairman and CEO of Halliburton Company and was associated with Brown and Root Company, which was engaged in gas exploration in Myanmar and Bangladesh. In 1996, India too was in search of natural gas to augment its energy sources. There were strong possibilities of surplus natural gas in Bangladesh and its probable availability for India. However, the Indo-Bangladesh political equations at that time were such that India was unlikely to get gas directly. There was also no way of getting natural gas from Myanmar through a pipeline passing through Bangladesh territory. One feasible option was to get natural gas from a third party engaged in exploring gas in Bangladesh. A commercial entity as the one headed by Dick Cheney could make the arrangement workable at a political level in Bangladesh.

Vijay Kelkar, Secretary Petroleum and Natural Gas came with Dick Cheney to the meeting with the PM. Since I was handling issues relating to this Ministry, I dealt with the coordination and covering the meeting.

We were in the waiting room, and Dr Kelkar introduced me to Dick Cheney. I was meeting Mr Cheney for the first time. He was on a business trip to India. A tall and heavily built person with an imposing personality, Mr Cheney informed me about the work his company was doing in Myanmar and Bangladesh and its possible economic benefits to India. He was quite clear about the sensitivities of Bangladesh in supplying gas to India through a bilateral arrangement.

Prior to the meeting, Kelkar told me that Dick Cheney was a popular and influential Republican politician in the USA and a probable for the Republican Party in the upcoming US presidential elections. As such his meeting with the PM could be very important for India and should be conducted properly.

While discussing this issue, Kelkar, perhaps jokingly, said, 'Sometimes while listening to others, our PM closes his eyes. This could give the impression that he is not interested in the topics being discussed in the meeting. This does not give good impression to the visitors'.

I said to Kelkar, 'The PM is always very attentive even though his eyes might be closed. Many persons close their eyes to concentrate all their efforts in listening attentively'.

Kelkar heard me and asked if something could be done to make sure that the PM did not close his eyes. I suggested that the best way to attend to this concern was to make the discussion interesting, make it two-way and keep it short. On a lighter note he suggested that I shake the Prime Minister's sofa when he closed his eyes. I just smiled and replied, 'No way'.

The meeting went off very well. Even though there was no surety of any such arrangement materialising, yet these options were being considered, explored, and discussed at high levels in the Ministry. Dick Cheney referred to the possibility of natural gas supply to India from Bangladesh and Myanmar, which never materialised eventually. But I was very much impressed by the way he started the discussion and systematically put across all his arguments. He kept the discussion short and to the point which was more businesslike.

MOU ROUTE FOR POWER PROJECTS – AN OPAQUE METHOD

During the first half of the 1990s, the country was facing serious power shortages. To meet the power shortages quickly, the earlier government headed by P. V. Narasimha Rao had decided to add power generation capacities by encouraging private sector investments in power generation. This was proposed through stand-alone independent power producers (IPPs) with funds from international financial institutions (IFIs). An IPP or non-utility generator (NUG) is not a public utility entity such as a state electricity board but these are owned facilities to generate electric power for sale to utilities and end users of different states. These IPPs were to then sign Power Purchase Agreements (PPAs) with states and Fuel Supply Agreements (FSAs) with Coal India Limited (CIL) and the Railways. As a first step in this direction, the government had decided to implement six IPP projects, important among these were Enron's Dabhol Power project, Hinduja's Visakhapatnam Thermal Power project, 1,000 MW plant of the Mangalore Power Company (MPC) funded by Cogentrix of the USA, etc.

The addition of power generation through the Memorandum of Understanding (MoU) route was an opaque method. According to this, prices, Engineering Procurement and Construction (EPC) cost, tariffs and other performance parameters of power-generating stations were not discovered by open tenders but were to be decided through discussions between different stakeholders after the MoUs had been signed. In fact, in one of the meetings in the PMO in December 1996, the Secretary (Power) mentioned that there were about 300 issues that would need to be resolved with respect to PPAs and FSAs. Of these about 46 issues were related to the Ministry of Finance which had to give counter guarantee. These were complicated issues that were difficult to resolve by discussions and thus the financial closure of each project was taking time.

Most of the IPP projects were in the state sector, funded by foreign investments, which required guaranteed repayments of loans in foreign currencies and protection of the interests of the investors. In such situations, the counter guarantees of the government of India were required to repay the loans if these were not paid by the concerned state governments. Among the unresolved issues, which needed resolution before the projects could take off, were the reasonableness of the costs including EPCs, tariffs offered by the projects, counter guarantee formats, agreements for coal supply by CIL and coal transportation by railways. The Dabhol Power Project of Enron was already attracting a lot of criticism because of the high cost of power supply and many stakeholders associated with the IPPs were apprehensive and thus reluctant partners.

During PM Deve Gowda's tenure regular discussions were held by the state governments, union ministries of Power, Coal and Railways with the IPPs. The Finance Ministry too was involved in most of the discussions. The focus of these meetings was on ways and means to reduces EPCs and hence power tariffs. Many meetings were held at the PMO to discuss and resolve outstanding issues of these IPP projects as well as problems in sharing risks between CIL and railways in the FSAs.

My colleague Pankaj Saran, who was Director in the PMO and handled power sector, assisted me in these meetings and discussions. Since the issues relating to costs, prices, tariffs, performance parameters, etc. were quite complicated it was difficult to resolve these through discussions. There were many loose variables which were to be decided and fixed. If these projects had been processed through competitive tariffs or open competitive bid methods, most of these issues would have been resolved in a short time. However, since it was the MoU route that was opted for, the discussions continued without any early or quick resolution in sight.

The main aim of these discussions at different levels was to complete financial closure and start the construction of these projects. However, the inability of the governments to resolve various issues and the public criticism of the Dabhol Power Project of Enron delayed the implementation of these projects further. This went against the government's plan of quick addition of power generation capacity in the country. With time, the government too realised its inability in reducing EPC costs and power tariffs in the absence of competitive bidding. The matter lingered on and some IPPs such as that of Cogentrix fizzled out. Except for two, all other IPPs got delayed and were forgotten as time passed. The Deve Gowda government continued with discussions on all IPPs but could not enforce transparency as the MoUs had been already signed by the previous government. There were too many loose ends and a lot of variables to be discussed and agreed to by different parties with opposite interests.

I will not be wrong if I say that the Narasimha Rao government's eagerness to add generation capacities was undone by the opaqueness of the MoU route adopted by it. In my later years in the PMO, during the tenure of PM Vajpayee, when one of these projects came to the Cabinet for approving counter guarantee by the government for the lenders of the project, there were differences between the then Minister, Secretary and Special Secretary (Power). The latter two were firmly in favour of competitive bidding for the EPC of an MoU route project but the Minister was not in favour of competitive bidding. However, both the PM and Finance Minister Jaswant Singh favoured and insisted on the competitive bidding for discovering the EPC costs for all MoU route projects.

STREAMLINING PADMA AWARDS

In the 1990s there was a lot of criticism about the way the Padma awards (Padma Bhushan, Padma Vibhushan and Padma Shri Awards) were being conferred. There was a feeling of subjectivity in selection of nominees for the Padma Awards. In February 1992, a writ petition was filed in the Kerala High Court questioning whether the civilian awards presented by the government of India were 'titles' as per the Article 18 (1) of the Constitution of India. The constitutional article states that 'no title, not being a military or academic distinction, shall be conferred by the State'. A similar petition was also filed in mid-1992 in the Indore Bench of the Madhya Pradesh High Court and a notice was issued on 25 August, which led to provisional suspension of all civilian awards from 1993. Soon, a Special Divisional Bench of the Supreme Court of India was set up with a panel of five judges that delivered the verdict on 15 December 1995 that the 'Bharat Ratna and Padma Awards are not titles within Article 18 of the Constitution of India'.

In 1996, a high-level Padma Awards Review Committee headed by Vice President K. R. Narayanan was set up, which in its report prescribed strict norms for deciding the awards, including limiting the total number of awardees to a maximum of sixty and setting a deadline of 1 October for receiving recommendations. The streamlined procedure included inviting names, setting up of an Awards committee under the cabinet secretary and inclusion of prominent persons in the Awards committee. The recommendations of the Awards committee were then required to be placed before the President for approval after obtaining the approval of the PM. This procedure for selection of the awardees was adopted in 1998 and the Padma Awards resumed once again after a brief hiatus between 1993-97.

5

GETTING TO KNOW THE NORTH-EAST

The Prime Minister's Office suggested a six-day tour of the states of the North-East in October 1996. It meant that the PM would be away from Delhi for at least a week, something that had not happened in the past. According to the proposed programme, the PM was to not just visit each of the north-eastern states but also halt in almost all of them. Since I oversaw the north-eastern states in the PMO, it was on me to prepare a detailed tour programme for each of the states. Soon enough I was busy preparing the schedules of meetings of the Prime Minister with important persons and the general public in each state.

G. K. Pillai, Joint Secretary (North-East) in MHA, worked on the minute-to-minute details of each meeting and event. He collected information about important ongoing and delayed projects in these states, and on issues which could possibly be raised by the states during the tour. After consulting all state governments and relevant authorities in the government, a detailed programme for each meeting was chalked out. As MHA has a single NE division for handling all matters of the North-East, Mr Pillai coordinated with all the states, while at the PMO,

I coordinated all matters relating to the visit.

The six-day tour reflected the sincerity of the Prime Minister in addressing the development concerns of these states. He was accompanied by Ram Vilas Paswan, the Railway minister, B. P. Baishya, Member of Parliament, H. K. Dua, media advisor to the PM, Home Secretary K. Padmanabhaiah, B.N. Yugandhar and G. K. Pillai along with PMO officials. The tour was arranged to give the PM adequate time to listen to and discuss genuine grievances of the people in each state and meet all chief ministers, councils of ministers and state government officials.

Before the tour, PM Deve Gowda had a preparatory meeting with important secretaries of the government. The MHA coordinated all matters relating to law and order and economic development. Based on the preparatory work done by Mr Pillai, K. Padmanabhaiah planned a presentation on general issues of the north-eastern states as well as specific issues of each state. Mr Yugandhar, given his experience in the government, developed the strategy for the economic development push. As soon as Mr Yugandhar saw the size of the MHA presentation, he advised the Home Secretary to reduce its size to not more than ten minutes. I was standing nearby when Mr Yugandhar pointed out that it would be difficult to keep PM's attention for more than half an hour in this meeting. After Mr Padmanabhaiah's ten minutes, the remaining twenty would be for discussions on points made by the secretaries and development of strategy for the North-East.

PICKING UP THE GAUNTLET FOR FARMERS

At the meeting, the Home Secretary presented on the prevailing law and order situation, the level of economic development as well as disparity of development within and outside the north-eastern region. The presentation was followed by a discussion on several of the pressing issues. These included steps to improve public services and to expedite infrastructure projects relating to railways, road transport and highways, air connectivity, telecommunications, health and education, agriculture and horticulture, power, petroleum, banking, etc.

While discussing matters relating to the increase of bank credit to the agriculture sector, the Secretary Banking (now called Secretary, Financial Services) informed that banks were reluctant to further lend to farmers in the North-East as they had huge unpaid outstanding loans. He quoted a figure of about Rs 85 crore as defaulted loans, which seemed too little keeping in view the large area of the region. I was sitting right behind the Prime Minister and saw him getting very angry at the reasons given by the Secretary against increasing credit flow to farmers. In an angry tone, he pointed out that the banks had not stopped lending even after the fiasco of Indian Bank, which lent more than Rs 1,200 crore to small corporates and exporters in the south India and had already become Non-Performing Assets (NPAs). He turned to Mr Satish Chandran and expressed his unhappiness with the attitude of Secretary Banking towards the people of the north-eastern states and asked him to be shifted out. However, due to heavy workload for the preparation of the tour I forgot to put up a note to the PM about this and the Secretary Banking remained.

The PM was right in quoting the example of the Indian Bank. While nobody would support farmers or other debtors to default on loan repayments, yet lending in the agriculture sector, especially in remote areas of the North-East, makes better economic sense for the country. The region has vast agriculture and horticulture potential and credit flow to the farmers is essential for expediting the tempo of economic development in rural and hill areas. Moreover, generation of additional employment was necessary to wean away the youth from militant activities, which has plagued the region for decades.

A POSITIVE VISIT

The PM's visit started on a positive note. There was a lot of enthusiasm among the people as it was the first time that any prime minister had planned a six-day tour of the region. I had listed important issues of each state and possible actions to be initiated on all important points. Outlines of talking points and brief speeches for important occasions were also prepared for the PM to use.

This was my first visit with the Prime Minister. There is a special airplane which takes him on internal and external tours of different states or countries. For internal journeys within the country, a small-sized Boeing was used while a big-sized Jumbo Boeing was used for tours abroad. The journey started from the technical area in the northern end of the Indira Gandhi International Airport. A list of people travelling for each leg of the journey and their seating arrangement is meticulously prepared by the PMO beforehand and firmed up in consultation with the state governments, air force officials, airport authorities, state police and MHA. There is a tour officer in the PMO who travels with the prime minister and ties up all logistics of the visit. Only those who are in the list given by PMO are allowed inside the technical area of the Indira Gandhi International Airport.

There is a separate machine to screen the luggage of those accompanying the PM. During this visit a strange thing happened. My wife and I had brought a set of six high-quality knives from the USA some years back and one of these was forgotten in the suitcase pocket. My wife happened to pack my clothes for the tour in the same suitcase but somehow it remained unnoticed. I do not know how, but surprisingly, the knife was not detected by the airport screening machines either. Whatever be the reason, it was indeed a security lapse. I discovered the knife after checking in to my hotel, in Guwahati. Once found I did not think it prudent to carry the knife through my journey and gave it to the Bellevue Hotel staff for their use in the kitchen.

MEETINGS IN ASSAM

The Chief Minister of Assam, Prafulla Kumar Mahanta's party was one of the constituents of the United Front government headed by PM Deve Gowda. Assam, the first state in the Prime Minister's tour agenda, is the largest among the north-eastern states. It is the gate way to all other states of the North-East except Sikkim. The PM halted for the night at Guwahati Raj Bhawan.

The Chief Minister and his Cabinet had long meetings with the Prime Minister and raised issues for economic development of the state and completion of ongoing projects. Many important projects were proposed relating to flood control, Jogighopa rail-cum-road bridge on the Brahmaputra river, completion of Numaligarh refinery, Assam Gas Cracker Project, funding infrastructure of universities, railway projects, expansion of Guwahati airport, etc. The issues raised by Assam government also included influx of foreigners, ineffective laws such as Illegal Migrants (Determination by Tribunal) (IMDT) Act and identity crisis of ethnic groups in the state. Each of the meetings were followed by officer-level meetings for concretizing the action plans on different points discussed with the PM.

TRIPURA GOVERNMENT'S CONCERN ABOUT INFILTRATION

Next day, the Prime Minister went to Tripura. He was given a traditional welcome by the different ethnic communities. The traditional welcome included songs and dances of tribal and non-tribal groups. After the welcome, the PM met Chief Minister Dasarath Deb of the CPI (M), a quiet and soft-spoken man.

The Tripura government was mainly concerned about the infiltration from Bangladesh and early completion of fencing on the international border with Bangladesh. The state government also raised issues related to infratructure such as the completion of the railway line from Kumarghat to Agartala costing Rs 525 crore, upgradation of facilities at Agartala airport, sanction of additional India Reserve Battalions to check infiltration from Bangladesh, completion of state highway from Agartala to Sabroom along the international border as well as generation of employment opportunities for the educated unemployed youth of the state. The PM later met the council of ministers too. The halt was in Agartala that night.

A SHORT VISIT TO MIZORAM

The Prime Minister left for Aizawl, the capital of Mizoram by a helicopter the next day. He received a very warm welcome there. The helipad was about seven kilometres away from the Raj Bhawan and people in colourful customary dresses had lined up all along the road through which his cavalcade passed.

The Mizoram Chief Minister led his delegation and presented various issues confronting the state and its people. Several important issues were raised before the Prime Minister, which included funding Phase II of Aizawl Water Supply scheme, funding of Tuirial Hydroelectric Project, improving air connectivity, construction of an airport at Aizawl and funding of Border Area Development Programme (BRDP) liberally and the removal of Assam Rifles from the heart of Aizawl.

The state government was quite emphatic that the Assam Rifles should vacate the big piece of land it was occupying in the heart of Aizawl town. They required it for town development and for constructing other state government buildings. The state had been offering the Assam Rifles an alternate land a little away from Aizawl for many years but the latter had not agreed to the proposal. After the meetings and discussions were concluded, the PM left for Manipur.

PUBLIC BANDH IN MANIPUR

Manipur has the maximum number of militant groups in the North-East. As and when there is a visit either by the PM or the President of India to the state, the militant groups would give a call for a bandh and issue threats to the public not to come out and welcome the visiting dignitaries. Prime Minister Deve Gowda too was welcomed by a public bandh when he arrived in Manipur. In fact, it would have been surprising if they had not given a bandh call.

The road from Imphal airport to Raj Bhawan wore a deserted look. This was in sharp contrast to the journey from the helipad to the Raj Bhawan in Mizoram.

When we reached the Imphal Raj Bhawan, we were quite tired. The accommodation for the Prime Minister was in the Raj Bhawan. For others in his entourage arrangements were made in a hotel about two kilometers away. However, the schedule demanded that we wait in the Raj Bhawan to assist the PM in his meetings and discussions with the Governor, the Chief Minister, council of ministers and other public representatives. We had no time to go to the hotel to freshen up. Home Secretary Padmanabhaiah and I sat in the main central drawing room of Raj Bhawan. We waited for about half an hour, but no one came to enquire if we required anything or even offer refreshments. I could see the Home Secretary getting very upset at the neglect by the Raj Bhawan personnel. He was sitting on the sofa with his legs crossed on the table in front. Suddenly, Governor O. N. Srivastva came out of his room into the central waiting room.

As soon as the Home Secretary saw the Governor he said, 'Who has made you Governor? We are in the Prime Minister's entourage. There is no place to rest and wash ourselves and no refreshments also'. To this the Governor replied, 'It is the duty of the state government to make arrangement for the Prime Minister's party. Raj Bhawan is neither responsible nor in charge of providing boarding and lodging to all persons in the PM's party. Please ask them'.

The Home Secretary did not move his feet from the center table as the Governor continued to stand. His retort was sharp, 'It is the responsibility of the Governor and his office personnel to look after Prime Minister's party as all meetings are scheduled only in the Raj Bhawan. The state government cannot provide refreshments in the Raj Bhawan; the Governor's office must do that. The Governor or his staff should have tied these up before the Prime Minister's visit rather than cutting a sorry figure'.

I heard this unpleasant conversation and felt embarrassed. The Home Secretary's rebuke was sharp, but it was to a very decent human being. I also felt that the state government's coordinator should have made all the arrangements. At least for the officers in the entourage, the visit to Manipur started on a poor note. After some time, we got some refreshments and also rooms to freshen up.

As in the other states, the PM's meetings were scheduled with the Chief Minister, the council of ministers, political leaders, public representatives, security personnel, business representatives and NGOs. The fragile security environment in Manipur where more than two dozen militant groups operated was the main cause of concern for the Central government. This was affecting growth of business and private investment in the state. The PM's visit was a good opportunity for NGOs and other organisations to present their views about the various issues confronting the state. However, the bandh prevented them from meeting the PM. Ordinary citizens too, who wanted to meet PM could not do so due to the bandh.

Manipur was planning to host the National Games in Imphal in 1997. The state needed funds to complete the sports stadiums and other associated infrastructure as well as the games village for athletes and games officials. Transportation of essential commodities was also disrupted by frequent disturbances on National Highway-2 (the then NH-39) from Dimapur to Imphal. The state government wanted expeditious completion of repair works on NH-37 (the then NH-53) from Jiribam to Imphal so that there was an alternative to the NH-2 available to the state. That night the PM halted at the Imphal Raj Bhawan.

A HALT AT KOHIMA

From Imphal, the Prime Minister left for Kohima by helicopter. The Nagaland government was very hospitable and welcomed the guests warmly. The Prime Minister was given a colourful welcome by the people of the state. Nagas, in their customary dresses, had lined up on both sides of the road through which the cavalcade passed.

The Prime Minister met all organisations, leaders and NGOs in the evening. The main issues projected by the state government included additional funds to complete Doyang Hydro Electric Project of NEEPCO, four-laning of the NH-2 (the then NH-39) up to Kohima, starting of a helicopter service from Guwahati to Kohima and Dimapur, additional funds for Nagaland University, gauge conversion of railway line between Dimapur and Guwahati, upgradation of hospital facilities at Kohima and direct air connectivity between Dimapur and Delhi.

The meetings were followed by a colourful dance programme. At the end of the day we were very tired from all the travelling and meetings. However, we still had to prepare actionable points and convey those to the appropriate authorities in the government the same day. At the same time the Prime Minister had to be briefed about his meetings and programmes for the following day. It was well past midnight when I was free. I reached the hotel after 1 a.m. and called it a day. I was dead tired but knew that I had to get up early to reach the helipad before 8.30 a.m., in time to hand over the material for the PM's folder for the Arunachal Pradesh visit.

VISIT TO ITANAGAR AND INTERIOR AREAS

The next morning, the Prime Minister left for Itanagar. His visit to Arunachal Pradesh included visits to interior areas of the state as well as to the state capital Itanagar. In the interior areas he visited some bridges and agriculture-horticulture work done by NGOs and villagers. The Arunachal Pradesh government had been making special efforts to improve connectivity of its interior areas by constructing motorable roads and bridges. The government realised that only after roads were constructed would the farmers be able to access markets for selling their produce as well as for buying inputs needed by them. The PM appreciated the efforts of the engineers involved in building bridges. Some of these engineers were from southern India and were engaged in upgradation of the infrastructure in rural areas of Arunachal Pradesh.

It was evening when we reached Itanagar. The PM held meetings with the Chief Minister and his council of ministers, political leaders, and other organisations as per schedule. The Arunachal Pradesh government requested him for several sanctions and approvals for projects. These included sanction of Itanagar and Naharlagun Water Supply scheme, construction of a new airport at Itanagar, extension of national highway from Itanagar to Gohpur, a special grant for construction of Arunachal Pradesh Legislative Assembly for which the late Prime Minister Rajiv Gandhi had laid the foundation stone in 1986, and the sanction of two India Reserve Battalions for checking the activities of militants in the districts adjoining Nagaland.

CONTOURS OF PM'S STATEMENT

In five days, the Prime Minister had visited six of the states of the North-East and broadly knew the issues confronting each of them. Only Meghalaya was left for the last day. After the visit, he was to address a press conference at Guwahati to announce the new initiatives which the Government of India would undertake to give a developmental push to the North-East. It was late evening when all the meetings at Itanagar got over. Mr Yugandhar asked Mr Pillai and me to prepare the contours of the statement the Prime Minister should make in the press conference at the end of his tour of North-East on 27 October 1996.

Mr Pillai, Mr Yugandhar and I met the PM and discussed with him the important points to be included in the press statement. The PM gave his general approval to the proposals to be included and the special measures needed to give impetus to the economic development of the North-East. When we were coming out from the drawing room, Mr Yugandhar gave us detailed instructions and stated that whatever should be announced at the press conference should be substantial and must be remembered in the coming years as the 'Deve Gowda Mantra' for the development of the North-East. These initiatives, according to him, should lay the foundation for increased fund flow to the North-East and upgrade the infrastructure.

Later developments during the PM Vajpayee's tenure, such as setting up of a separate Ministry of Development of North Eastern Region (MDoNER) and a separate Non-Lapsable Central Pool of Resources (NLCPR) were based on the 27 October 1996 press statement of Prime Minister Deve Gowda at Guwahati.

Mr Pillai and I worked overtime to prepare the statement for the press conference. We wanted to ensure that all specific issues agreed to by the PM in all states as well as the general concerns of states and the Government of India were covered in it. Prime Minister Deve Gowda's visit had raised high expectations in the North-East. Former Prime Minister Narasimha Rao had visited the region only once, and that too up to Guwahati, during his five-year stint. There were sharp comparisons between the approaches of the two prime ministers towards the North-East. It was clear to all that PM Deve Gowda favoured the development of rural areas.

From Itanagar to Shillong, we travelled by helicopters and the press statement of PM was finalised partly during this journey. It was during this flight that I included the Maram to Phaibung road (later changed to Senapati to Phaibung) after consultation with G. K. Pillai. This road in Senapati district would connect remote areas called Lepaona and Chilevai areas of the Senapati district of Manipur. L. Jonathan, a local MLA and Minister who represented these areas had pressed for this road during PM's visit to Manipur. This road proved to be the most important infrastructure component which helped in the opening up of and the development of the remote areas of Manipur.

After landing at the air force base at Shillong, we were to be taken to the Raj Bhawan by road. The transport arrangements were not properly made by the state administration and were quite haphazard. A few of us were left behind and had to travel by a bus to Raj Bhawan. As Shillong did not have any bypass roads, all traffic had to per force pass through the Shillong town. Unfortunately, to keep up with the Prime Minister's convoy our bus driver too drove fast and once so recklessly that we almost met with an accident. I felt relieved when we finally reached the Raj Bhawan.

At the Raj Bhawan, the Prime Minister met up with the Chief Minister and his council of ministers, public representatives, NGOs, security personnel and state government officials. The state government requested for funds to complete the North Eastern Indira Gandhi Regional Institute of Health and Medical Sciences (NEIGRIHMS), for which the foundation stone was laid in 1986, funds for Shillong bypass road, upgradation of Umroi airport, extension of railway line in Meghalaya, widening of national highway up to Tura, construction of Dawki bridge connecting Meghalaya with Bangladesh, etc. At Shillong, we got the Prime Minister's press statement retyped and made copies for the press conference at Guwahati that evening.

6

NEW INITIATIVES FOR NORTH EASTERN REGION

The Prime Minister's press conference took place at the Guwahati airport on 27 October 1996. I had given a corrected version of the press statement to the PM's personal secretary. Unfortunately, in the hurry, some pages were photocopied upside down. The correct copy meant for the PM's speech was passed on to Ram Vilas Paswan and the PM got the one that was stapled wrong. He, however, did not lose his cool and read out some portions of the press statement. All media personnel received copies of the statement.

Even though the press conference was held in a makeshift arrangement near the tarmac, the impact of the press statement was huge. It was the beginning of new initiatives for the development of the North-East. People at the press conference were very happy and applauded the PM for his new and bold initiatives. The six-day tour of the North-East had been successful. The questions and answers in the press conference reflected it clearly.

The PM's statement entitled 'New Initiatives for North Eastern Region' contained major policy initiatives on important issues raised by the various states and other stakeholders with the Government of India from time to time. PM Deve Gowda's 'New Initiatives' requested for cooperation of all sections of the society and appealed to the youth to shun violence and come forward for discussion with the government. He gave an open invitation to all groups and individuals, including militant groups, to meet him without any preconditions and discuss their legitimate demands. At the same time, he firmly stated that violence would not be tolerated and would be put down with a heavy hand. He very rightly referred to the feeling of a loss of identity among various ethnic groups and of getting a stepmotherly treatment from the Government of India. He said he wanted to bridge the gap in the infrastructure development of the North-East and the rest of India.

There were state specific projects that were projected before the PM during the visit. The estimated cost of completion of the projects and schemes covered in the 'New Initiatives' was around Rs 6,200 crore. In addition to state specific schemes, the policy initiatives announced by the PM included:

- Setting up of a high-level commission to determine gaps in infrastructure and backlog in basic minimum services, and provision of additional funds to remove the gaps
- Setting up of a high-level committee to examine and study reasons for high level of unemployment among educated youth in the North-East and suggest specific measures for promoting employment among educated youth
- All Central ministries and departments to earmark at least 10 per cent of their budgets for specific programmes in the North-East
- Ministers and Secretaries of the Central ministries and departments, especially social sectors, petroleum, surface transport, railways, civil aviation, tourism and water resources would tour north-eastern states at least once in a quarter
- Improvement of railway services and completion of ongoing railway projects
- Full funding of important projects concerning highways, railways,

power and Numaligarh Refinery

- Increasing credit flow and setting of a special cell under deputy governor RBI to monitor increased credit flow in the North-East
- Strengthening of Central agencies engaged in promotion of agriculture, trade and industry such as NABARD
- A New Industrial Policy for the North-East
- Comprehensive water management and flood control measures
- Extension of Employment Assurance Scheme to all Blocks by 31 March 1997
- Extension of Border Area Development Programme to more areas
- Preparation of an Integrated Tourism Development Plan for the whole region
- An export promotion policy for the North-East, especially aimed at promotion of trade with South-East Asia
- Strengthening of institutional arrangements for control of AIDS, narco-trafficking and drug addiction

NABARD AND RIDF

The North-East is mostly an agriculture-based economy. In such regions, banks such as NABARD (National Bank for Agriculture and Rural Development) should have played a major role and funded agriculture and horticulture-based economic activities. Surprisingly, the funding from NABARD was very insignificant. During his visit, the Prime Minister realised this and specially desired that NABARD should increase its funding under Rural Infrastructure Development Fund (RIDF) to these states. He directed NABARD to fix targets of yearly loan disbursements so that the PMO could monitor the efforts made by its management in this regard.

A special cell was also set up in the RBI under Deputy Governor to suggest ways and means to increase credit flow to agriculture, industries and self-employment programmes in the North-East. RIDF credit proved very helpful to farmers and the states. This credit directly helped in improving rural infrastructure which increased agriculture productivity.

NORTH EASTERN DEVELOPMENT FINANCE CORPORATION (NEDFi)

To cater to the economic development needs of the North-East, the I. K. Borthakur Committee Report had recommended the formation of a North-Eastern Development Bank. Based on the recommendations made in this report, the then Finance Minister, Dr Manmohan Singh, in his Budget speech in March 1995 announced the setting up of a development bank for expediting the economic development of the north-eastern states of India. Pursuant to this, the North Eastern Development Finance Corporation Ltd (NEDFi) was formed on 9 August 1995 and formally inaugurated by Prime Minister Narasimha Rao on 23 February 1996. The Corporation was inaugurated with much fanfare and raised expectations of the people of the North-East.

NEDFi was created to provide financial assistance to micro, small, medium, and large enterprises for setting up industrial, infrastructure and agri-allied projects in the north-eastern region and microfinance through MFIs and NGOs. Besides financing, the Corporation was also to offer consultancy and advisory services to the state governments, private sector, and other agencies. NEDFi was also required to conduct sector or state specific studies under its Techno-Economic Development Fund (TEDF).

During PM Deve Gowda's tour it was noticed that activities of NEDFi were almost non-existent. None of the states mentioned anything about NEDFi and its usefulness. This was surprising since NEDFi was set up to play an important role in the economic development of the region. It became quite apparent that NEDFi was not playing its role as was conceptualised and its activities were mostly confined to Assam. Its annual lending was just about Rs 10 crore and there was an urgent need to scale up its operations several times if it had to make any contribution.

After the PM's visit, an increased target was set up and NEDFi was asked to submit monthly targets. It was made clear to its management that if it was lending Rs 20 crore or less to the region, there was no need of a separate organisation. A close watch was kept by the PMO on the progress and activities of NEDFi. As and when the progress of projects of the North-East was reviewed, the progress of NEDFi was invariably taken up. The increased emphasis from the Prime Minister pushed it to perform better and steadily lending by NEDFi also picked up.

FOLLOW-UP AT PMO

The North-East division of MHA printed about 50,000 copies of the 'New Initiatives for North Eastern Region' and distributed to all stakeholders, states and important agencies. A strict time frame was put in place for action under each point and important issues were monitored by the Secretary to PM. A cell was set up in PMO to regularly review and monitor the progress of these initiatives. The North-East division of MHA under G. K. Pillai actively reviewed and pursued the projects and schemes and provided monthly feedback to the PMO. Special meetings were convened with Secretaries of departments and heads of organisations in charge of projects and schemes and monitorable action plans were prepared and circulated to all state governments and concerned departments. Monthly progress reports were circulated to all states to know the correctness of the progress, as well as to solicit their cooperation for removing any bottlenecks in implementation.

Targets were fixed for credit for NABARD under RIDF and soon credit flow started increasing. An increased target was fixed for NEDFi for credit disbursement and it was advised to visit each state and create entrepreneurial awareness among the people for availing credit. The Employment Assurance Scheme and the Border Areas Development Programme were extended to more areas. This provided employment opportunities to the unemployed in the rural and hill areas.

An integrated tourist circuit was planned and put in place for increasing the flow of tourism to the area. The Ministry of Tourism had prepared special packages for tourists for the North-East. Special packages were prepared for government employees who were interested in availing leave travel concessions to visit any part of the country. Special emphasis was given to control drug trafficking and its regional structure was strengthened. Ministry of Health and Family Welfare increased fund flow for AIDS control and prepared specific plans for the vulnerable areas of the North-East.

Technology Mission on Horticulture consisting of four mini missions was started with full vigour. The purpose of the Mission was to develop better and high yielding varieties of fruits suitable for different areas of North-East, increasing acreage under fruits' cultivation, improving marketing and preservation of fruits, and setting up of fruit processing plants at different places in the region.

The Rajdhani train began its service from Dibrugarh to New Delhi. This was not only a boon for the people of Nagaland and Manipur but also for the officials in Delhi as senior officers started visiting the North-East frequently. Except for one or two schemes, all state-specific schemes were approved and their implementation started. Cooking gas bottling plants were set up in all states. The Numaligarh refinery, where work had come to a standstill due to lack of funds, was provided Rs 1,200 crore, leading to the restart of work and completion of the refinery. Some projects such as the Lower Subansiri Hydroelectric project were delayed because of environmental and forest clearances. However, the thrust from the PMO continued.

The 'New Initiatives for North Eastern Region' laid the foundation for expediting the development of the region. It continued as the guiding principle for development in the later years too, even after the addition of new schemes. The all-important fund called Non-Lapsable Central Pool of Resources (NLCPR), now the main resource available for funding infrastructure projects in the North-East region was created because of the guidelines laid down in the New Initiatives even though the population of the North-East was less than 5 per cent of the population of the country, the land area is about 8 per cent of the total area of the country. It was B.N. Yugandhar's suggestion that at least 10 per cent of Central funds should be spent in the North-East for reduction of infrastructural deficiencies in the region.

Later in 1999, during the tenure of PM Vajpayee, when NLCPR was constituted, the same arguments and concepts as were enunciated by PM Deve Gowda were used. The then Deputy Chairman of the Planning Commission, Jaswant Singh, was the one who suggested the concept of a Non-Lapsable Central Pool of Resources for the North-East and PM Vajpayee approved the same.

In pursuance of the Prime Minister's announcement, a high-level commission was appointed under the chairmanship of S.P. Shukla, Member, Planning Commission. The Commission was required to critically examine the backlog in respect to Basic Minimum Services in the seven north-eastern states and the gaps in important sectors of infrastructural development in the region, especially in power, communications, railways, roads, education, agriculture, etc. It also had to suggest policies, programmes and requirement of funds to bridge the gaps in infrastructural sectors. Mr Yugandhar was very particular about the progress of the BMSs, comprising of seven essential services primarily for rural and backward areas. These BMSs were regularly monitored in the PMO. The PM, too, was particular that different services under the BMSs were fully funded and the ministries and departments concerned of the government monitored them regularly.

The Shukla Commission submitted its report on 7 March 1997. It recommended an indicative outlay of Rs 93,619 crore for power, roads, railways, irrigation and flood control, agricultural research, commodity boards, broadcasting, handloom and handicraft, design and exhibition facilities, tourism, renovation of cultural sites, higher education, external trade, etc. The Commission also recommended Rs 17,995 crore for all the seven states during the Ninth Five Year Plan. The Commission's report included all projects and schemes both in Central and state sectors which were of priority. The Planning Commission also started providing funds for these projects and schemes recommended by the Commission.

The 'New Initiatives for North Eastern Region' was the result of the concern and dedication of H. D. Deve Gowda for the upliftment of remote and rural areas of the North-East. No PM had ever visited North-East for this long at one stretch, or listened to the concerns of the people. B.

N. Yugandhar helped in preparing a document, which till today is quoted as the basic document for the economic and infrastructural development of the region. As a result, the fund flow to the North-East increased substantially. Many Central ministries and departments started paying special attention to the projects and schemes in the North-East.

It would not be wrong to say that the initiative of PM Deve Gowda opened the door for accelerated development of the North-East. It really became a 'Deve Gowda Mantra' for development of the North-East, as had been rightly suggested by Mr Yugandhar in Itanagar on 26 October 1996.

PRIME MINISTER I. K. GUJRAL

(APRIL 1997 – MARCH 1998)

Author's Take

"

I. K. Gujral was a political lightweight. His main strength lay in external affairs. A number of Indian Foreign Service officers were appointed to assist him as soon as he took over as the PM. Since he had not worked in any state government, he depended on the expert advice of two senior retired Indian Administrative Service officers of the Punjab cadre—his Principal Secretary, N.N. Vohra IAS (Retd.) and T.K.A. Nair IAS (Retd.) Secretary to PM. He continued with the initiatives taken by his predecessor H.D. Deve Gowda. A soft-spoken man, he was a true democrat and a thorough gentleman. He had a soft corner for Punjab and did whatever he could do to help the state of Punjab.

"

7

PM GUJRAL: THE KIND-HEARTED DEMOCRAT

H.D. DEVE GOWDA LOSES CONFIDENCE VOTE

By the end of March 1997, it was becoming clear that relations between Sitaram Kesri, president of Indian National Congress (Indira) [INC (I)], and Prime Minister Deve Gowda had soured quite a lot. It was clear that Sitaram Kesri could pull the plug on the government any time. In April 1997, the Congress party withdrew its support from the United Front government led by PM Deve Gowda on the ground that the Prime Minister did not consult them on important matters relating to governance. The confidence vote was discussed in the Lok Sabha where PM Deve Gowda gave a spirited reply. On 11 April 1997, he lost the confidence vote in the Lok Sabha by a big margin as the INC(I) voted against the government. There were 190 ayes against 338 noes in the vote of confidence.

In this process, both the main players, Kesri and Deve Gowda proved to be the biggest losers. While Kesri, who had hoped to lure away some partners of the United Front, was unable to make any dent in the unity of the United Front, Deve Gowda who had hoped to split some INC(I) members to his side, could not do so too. The INC(I) did not have any other alternative of forming a government and agreed to support another United Front government under a new leader on the condition that it would be consulted before any important decision was taken and would not be marginalised.

H. D. DEVE GOWDA – PM FOR RURAL AREAS AND FARMERS

Prime Minister Deve Gowda was not only pro farmers but also pro rural areas. Though he was not fluent in Hindi and needed assistance while speaking in the Hindi belt states, he focused on development of all rural areas to improve the condition of the farmers and remove infrastructural deficiencies of hilly and backward areas such as the North-East, Jammu and Kashmir, etc.

I. K. GUJRAL TAKES OVER AS PRIME MINISTER

After the vote of confidence there was hectic activity to elect a new leader of the United Front. As chairman of the United Front Steering Committee, Chandrababu Naidu's role was crucial in any discussion or government formation. The political activities of government formation shifted to Andhra Pradesh Bhawan in New Delhi. After a few days, the United Front elected Inder Kumar Gujral as their new leader and he was sworn in as Prime Minister on 21 April 1997. He was acceptable to the INC (I) and other parties for his non-controversial nature as against strong contenders like Lalu Prasad Yadav and Mulayam Singh Yadav.

These were the days when the CBI had become very active and several cases were being investigated by CBI against important politicians, including Lalu Prasad Yadav. In fact, the way CBI cases were appearing daily in newspapers it was creating fear among politicians and bureaucrats. With a coalition government at the helm, the political situation was not stable. Mr Naidu coordinated with the various United Front constituents on important issues to ensure the survival of the government.

DESTABILISING FACTORS

When I. K. Gujral became Prime Minister, there were many factors that could easily destabilise the government. The foremost being that it had many constituents and most of them had their regional agendas. Moreover, the government was surviving on the outside support of the INC (I), which had its own national and regional agenda. At the state level, many of the regional constituents of the United Front found INC (I) as their opponent political party. These contradictions were making the running of the government very difficult.

With the CBI investigating high profile cases, including some against high profile people in the government, the Supreme Court was keeping a close watch on these cases. It was difficult for the government not to give the prosecution sanction under any circumstances. At the same time public opinion was building up for free and fair investigation of these cases so that the politically powerful would also face the law.

Several applications had been filed in the courts for freeing CBI from the control of the Government of India. To make matters worse, Vineet Narain, a prominent journalist and anticorruption activist, had filed a Public Interest Litigation (PIL) in the Supreme Court demanding full autonomy for the CBI so that the cases against important persons could be investigated and prosecution sanctions were not delayed. His PIL was being heard on a regular basis in the Supreme Court. It was also during this period that the Governor of Bihar had given the prosecution sanction against Lalu Prasad Yadav on the request of the CBI. The corruption case against a heavy weight like Lalu Prasad was proving to be too embarrassing for the government to handle.

The Jain Commission inquiring into the conspiracy theory in the Rajiv Gandhi assassination had submitted its report to the government in August 1997. There were allegations that a portion of the Report was leaked. There were also reports that the Jain Commission had blamed the Dravida Munnetra Kazhagam (DMK) amongst others for tacitly supporting the Tamil militants accused in Rajiv Gandhi's assassination. In brief, there were too many destabilising factors for the Gujral government from the day it took office. The political environment, the relations between the INC (I) and some partners of the United Front was filled with too much animosity for the government to last long.

N.N. VOHRA TAKES OVER AS PRINCIPAL SECRETARY

When I. K. Gujral took office, many IFS officers joined the PMO. These officers had either served with the PM earlier or served with senior officers who had served with the PM when he was Minister of External Affairs in the Deve Gowda Ministry. N. N. Vohra belonged to Punjab cadre. He had the distinction of serving as the Defence Secretary as well as Home Secretary of India in the span of his career. He took over as Principal Secretary to the PM. This was my first opportunity to work with him. I had heard that he was a very hard task master and meticulous in his work. He seemed to be ideally suited to serve the post at that time.

N. N. Vohra's appointment was all the more important as the PM had mostly served either in MEA or in Ministry of Information and Broadcasting (I&B) and did not have experience of working in the social and infrastructure sectors, which is important for running a government. My working experience with Mr Vohra was very pleasant. I found that he never minced words while giving suggestion or taking decisions. T. K. A. Nair, an officer of the Punjab cadre, also joined the PMO as Secretary to PM.

About the same time, a certain DIG-level IPS officer of the Haryana cadre also began working as Officer on Special Duty (OSD) to the PM. I had not seen any order issued by the establishment branch of the PMO about the appointment of this OSD. It seemed that the IPS officer had joined PMO through some personal acquaintances of the PM. I also heard that the MHA was not in the loop about this IPS officer joining the PMO. Since MHA is the cadre controlling authority for deputation of IPS officers, the appointment of this IPS was irregular. MHA should have been involved in his posting in the PMO.

The said officer met me a few times in my office, and on one occasion wanted to know about some case referred to the PMO by MHA. Even though he seemed a decent person and always well behaved, yet, there is a natural tendency to be cautious when someone asks for specific sensitive case. It rang alarm bells in my mind. Neither did I tell him anything about the case nor showed him anything. On an earlier occasion, while talking with some of my colleagues I had come to know that there were instructions from the Principal Secretary to not show any file or discuss such cases with any OSD or anyone else as they could leak out information.

During 1996 and 1997, many sensitive cases were appearing in the newspapers on a daily basis and I was dealing with some of them. We used to send files and papers to the Principal Secretary who would then send them to the PM or decide at his level. If any person saw any file when it was with the personal staff of the PM, it was their problem. We were very careful in maintaining secrecy of sensitive papers. A serious and sensational case of the mid 1980s in the PMO during the tenure of Rajiv Gandhi had raised caution in the PMO. The key personnel in that case were from the office of P. C. Alexander, Principal Secretary to the Prime Minister. Documents were photocopied and passed on to adversaries. That case had spread to the Ministries of Finance and Defence too. Thereafter, PMO had become very careful in maintaining secrecy of its documents. So much so that photocopying of papers in the PMO now requires the signatures of senior officers.

VINEET NARAIN CASE

The matter regarding freeing CBI from government influence used to appear in newspapers daily. The public opinion was in favour of free and fair investigation of corruption cases against heavy weight politicians. The Supreme Court was hearing Vineet Narain's PIL on the investigation of high-profile cases by CBI. The PIL made a strong case for insulating CBI from government influence. During the hearing, the Attorney General of India represented the government. The Supreme Court wanted the government's position on all issues and matters relating to structure, appointment of Director of CBI and other officers as well as functioning of the CBI. The Attorney General presented the government's position after the views were firmed up by the Prime Minister's Office.

As Joint Secretary, I used to service the meetings taken by Principal Secretary with Home Secretary, Secretary Personnel, Secretary Law and Director CBI for formulating Government of India's position before the Supreme Court. The issues relating to autonomy for CBI had many pros and cons and the discussions spread over several meetings. During one of those meetings the Director CBI R. C. Sharma came on crutches having met with an unfortunate accident in Guwahati. When the matter relating to autonomy for CBI was under discussion, I remember hearing him telling the other members clearly that complete autonomy for CBI from government would not be appropriate. According to him, there were reports that 20-30 per cent of the lower staff in CBI was not honest and full autonomy would create serious problems for functioning of the government officers.

Within a few weeks, the government's position on the various issues was placed before the Supreme Court. It was a watered-down version of the autonomy for CBI. The view was to place the CBI under Central Vigilance Commission (CVC) and appointment of Director to be done through a high-level committee under the prime minister. The Supreme Court took into consideration the advice of the Attorney General and announced its judgment broadly as per the views formulated by the government. In any case it was a good beginning for the working of CBI with least influence from the government.

CEASEFIRE WITH NSCN (IM)

Since mid-1995, the government, at the highest level, had been in touch with NSCN (IM) leadership. As a result of discussions and talks between the two, on 25 July 1997, a ceasefire agreement was signed between the Government of India and NSCN (IM). This was one of the biggest achievements of the Gujral government. NSCN (IM) was the largest, well-armed and strong militant organisation in the North-East. As per reports they had supported other militant groups too. The general assessment was that when the settlement with NSCN (IM) was finally concluded, there would be peace in the North-East. The ceasefire has been extended from time to time and continues to be in force. The talks and its details are kept secret. To help in the talks, a senior person acceptable to both parties has been working as an interlocutor. There is also a chairman of the Ceasefire Monitoring Group who looks into complaints of ceasefire violations by either party.

Even though I was in charge of matters relating to MHA, the issues relating to talks were directly handled by the interlocutor with the Principal Secretary to PM. After the ceasefire agreement was signed, I compiled all papers and files available in the PMO and shared it with the interlocutor so that he had full information about the discussions with the NSCN (IM).

The first notings related to the first meeting of former Prime Minister Narasimha Rao with NSCN (IM) leaders in 1995, somewhere in Europe. The then Principal Secretary had written the brief record of that discussion behind the file cover with ball point pen. The people present or mentioned in the discussion were mentioned by their initials. This first meeting had recorded two important points, which I will mention here, as these do not make any difference to the progress of talks which are underway between the government and NSCN (IM). The first point was that talks would be held at the highest level (prime ministerial level) in the government, which means the person taking a view on NSCN (IM) demands would be the prime minister and nobody below him. The second was a reference to the statement of former Prime Minister Morarji Desai about the Nagas. I do not want to write anything else in this book about the talks.

THE AIR VICE MARSHAL CASE

Prime Minister Gujral used to visit Jalandhar quite often. He had decided to contest from Jalandhar Lok Sabha constituency during the parliamentary elections. One day, I received a telephone call from the PM's personal staff camping at Jalandhar. I was told that the PM had asked for a particular Air Vice Marshal belonging to the Sikh community, who was not recommended by the Ministry of Defence, to be included in the panel of approved officers for promotion in the PMO. This was not correct. If this was done in the PMO, it would be called manipulation, attract widespread criticism, and the matter could land in a court for scrutiny too.

If the Services Board of the Ministry of Defence and the Cabinet Secretary had not recommended his name, there was no way it could be inserted in the list in the PMO. I immediately went to Mr Vohra and briefed him about the telephone call. Mr Vohra told me firmly, 'No way. If the old man (referring to the PM) wants to include any new name in the approved list, which has not been recommended by the Ministry of Defence and Services Board, let him write in his own hand in the PMO file and give reasons himself for including a new name in the list. Officers in PMO cannot do this'. I conveyed back this message to Jalandhar. There was a sudden silence on the other side. It seemed the people lobbying for promotion of the Sikh officer developed cold feet and did not want to pursue the matter further. The matter ended there.

I too am a Sikh, but my religion has taught me to fight for truth. I was sure that the PM would never ask such a thing on his own. There must be people in Jalandhar who must have lobbied with him and pressurised him. Later, in March 2002, I read in the newspapers about the same Sikh officer when he was compulsorily retired from the Air Force for using political patronage to further his career. He got a letter written by a political person from Punjab for a posting in the Western Command. I felt bad when I read the news. It seemed the officer was a habitual manipulator and that his conduct was not suitable of the position he was holding. If I was in Jalandhar when such a request was made, I would have advised the PM not to encourage such manipulations by the officer and nipped the matter in the bud. Since it was not done, the officer used the same tactic to get a better posting, and finally had to face the sack.

KGOE

The PMO, as mentioned earlier, is a zero-error place and those who are not careful with facts and figures could have difficulty in advising the PM properly. A tiny example illustrates this well. The Prime Minister was to address the Parliament on various issues, including energy matters. Based on written materials received from the ministries of Petroleum and Natural Gas, Coal and Power I prepared a brief speech for him. I was aware that he should speak in a language that most parliamentarians could understand and appreciate. Since the units of energy in Electricity, Petroleum and Coal are different, to establish equivalency and make the comparisons as well as aggregation easy, there are equivalence units in energy that are used often. One such unit often used wherever coal is compared to petroleum is called kilogramme of oil equivalent (kgoe), in which the energy contents of petroleum and coal could be compared.

The draft of the PM's statement was prepared and sent to his personal staff. However, I did not want to take any chance so I went to the parliament house to check if any assistance was needed while briefing the PM. I was pleasantly surprised when told that 'KGOE' was a spelling mistake and hence all sentences with those words had been deleted. I told them that the 'KGOE' had been expanded in the first sentence and would need to be expanded wherever these words appear. Without establishing equivalence between coal and oil/petroleum, the whole concept of substitutability and aggregation of the total energy requirement of the country would not be explained with clarity. India has enough coal reserves and a part of the statement was laying emphasis on coal exploration and indicating equivalency of coal quantity with petroleum products and natural gas. The Prime Minister's speech would be meaningless in Parliament without these words.

I realised that if freshers among the prime minister's personal staff handled paperwork, there were chances of serious mistakes happening. From then on, I made sure to check with the personal staff about the issues which they felt I should brief the Prime Minister. I did not want any incorrect facts or figures or statements coming out from the PMO.

PETROLEUM PRODUCTS vs CRUDE OIL

In 1997, India was importing crude oil and petroleum products. A large quantity of these entered India through Mumbai Port. Some newspapers reported unusually long delays in the offloading of crude oil and petroleum products at the port. It appeared that the port lacked quick or mechanised off-loading facilities. As a result, higher demurrage charges were being paid for tankers waiting at sea for their turns for unloading.

I analysed this based on the data obtained from the Ministry of Petroleum and Natural Gas. I found out that the expenditure incurred as demurrage in respect of crude oil per barrel was less than one third of demurrage charges paid for petroleum products per barrel. It meant that the Mumbai Port did not have smooth mechanism to off-load petroleum products. This was possibly because of the changes of tanks and pipelines required for different products such as HSD and Petrol etc. More time was required to offload petroleum products as compared to the time taken to offload same quantity of crude oil. I briefed the Secretary, Ministry of Petroleum and Natural Gas about this issue. The Ministry initiated action with relevant port authorities to improve the offloading of petroleum products. I was also informed that within the next few years, petroleum refining capacity in India would increase substantially, and possibly exceed our demand and there would be no import of petroleum products into the country after that.

8

VISITS TO J&K AND THE NORTH-EAST

WANDHAMA MASSACRE

The Prime Minister wanted to visit the Wandhama village in Ganderbal district of Jammu and Kashmir where twenty-three Kashmiri Pandits were massacred on the night of 25 January 1998. Of the 24 males in the village that night all, except a young boy, were killed. The journey to Wandhama had a night halt at Udhampur. From there the journey was by helicopters through a very rugged terrain. The Governor and the Chief Minister of Jammu and Kashmir accompanied the Prime Minister.

During the stopover at Udhampur, the Prime Minister took me aside and placing his hands on my shoulders, asked me to relook at the ex-gratia payments being given to the families of the victims of terrorist violence in Kashmir. He wanted to increase this as the existing ex-gratia was too low and referred to those victims who were the earning members of their families. I could sense his sincerity and concern on these issues.

The Wandhama village is surrounded by hills on three sides with a small rivulet flowing on the fourth. When we reached the village, there was an eerie calm. The villagers who came to meet the Prime Minister said that the Kashmiri Pandits in the village had stayed on in spite of tremendous threats and were a symbol of communal harmony in the village. They had resisted migration at a time when other Pandit families were leaving the violence-hit state. PM Gujral met the lone surviving boy who had hid himself under wood and haystacks that fateful night. Even if any grant or assistance was to be given, there was nobody left in the families to whom the ex-gratia grants could be given. It was a very painful sight to see the burnt down houses of the Kashmiri Pandits. The militants intended to completely remove the community from this region. The government feared that this massacre was sending a message loud and clear to Hindus in interior areas of the state to leave. It was also exposing the helplessness of the government in protecting the Pandits living in isolated pockets.

It was indeed difficult for the government to protect every family. On the flight back to Delhi, I met the PM in his cabin. He was worried and was wondering how to control such killings. He pointedly asked me, 'Can anything be done to stop such massacres in the interior areas of Kashmir?' My reply was, 'Sir, the Kashmiri Pandits stay in small numbers in villages in interior Kashmir. The government and its agencies cannot protect each village. The Muslim majority in these villages would have to provide the protection to the Kashmiri Pundits.' The Prime Minister concurred. His visit to this remote village, witness to a massacre, showed the government's support and sympathy. Other than that, there was no immediate solution to the killings in remote villages.

MANIPUR BOYCOTTS PM'S VISIT

Prime Minister Gujral, like his predecessor, was keen to visit the North-East. His visit was planned to Assam, Tripura and Manipur. He was accompanied by the Union Home Minister Indrajit Gupta. The visits to Tripura and Assam were routine and the states requested adequate funds to complete the ongoing projects. Just before leaving Agartala for Manipur, the Home Secretary, who was travelling with us, informed that the militant groups in Manipur had given a call for a bandh and boycott of the PM's visit as had been done during PM Deve Gowda's visit. The road from Imphal airport to Raj Bhavan was spilled with lubricating oil. The state government, however, informed that the oil spill would be cleaned by evening and there was no threat to the visit. It was late afternoon when the PM reached Imphal. The roads were heavily barricaded and only a handful of spectators stood waving flags to welcome him.

In the evening, both the Prime Minister and the Home Minister met with state political leaders and representatives of NGOs in the banquet hall of the Raj Bhawan. They went around meeting everyone present, shook hands and discussed the issues they wanted to raise. In the morning, a press conference was arranged in the dining room of the banquet hall. As is the protocol, based on MHA's prepared list, the PM was briefed about some sensitive questions that could be asked in the press conference. I too advised the PM to be very careful while answering questions about Manipur's territorial integrity and the on-going peace talks with NSCN (IM).

The press conference led to a bit of confusion due to the incessant questions from the press. The Prime Minister was seated in the centre of a long table. While answering queries posed by journalists to his left, he was also asked a question by a journalist from his right side about his views on territorial integrity of Manipur in the light of peace talks with NSCN (IM). As it was bound to happen, he could not hear the question properly. His reply that the government would look into this. This reply led most mediapersons present there to assume that the Government of India was unable to give categorical assurance about the territorial integrity of Manipur and that it was still a negotiable issue. This led to uproar. The PM's clarification in the end pacified the situation.

JAIN COMMISSION REPORT

On 28 August 1997, the Commission under Justice M. C. Jain set up to look into the circumstances of and the conspiracy leading to Rajiv Gandhi's assassination, presented its report to Indrajit Gupta, the Union Home Minister. After a few days, the Prime Minister was asked if the report could be processed in consultation with different line departments. The PM was quite clear on its processing. He knew that the findings of the Commission could destabilise his government and said, 'Before jumping into the ditch, I want to know how deep the ditch is?' He did not want the Report to be circulated as he wanted to understand its contents and its implications for his government. He wanted to screen the Report through his close confidantes before proposing a course of action. Already some findings of the Report were leaked to the media. Since some of the critical findings, such as encouraging and giving safe sanctuary to LTTE cadres in Tamil Nadu faulted DMK, the main ally of the United Front government, serious problems were in store for the Gujral government.

The Jain Commission Report was tabled in the Parliament on 20 November 1997. The Parliament witnessed angry scenes. The INC(I) demanded the sacking of DMK ministers from the Union Cabinet as the Report partially blamed DMK for encouraging the growth of LTTE cadres in Tamil Nadu, responsible for the assassination of the former prime minister. Prime Minister Gujral did not agree to the demand and as a result the INC(I) withdrew its support to the government. I.K. Gujral resigned, and in his letter to President K.R. Narayanan he said, 'My government has lost its majority and does not want to continue in office on moral grounds'. While resigning the Prime Minister did not call for the dissolution of Lok Sabha. The President accepted the resignation but asked him to continue in an interim capacity.

Chandrababu Naidu had already stated that all the constituents of the United Front would neither support the INC(I) nor the BJP. The President of India had no option but to dissolve the Lok Sabha on 4 December 1997 and triggering snap elections. I. K. Gujral continued as interim prime minister during the conduct of elections.

THE KIND-HEARTED DEMOCRAT

Working with Prime Minister Gujral was a very pleasant experience. He would listen carefully to all the suggestions given and give each of them due consideration. I found him to be a hardcore democrat who cherished democratic values and believed in the rule of law. During the course of a closed meeting with senior security officials, one of them informed that the leader of a militant organisation from India and living in a foreign country was giving orders to militants operating in India and inciting violence against security forces. He said to the Prime Minister, 'Sir, the foreign government, where that particular leader is staying, has given a hint that he could be bumped off in a vehicular incident if the Government of India so desired. The violent incidents in India would then reduce substantially.' The Prime Minister shot back, 'India is a democratic country where rule of law prevails. The Government of India would follow the due process of law and not resort to any unlawful means to eliminate militants as otherwise there will not be any difference between the Government of India and the militants.' Closing the discussion, he said, 'Peace achieved through democratic means lasts forever as compared to peace imposed by use of force.' There was no more talk on that topic.

As I came out of that meeting, I was full of praise for the Prime Minister as a person who had a strong grounding in the democratic system of governance. He was fair in his dealings with friends and foes alike. To me it appeared that he did not have any foes. He was more like a fatherly figure who could not punish and penalise anybody. But politically he was a lightweight and many people tried to take advantage of this weakness.

PRIME MINISTER
ATAL BIHARI VAJPAYEE – I

(MARCH 1998 – OCTOBER 1999)

Author's Take

"

Politically powerful, Atal Bihari Vajpayee was not only the unchallenged leader of Bharatiya Janata Party but was also equally at ease with leaders of all political parties. He was an excellent listener. He heard every point of view carefully, rarely interrupting. He was genuinely interested in taking all political parties along in important government decisions. He inducted seasoned bureaucrats into the PMO, which helped in taking far-reaching decisions in opening important sectors of economy. He took great initiatives to normalise relations with Pakistan. Nuclear tests at Pokhran which is generally referred to as Pokhran II was the most important decision of his period.

"

9

ATAL BIHARI VAJPAYEE TAKES OVER AS PRIME MINISTER

FRESH LOK SABHA ELECTIONS

After the United Front Government headed by Prime Minister Gujral collapsed, the three main political blocs, the United Front, the INC(I) and the BJP failed to form a realigned coalition government. President K.R. Narayanan dissolved the Lok Sabha on 4 December 1997 and called for general elections to the Lok Sabha. The Election Commission issued a notification to hold elections in February and March 1998.

RESULTS OF ELECTIONS TO LOK SABHA

The general elections saw a three-way fight between INC(I), the United Front and the BJP. The main campaign issues were how to achieve political stability, tackle corruption and rejuvenate the country's economy. For improving the economy, the INC(I) adhered to its pro-reform platform of recent years, favouring foreign investment and loosening of state controls on the insurance sector. The BJP, for its part, championed economic nationalism and promised to shield domestic industry from international competition. It advocated restricting direct investment to non-priority areas. Local, down-to-earth issues such as creation of employment opportunities, improving public services, safe drinking water, electricity, etc. assumed equal importance in the minds of the voters across the country.

Opinion polls initially favoured the BJP, but the INC(I) also made a comeback when Sonia Gandhi, widow of Rajiv Gandhi, entered the fray and campaigned for the party. Some forecasters predicted another hung parliament with no single party or a political bloc securing an absolute majority. When the elections results were announced, the BJP and its allies won a total of 252 seats while the United Front and its allies got only 97. The INC(I) led by Sitaram Kesri and its allies secured 165. Subsequently, the BJP got support from other parties and increased its strength to 286 and staked claim to form the government.

A BJP-LED GOVERNMENT

On 19 March 1998, a BJP government led by Atal Bihari Vajpayee was sworn in. This was the first time that I would work under a BJP dispensation. In May 1998, the National Democratic Alliance (NDA)—a coalition of 13 political parties led by BJP—was formed. When Vajpayee took over, the main topic of discussion in PMO was about the choice of Principal Secretary to PM. Everybody in the PMO was ready to hazard a guess. Most of the old hands in PMO had expected Bishan Narain Tandon who was Principal Secretary to PM Vajpayee during his 13-day government to assume the post. Some others pointed out that his advancing age would not make him eligible. Even in 1996 when he was principal secretary, the officers who worked with him found him too old to perform his duties efficiently. The appointment of principal secretary and the private secretary to the PM are very important for the joint secretaries, directors and deputy secretaries working in the PMO.

These are key positions and the people holding these positions make a lot of difference in the functioning, disposal of work and decision-making in PMO. Naturally, all PMO officers were eagerly waiting for the appointment.

This time, the BJP-led NDA government was likely to be in power for a long period. In 1996, the officers in PMO as well as the general public knew very well that the BJP government would not last long as the INC(I) along with the United Front had a big majority. In 1998, however, there was a sea change. The BJP won a sizeable number of seats. Some PMO officers expected the influence of RSS and its affiliates in the functioning of government and more so in the working of the PMO. One way the RSS agenda could be implemented was to replace the existing officers with officers who were more sympathetic to RSS and BJP. Hence, people at the PMO thought there would be possible transfer of officers from the PMO to other ministries, departments or to their parent cadres.

I had joined PMO about a year and half back and wondered about my transfer to any other ministry or organisation. At that time, we were not aware that the PMO under PM Vajpayee would function in a fair and apolitical manner. I still remember the fearless way in which we worked in the PMO under him. We never hesitated to give our views or advice, or write notes on PMO files, which we felt were correct for the use of the PM, and these were all appreciated by PM Vajpayee. The atmosphere in the PMO under PM Vajpayee helped us in giving our best. These were my best years in service.

A NEW PRINCIPAL SECRETARY

Brajesh Mishra took over as Principal Secretary. Nobody in the PMO knew him or had speculated that he would assume the post. Brajesh Mishra had joined the IFS in 1951. He served as Chargé d'affaires in Beijing after the 1962 Sino-Indian War and was later India's Ambassador to Indonesia. He was also Ambassador and India's Permanent Representative in Geneva apart from serving as India's Permanent Representative to the

United Nations from June 1979 to April 1981. In April 1991, Brajesh Mishra joined the BJP and became head of its foreign policy cell. Before becoming Principal Secretary, he resigned from the BJP.

I found Brajesh Mishra to be very clear-headed and forthright in his approach. He was very accessible and listened to whatever points were being made in meetings. As he had served in the IFS throughout his life, he did not need much advice from MEA about issues relating to external affairs. He gave us a lot of freedom to handle ministries and departments which we handled with the support of the Secretary to PM. He always supported us and encouraged us to perform better. Brajesh Mishra was very quick in decision-making. I never saw him delay any file or case for more than a few minutes. He was very powerful, and many Cabinet ministers used to meet him to seek his advice or even his blessings on important matters. By the time PM Vajpayee's tenure was ending in 2004, Brajesh Mishra was considered one of the most powerful principal secretaries the PMO had ever seen.

SECRETARY TO PM

T.K.A. Nair, who was Secretary to PM I.K. Gujral, continued working with PM Vajpayee. After some months Nair left PMO and joined as Chairman of Public Enterprises Selection Board (PESB) and N.K. Singh was appointed as Officer on Special Duty in PMO.

PRIVATE SECRETARIES TO PM

During his six years, there were a number of private secretaries who assisted the PM. By this time, a tradition had been set to have one of the private secretaries from the IFS. The other could be from IAS or any other Central service with preference given to IAS. This system was quite useful as IFS officers were able to coordinate matters of foreign affairs, visiting dignitaries and protocol matters. The first private secretary who came along with PM Vajpayee was Shakti Sinha, an IAS officer of AGMUT (Arunachal Pradesh–Goa–Mizoram–Union Territories) cadre, who had a distinguished career in the service. Shakti Sinha had full confidence of the PM. It was given that Shakti Sinha would be PS to PM. He was a very pleasant person and welcomed officers in his chamber. I always found him smiling despite his busy schedule. A few years later, he went on deputation to a World Bank posting in Washington and then a UN mission in Afghanistan. Other private secretaries included Ajay Bisaria IFS, Anandrajan IRS, R.P. Singh IAS, etc.

PMO A NON-POLITICAL OFFICE, SAYS PM

After a few days of taking over, Prime Minister Vajpayee met all officers in the meeting room next to his office in South Block. After introductions and pleasantries, we broadly informed him about the work we handled. He encouraged us to work sincerely and with dedication. I clearly remember a few lines that he spoke about working in the PMO. Speaking in Hindi he said, 'I had thought that the PMO functioning was more like a political office, but I have seen that the PMO works like any other government office without any political influences. I want the PMO to work that way and I am happy. When I was outside the PMO, I had a different perception of its functioning. Congratulation to all of you and keep on working that way.' His words indeed had a profound impact on our performance and morale.

The Prime Minister did not want the PMO officers to be exposed to the media. He might have had his own reasons for this. One incident reflected his approach. In relation to a news story in a southern magazine in March 2001 about overindulgence of PMO in some projects, the Principal Secretary and N.K. Singh, OSD to PM, decided to hold a press conference and provide clarifications on the issues mentioned. N.K. Singh took one of my colleagues and me to a press conference in the PIB room in Shastri Bhawan. After the press conference, I was told that the PM had expressed his unhappiness to Brajesh Mishra over the presence of two joint secretaries in a press conference. He wanted the PMO officers to be away from public gaze.

ASHOK SAIKIA IAS

Ashok Saikia, an IAS officer of 1971 batch of Assam-Meghalaya cadre, had held important assignments within and outside India and worked with distinction. He was the only Joint Secretary who was brought in by the Prime Minister to the PMO. All other officers were retained as they were. Saikia had worked in social and agriculture sectors in India and was always well informed about daily happenings in Indian bureaucratic circles. He was close to the PM, who we came to hear was his local guardian when Saikia was a student in Delhi. In fact, Saikia was the only person in PMO who did not need PM's approval to enter his office.

Saikia was always conscious about issues which could adversely affect the image of PMO and acted firmly and swiftly when he sensed something wrong was happening. He was closer to the PM, perhaps, even more than Principal Secretary Brajesh Mishra.

Saikia had a soft corner for north-eastern states with respect to all issues, be they related to sanction of economic development projects or helping officers of NE cadres in getting postings in Delhi or any other miscellaneous purpose. I always enjoyed working with him. He was pleasant to talk with and helpful in sorting out complicated issues. I saw many officers visiting him and lobbying with him for better postings in the government and abroad. Many politicians from the North-East used to visit him and his sources of information were very diverse. I also used to see some ministers sitting with him in his office. Even though I was the Nodal Officer for coordination of various issues of the north-eastern states, he never asked me to do any favour for any person from North-East or Assam. He always supported my initiatives for development of North-East. Whenever junior officers had problems, they approached him for help. His posting as Joint Secretary and later on as Additional Secretary reduced the influence of the private secretary to PM.

TWIN ROLES FOR PRINCIPAL SECRETARY

In November 1998, Brajesh Mishra was also appointed as National Security Advisor (NSA) to PM. This seemed a correct decision, primarily because a single decision-making focal point in the PMO, with respect to external affairs matters and security issues seemed a better approach. The Principal Secretary could consult Secretaries and other officers of MEA, MHA and Ministry of Defence. Since Brajesh Mishra was well experienced and had excellent relations with all, he was able to advise the PM much better in his twin roles.

Every year the Principal Secretary used to host a lunch in the lawns of his official residence in the month of December, where he used to invite diplomats, ministers and senior officials. This would give an opportunity to diplomats and officials to know more about one another. I found these lawn luncheons to be one of the best opportunities where informal discussions took place on foreign relations, economic development and security related issues. I attended four to five such lunches and still carry pleasant memories. In the course of these lunches, ministers could be seen discussing matters with diplomats of the USA, China, Russia, etc., in the warmth of the December sun. These lunch parties highlighted the personal rapport, vast influence and diplomatic skills of Brajesh Mishra.

THE NON-EXISTENT INFLUENCE OF RSS

When we are outside the PMO, we do not know its functioning and imagine many things about its working, file processing and method of decision-making. I too had imagined that with the BJP-led government coming to power, the RSS would exert its influence in the functioning of PMO. There were also fears that the decision-making in PMO under BJP could be influenced by RSS thinking directly or indirectly. After working for a few months under the government, I realised that there was no difference in the functioning of PMO. The Vajpayee tenure was same as it was during Deve Gowda and Gujral periods. In fact, during the Vajpayee period the decision-making was much quicker and firm. The coalition partners of the NDA were under a party, which had majority seats in Parliament. Moreover, Prime Minister Vajpayee commanded overwhelming respect as a statesman and was acceptable even to Opposition parties.

The absence of overt influence of RSS functionaries was a pleasant surprise to me. While the members of RSS could be meeting the PM as other citizens, I never noticed any attempt being made to meet the PM regularly to influence his, or the PMO decision-making process. I think the credit for this goes to the Prime Minister, who wanted to provide governance as per the Common Minimum Programme (CMP) agreed to by NDA partners.

AN ERA OF QUICK DECISION-MAKING

Within a month or so, the decision-making in PMO picked up speed. I found the ACC proposals cleared on the day of their receipt. Regarding routine matters or where PMO could not add value to decisions, or where the proposals used to reach it through a well-laid-out procedure, the PM as well as the Principal Secretary were very fast in clearing these proposals. Only in those cases, where there were some differences among different ministries, departments, agencies of the government, or where PMO had a different view on the matter, the decision-making used to be somewhat delayed or took time, as these required proper examination.

A few officers in the PMO, who were there during the Narasimha Rao government and continued working during the Vajpayee government, used to compare the average time taken in simple personnel matters relating to ACC during the tenures of both governments. The proposals which used to take weeks and months during the Rao period were being cleared in a matter of days in the Vajpayee tenure. The quick decision-making in all matters accelerated the speed of government functioning, yielded dividends, and ministries too moved fast.

The meetings conducted by the Principal Secretary were business like, the decisions clear, to the point and quick. In fact, a proposal for the extension of service of a Chairman and Managing Director (CMD) of a Navratna Company was approved by PMO even though the minister concerned was holding on to the file waiting for favours from the officer before clearing the case. As the CMD had an outstanding performance to support his case, PMO had no hesitation in extending his service.

Such instances created good working atmosphere in the government and its agencies. I too am used to quick processing of files and decisions, therefore, the fast-paced PMO suited my temperament.

A POWERFUL PM

PM Vajpayee was powerful, and this helped in pushing the development agenda of the government at full speed. Since BJP had the largest number of MPs in parliament and the NDA had its steering committee with all constituted members, decisions were fast, and the PM had full authority to take decisions. Many times, I used to be surprised to see that PM was very considerate towards Opposition parties and their concerns. Most of the time, he took care that Opposition party leaders were given due respect at all levels. I especially found this when the case for appointment of P.C. Sharma IPS (Retd.) as Member of National Human Rights Commission came up for discussion, where even the Opposition party agreed with the government position.

Another high profile, but not so appropriate case, related to the extension of deputation of Pulok Chatterjee, an IAS officer, and allowing him to continue working with Sonia Gandhi, the then Leader of Opposition in Lok Sabha. The PM approved the extension of his deputation as private secretary to the Leader of the Opposition as he felt that it should be of her choice. During the processing of this proposal, I heard some BJP ministers discussing this and opposing the extension of the deputation. But they had no courage to speak against the decision of the PM. That was the liberal and inclusive style of working of PM Vajpayee. Most of the time in the meetings, he would listen carefully to the views of all participants and speak only after he had heard all of them. He was very patient and considerate of the views of all.

KARGIL WAR

A lot has been written about the Kargil War. I was not handling matters relating to the war on a day to day basis in the PMO, though I will write here about one aspect of this. The war took place between May-July 1999. The conflict was believed to have been orchestrated by the Pakistan Army Chief, General Pervez Musharraf, without the knowledge of Prime Minister Nawaz Sharif. It started with the infiltration of Pakistani troops, and terrorists into Indian territory. The infiltrators positioned themselves in key locations that gave them a strategic advantage during the start of the conflict. India declared the operation successful on 26 July. The Indian victory came at a high price as official death toll on the Indian side was 527, while on the Pakistani side there were varying guesses about casualties.

RAW REPORTS SCREENED

A number of defence and security experts had on many occasions voiced their concern about the incompetence of the Research and Analysis Wing (RAW) in alerting the Centre about the presence of so many Pakistan army personnel and terrorists, so deep in Indian territory for such a long period. It reflected very poorly on the working of the RAW. Even the Intelligence Bureau was unaware of this deep intrusion and it was the complete failure of the functioning of the RAW. I heard that there was some enquiry going on about the extent of failure of the RAW in providing information about the intrusions in Kargil.

About a week after the Kargil war, Principal Secretary Brajesh Mishra asked me to check all RAW reports sent to the PMO and see if there was any mention of intrusions into India in Kargil. I checked all reports from January 1999 onwards, especially, the RAW reports of a few months preceding May 1999. Surprisingly, there was no information of intrusions, either before or after, in the reports. I informed him that no such information was given by RAW to PMO in writing. I also told him that I did not know if Secretary, RAW had verbally informed anyone about these intrusions.

A few days later, the Principal Secretary again asked me about a specific-dated report from among the RAW reports. It seemed to me that some senior person in the RAW had told him about a specific report with information about intrusion by Pakistan army and terrorists in Kargil. I checked that report and informed him that there was nothing in it about the intrusions.

By this time, it became clear that the RAW failed in its duty to provide information about Kargil intrusions. It was the failure of RAW as an organisation and of its top officials. Surprisingly, nobody was punished for the serious lapses in which about 527 soldiers sacrificed their lives and a number of others were wounded. The gentleman who headed RAW at that time was rewarded with governorship of a state in the North-East.

When I took over as Chief Secretary of Manipur in August 2004, I was informed by the then Governor Dr S.S. Sidhu that his predecessor was very unhappy with me. I informed him that his predecessor had reasons to be unhappy with me as I held the view that he should have been held accountable and punished for the Kargil fiasco, rather than being rewarded with the post of a governor.

POKHRAN NUCLEAR TESTS AND LAHORE BUS DIPLOMACY

After 24 years of conducting its first nuclear tests in Pokhran, India carried out five underground nuclear tests in May 1998. These nuclear tests, called Pokhran-II, took place just a month after the Vajpayee government assumed power. In late 1998 and early 1999, PM Vajpayee pushed for a full-scale diplomatic peace process with Pakistan. With the historic inauguration of the Delhi-Lahore bus service in February 1999, he initiated a new peace process aimed towards permanently resolving the Kashmir issue and other conflicts with Pakistan.

The Lahore Declaration espoused a commitment to dialogue, expanded trade relations and mutual friendship, and envisaged a goal of denuclearized South Asia. This eased the tension created by the 1998 nuclear tests not only between the two nations, but also in South Asia and the rest of the world. These were wonderful achievements of the Vajpayee government.

10

BIG DEVELOPMENT PUSH FOR NORTH-EAST

Right from the word go, the government focused its attention on north-eastern states. The initiatives taken by the Deve Gowda government to increase fund flow to the region, helped maintain the momentum of economic development. Some of the projects and schemes initiated by the previous governments were getting completed and bearing fruits.

India had adopted the Look East Policy to promote trade and commerce. As a first step, it was necessary to develop infrastructure in the region so that individual states could take full benefit of possible trade with countries towards the east of India. The government increased emphasis on development of infrastructure such as roads, bridges, power, telecommunications, railways, etc., in North-East. The upgradation of the infrastructure for education and health sectors was also given priority.

PM VISITS ASSAM

On 14 April 1998, the PM arrived in Assam. This visit to Assam and the North-East, immediately after taking over, was an indication of the new government's priority for the development of the region. At Guwahati, PM had a series of meetings with public leaders, security officials and government officials. He also had an important meeting with the council of ministers of Assam. At the outset, PM allayed their fears of the government going back on any of the announcements of United Front governments. In fact, he assured them that all projects and programmes announced by previous governments would be expedited and implemented with full gusto.

The Prime Minister specifically mentioned the projects and schemes listed in the Shukla Commission Report. He informed that all recommendations of the Commission would be examined, and proposed projects would be taken up in consultations with the concerned state governments. The council of ministers from Assam raised issues relating to provision of jobs to ex-militants who had come over ground and joined the mainstream, assistance for members of Surrendered United Liberation Front of Assam (SULFA), waiving off Rs 6,000 crore debt liability of the state, expanding the list of items covered for reimbursements under the MHA scheme of Security Related Expenditure (SRE), and special care of the north-eastern states. The Prime Minister was very sympathetic, and assured increased assistance to the states.

MEETING THE DELEGATION OF REGIONAL POLITICAL PARTIES

In the course of the visit, the PM met different delegations and heard their concerns. Among them was a delegation of all north-eastern regional political parties. They welcomed the PM's initiatives for the socio-economic development for their region. These regional parties represented the states of Nagaland, Assam, Mizoram, Manipur and Meghalaya. They assured the PM of their support for any initiative the government took for the economic development of the region. They emphasised on the restructuring of Centre-State relations, talks with insurgents, problems of infiltration, issue of Chakma refugees in Arunachal Pradesh, writing off the old debts of all states, development and use of inland waterways, opening of trade routes with Myanmar and Bangladesh, and representation of the North-East in Union Public Service Commission (UPSC).

One of the most important issues raised by them was the opening of a non-bureaucratic Cell for the North-East in the government, and possibly setting up of a separate Ministry for the region. These issues had also been raised at different levels by the state governments and some action had been taken by the Government of India. The major political parties, including Congress and BJP too had raised these issues. Congress had also voiced its concern against scrapping of Illegal Migrants (Determination by Tribunal) [IMDT] Act.

INAUGURATION OF JOGIGHOPA BRIDGE

The 2,284-metre-long Jogighopa rail-cum-road Bridge was the third bridge over the mighty Brahmaputra. In October 1996, when Prime Minister Deve Gowda visited the North-East, the progress of work on this bridge was dragging on for want of adequate funds. The Deve Gowda government announced a provision of Rs 55 crore additional funds in 1996-97, and Rs 120 crore in 1997-98 for the completion of the bridge. By end of March 1998, the bridge was ready for inauguration. This was a big boon for the economic development of Assam and its neighbouring states.

On 15 April 1998, Prime Minister Vajpayee inaugurated the Jogighopa Bridge, renamed as the Naranarayana Setu after Nara Narayan, a sixteenth-century Koch king. It was a very hot and a humid day and we were sweating in the tents set up by the state government. A large crowd cheered the PM en route to the venue and during the inauguration. I was sure that had PM Deve Gowda not announced provision of additional funds way back in 1996, under the 'New Initiatives for North Eastern Region', this bridge would not have been completed by 1998. PM Vajpayee was pleased to see the enthusiasm of the people who had gathered to greet him and watch the inauguration. It was a very auspicious occasion and was a boon for people living on either side of the Brahmaputra.

BIRTH OF NON-LAPSABLE CENTRAL POOL OF RESOURCES [NLCPR]

Before the inauguration of the bridge, the Prime Minister had a short meeting with me and other PMO and MHA officials. He wanted to know about additional funds that could be made available to the North-Eastern states to upgrade infrastructure, in addition to the assistance provided in the 'New Initiatives for North Eastern Region'. I informed the PM that as per the New Initiatives, the Central ministries and departments were required to spend at least 10 per cent of their budget allocations in the North-East. But some ministries and departments were spending as little as 2 per cent on the grounds that they were not able to identify projects in their sectors in this region. This appeared to be a laughable excuse. It was obvious that adequate efforts were not being made by them to prepare projects here, thus undoing Prime Minster Deve Gowda's effort.

Prime Minister Vajpayee directed me, and the other officials to immediately consult the Planning Commission about the unutilised funds of ministries and departments. He wanted to know how could these funds be kept as additional resources to fund infrastructural projects such as those of railways, roads, bridges, power, telecommunications, etc. and various projects of the state governments. I immediately passed on the message to the Planning Commission and requested for an urgent reply about the PM's concern.

The next day, when PM was inaugurating the Jogighopa Bridge, we got a printed message from the Deputy Chairman Planning Commission proposing the creation of a 'Non-Lapsable Central Pool of Resources' (NLCPR), with the unspent funds of the ministries and departments. This was a brilliant idea, and also a double-edged weapon. First, it would put pressure on ministries and departments to spend their budgetary allocations in the North-East by making special efforts to increase their presence in the region, and formulate projects. Second, if they did not spend their budgets, the shortfall in spending would get transferred to a non-lapsable pool of resources.

The non-lapsable character of the resources added a brilliant dimension to it. It implied that the funds would not lapse with the ending of the financial year. Instead it would keep on accumulating if the annual unspent funds of ministries or departments were more than the annual withdrawals of funds from the pool of resources. It was also decided that the projects of different states dealing with infrastructure could be funded from this accumulated pool. PM approved the concept and asked for Cabinet approval so that the NLCPR, as suggested by the Planning Commission, could be established. The NLCPR was born on 15 April 1998 near the Jogighopa Bridge. The credit for this goes to Deputy Chairman Planning Commission Jaswant Singh and PM Vajpayee, while the foundation for this was laid by H. D. Deve Gowda on 27 October 1996 at the Guwahati press conference.

PM'S GUWAHATI PRESS CONFERENCE

Prime Minister Vajpayee held a press conference at the end of his visit. This was significant as it was his first visit as Prime Minister to Guwahati. The people and the political parties had a lot of expectations from him and he did not disappoint them. He announced that the Government of India was willing to hold unconditional talks with all militant and other groups within the four corners of the Constitution. He announced measures to build and improve helipads in Arunachal Pradesh and improve other infrastructure required by security forces. He also said the Government of India would bear the states' expenditure on Counter Insurgency (CI) operations and other security related matters and that all political parties would be consulted before taking action on IMDT Act. He announced that the existing package for schemes announced by PM Deve Gowda would be increased and other schemes, suggested by state governments, would be included.

He was categorical in stating that there would be no separate state for Bodos while informing that the Minister of Defence had opened a channel to Bodos and would discuss their demands. Allaying fears, he said that the talks with NSCN (IM) would be held soon and efforts would be made to resolve various issues across the table.

CLOSE MONITORING IN PMO

In the PMO, a special mechanism was established to monitor the progress of all schemes and projects announced by the PM. The monthly progress of all these was shared with the state governments as well as with the ministries and the departments of the Government of India. These progress reports were uploaded on the PMO website every month. The state Chief Secretaries and the Resident Commissioners of all North-Eastern states in Delhi were asked to apprise their state governments of the availability of the progress reports on the PMO website. The states were asked to inform PMO about any inaccuracy in the information about progress of any scheme. Despite repeated reminders to the states to share information about status of implementation of schemes, the PMO rarely got any feedback. This was a big negative factor in monitoring the progress. If states had been more proactive it would have made the monitoring easier and implementation more effective.

PRIME MINISTER
ATAL BIHARI VAJPAYEE – II

(OCTOBER 1999–MAY 2004)

Author's Take

"

A liberal democrat, PM Vajpayee gave full freedom to his officers to take initiatives in governance. His second tenure was more stable as the NDA had a majority in the Lok Sabha. The Vajpayee period could be termed as the 'Golden Era' for infrastructure and economic development in the history of India. Major initiatives were taken in all sectors of the economy, particularly in petroleum and natural gas, surface transport, telecommunications, civil aviation, finance and power. Development projects in the North-Eastern states, constitution of Non-Lapsable Central Pool of Resources, India's race to Moon (Chandrayaan I) too were noteworthy. In this tenure, special emphasis was given to social sectors such as health, education and social empowerment. The decision-making in the PMO was quick and no ministry or department had the courage to challenge the PMO decisions. This improved the comfort level of officers working in the PMO.

"

11

A SINGLE-VOTE DEFEAT BUT BJP STORMS BACK TO POWER

FALL OF VAJPAYEE GOVERNMENT

The Vajpayee government was surviving with the support of different political parties. Some in the coalition were not stable partners. Within 13 months of having taken over, All India Anna Dravida Munnetra Kazhagam (AIADMK), a key coalition partner, withdrew its support. The Prime Minister moved a motion of confidence and the voting took place after two days of colourful debate on the failures and achievements of the government. In the end, Lok Sabha Speaker G. M. C. Balayogi declared the motion of confidence as defeated. The Vajpayee government was voted out in the Lok Sabha by a margin of one vote—the ruling coalition secured 269 votes and the Opposition, 270.

The Bahujan Samaj Party (BSP) and Saifuddin Soz of the National Conference voted against the government, tilting the balance in favour of the Opposition. The floor managers of BJP thought the BSP would abstain from voting, but their calculations went awry. Soz voted defying the party whip. There was criticism about the vote of Congress MP Giridhar Gamang, who had just become the chief minister of Orissa but was yet to resign from the Lok Sabha. He voted against the Vajpayee government. That made all the difference. Had he not voted, both sides would have equal votes, and the Speaker, who was from TDP, would have supported the government.

SURPRISING 'ABSENCE' OF CPI MP FROM LOK SABHA

I have known the members of Communist Party of India (CPI) and Communist Party of India (Marxist) [CPI(M)] to be well disciplined, and not the people to be tempted to go against their party lines in the parliament voting. However, on 17 April 1999, a CPI MP did not participate in the voting. I knew of the MP from casual discussions in the PMO. I learnt later that the MP was admitted to a clinic on the day of voting and kept in safe house so that the CPI members would not locate the MP. I also learnt that Rs 1 crore was paid to the MP before the confidence vote, and another Rs 1 crore thereafter.

After the government lost the confidence vote, two ministers went to hand over the remaining amount to the MP in the clinic. Seeing this, one of my colleagues remarked, 'Look, two foolish persons are going to deliver the remaining half of the promised amount even after losing confidence vote.' Maybe, they wanted to be honest in their dealings even in such matters.

Before this incident I believed that CPI and CPI(M) MLAs and MPs were well disciplined and could not be lured by money power. My belief was based on the fact that almost all of them rose from the cadres of their parties. Many of their public representatives have lived a very simple and austere lifestyle as compared to the luxurious living styles of representatives of other political parties. Both these political parties have strong disciplined cadres as compared to other political parties. But this incident changed my belief. The then Lok Sabha representative of my constituency, Sangrur in Punjab, Bhan Singh Bhaura of the CPI was known to be simple and strict. A trend was perhaps set by this new MP, who had not risen through the ranks as is the case of most communist MPs and MLAs.

NO CARETAKER GOVERNMENT AT THE CENTRE

The next general elections to Lok Sabha were announced for September and October 1999. The new Lok Sabha would thus be constituted only by second week of October. Therefore, the Vajpayee government would have to govern the country for about six months before the next government could take office.

Different views began to appear in newspapers about the competency of the Vajpayee government to take policy decisions. Some suggested that since they had lost the confidence motion, they could function only as a caretaker government, though there is no such provision in the Indian Constitution.

The PMO made a reference to the President of India to know if the government should work as a caretaker government and take routine decisions, or if they could take policy decisions which could not be postponed. A quick reply from the President's Secretariat settled the matter. There was nothing such as a caretaker government at the national level even though at the state level there is such a provision. Therefore, the existing government could function like a normal government, while being sensitive to the issue of the upcoming Lok Sabha elections, refrain from taking decisions that could be postponed without any adverse consequences. The communication was internally circulated among PMO officers.

1999: A FIVE-PHASE LOK SABHA ELECTION

The Presidential proclamation of 26 April 1999 dissolved the 12th Lok Sabha, and the Election Commission of India announced a five-phase Lok Sabha poll. It was also announced that a new Lok Sabha was required to be constituted in time to meet before 21st October. The BJP-led NDA was then a coalition of over 20 parties. Several other parties, not a part of the NDA, also committed themselves to supporting a BJP-led government in the election. The main Opposition parties were led by the INC(I). The Opposition coalition had fewer parties and its alliances were much weaker than those of the NDA. The United Front was the third force comprising Left-wing, Socialist and Communist parties, but it was not a strong electoral alliance.

The election campaigns were conducted on a few specific issues. The BJP campaigned on the leadership qualities of Vajpayee and compared it with the possible leadership in the Congress. While Vajpayee had experience of four decades, Congress president Sonia Gandhi was new to politics. Moreover, her leadership was challenged by Sharad Pawar, a senior leader with a powerful base in Maharashtra, on the grounds of her Italian roots. This led to an underlying crisis within the Congress that persisted during the elections and was capitalised by the BJP.

Another issue in BJP's favour was the positive view of Vajpayee's handling of the Kargil War, and its affirmation and strengthening of the Indian position in Kashmir. Further, in the previous two years, India had posted strong economic growth, on the back of economic liberalisation and financial reforms, as well as a low rate of inflation and a higher rate of industrial expansion. The BJP campaigned strongly on these achievements, as well as cultivating some sympathy for the predicament, which had led to the government's downfall. Overall, it appeared that the BJP-led alliance was leading in the pre-poll opinions.

Dr Manmohan Singh was a candidate from the South Delhi Lok Sabha constituency against V.K. Malhotra of the BJP. Dr Singh had been RBI Governor, Planning Commission Deputy Chairman and the Finance Minister during the Narasimha Rao government. People of India knew about his contribution in rejuvenating the Indian economy, which faced its worst crisis in 1991-92. The South Delhi Lok Sabha constituency from where he was contesting consisted of the educated elite of India. But this Lok Sabha constituency was a stronghold of the BJP since 1989, having won it four times. Many among the intelligentsia supported Dr Singh during the election campaign. The campaign was smeared by derogatory personal statements allegedly made by

Malhotra against Dr Singh. This upset Prime Minister Vajpayee, and he immediately called for Malhotra. He wondered how politicians could utter such things about opponents in elections and that too from a public platform. I was present at 7 Race Course Road at that time. The PM felt that Malhotra had crossed the line and needed to be advised to campaign on the BJP government's achievements and programmes instead.

Dr Singh lost the election to Malhotra by over 30,000 votes and BJP retained the Lok Sabha seat. When we compare this incident with what is happening today, we find many politicians stoop very low while criticising their opponents. Some politicians use words one cannot even mention. PM Vajpayee wanted his party members, particularly senior members to be decent in their utterances, more so when speaking against senior functionaries of other parties. He wanted the election campaign discourse to be decent and pleasant.

AND THE WINNER IS…

The results were decisively in favour of the BJP and the NDA. The NDA won 269 seats, and a further 29 seats came from its ally the TDP. The Congress party lost 23 seats, and its two key regional allies performed worse than expected. The Congress, however, regained some ground in states such as Uttar Pradesh. The Left parties fortunes continued to decline with the CPI dropping to just four seats and losing its official status as a national party as per the criteria fixed by the Election Commission. The decisive victory for NDA and its allies placed more responsibilities on the alliance partners to deliver the election promises made by the NDA.

A PM FOR THE THIRD TIME

Vajpayee took oath as Prime Minister of India for the third time on 13 October 1999. With a continuity of government post elections, the PMO continued with the same officers and their work allocations. There were changes in the Planning Commission with K.C. Pant as the Deputy Chairman. The new NDA government wanted to take up major initiatives in infrastructure, rural development and social sectors in a big way. The PM had a few sessions with Deputy Chairman, Planning Commission, and other officers of major infrastructure ministries.

After discussions, a list of initiatives was prepared which were required to be taken up in a time-bound manner during the tenure of the NDA government. These included investing in national highways, infrastructure sectors, emphasis on rural roads, increase in allocation from oil cess, dismantling of administered price mechanism of petroleum products, implementation of the Hydrocarbon Vision 2025, and amendments to Coal Nationalization Act and Foreign Exchange Management Act. High on agenda was also the need to set up cells in PMO, Cabinet Secretariat and Finance Ministry for a quick examination of proposals of disinvestment, formation of Expenditure Management Commission to suggest allocable efficiency in different components of expenditure items, targeting of subsidies on fertilizers, kerosene and other important items, expediting report on Telecom Regulatory Authority of India (TRAI) by Group of Ministers, removal of restrictions on movement controls in the rural economy, particularly on food grains, and emphasis on surface and telecommunications projects in North-East and Jammu and Kashmir.

These well identified priority sectors were pursued with vigour and became the major initiatives of the government during the next five years. Since the NDA government had a fresh and increased mandate of the people, its responsibilities to deliver on these promises also increased.

12

SURFACE TRANSPORT SYSTEMS

The development of surface transport systems consisting of roads, railways and inland waterways were identified as the priority sectors of the Vajpayee government. Immediately after the government took office again in October, plans were formulated to start work on improving road network and railways and arranging funds for the same. After a few meetings it was decided to levy cess on petrol and High Speed Diesel (HSD), the main fuel used in road vehicles. It was decided to fund construction of rural roads, national highways through National Highways Authority of India (NHAI), complete double railway tracks in the Golden Quadrilateral, strengthen rail connectivity to ports, replace old bridges and improve unmanned railways crossings from the fund collected from this cess.

The key people responsible for this were K.C. Pant and N.K. Singh. I handled some of these sectors from time to time. Looking back today, I find this was one of the best initiatives taken by the government. After more than 18 years, it is making waves in the infrastructure sectors of the country.

A NON-LAPSABLE CENTRAL ROAD FUND

The government decided to create a Central Road Fund (CRF) by imposing a cess on motor spirit, commonly called petrol and HSD to fund the construction of the roads. The Central Road Fund Act 2000 was enacted to create a Central Road Fund (CRF) under Section 6 of the Act out of a cess imposed by the Union government on the consumption of HSD. This CRF was used to develop and maintain national highways, state roads (particularly those of economic importance and provide inter-state connectivity), rural roads, and railway under and overbridges. It may be mentioned here that such road funds have been used world over for development of road infrastructure.

The CRF is a non-lapsable pool and an excellent source of funds for this important sector in India. The work on National Highway Development Programme (NHDP) and the Pradhan Mantri Gram Sadak Yojana (PMGSY) progressed at a fast pace. An important factor that enabled the country to fuel the 'road revolution' was the support from these internally generated funds to finance such projects. A welcome and interesting feature of the CRF has been that its revenue was increasing at a significant pace over the years due to increasing traffic on roads.

IMPLEMENTATION OF RURAL ROADS UNDER PMGSY

Ministry of Rural Development initiated a new scheme called Pradhan Mantri Gram Sadak Yojana (PMGSY) with one third of the fund it got from the cess on petroleum and petroleum products. M. Venkaiah Naidu, the Minister for Rural Development, was very enthusiastic to cover as many roads as possible under the PMGSY. Since this was a new scheme, a new approach was adopted to plan and implement the roads under it. A master plan called a Core Network was prepared for each district. This would first link villages with higher population and later villages with a lower population. The population slabs started from 1000, going down to 250 in the hill areas or remote rural areas. This approach was necessary to ensure that the fund flow to the PMGSY roads would be based on population and not manipulated by political considerations.

As more funds became available to the Ministry, it would cover villages with lower population too. The roads under PMGSY were planned to be built as per the Core Network Plan prepared for each district by the concerned State Rural Roads Development Agency and approved by the Ministry. The expertise of the Central Road Research Institute was also used to vet the District Core Networks of the roads. The Ministry also developed a better method for tendering, bid evaluations and construction of roads. It specified the project approval and implementation committees at the state levels. In a way, the PMGSY initiated by the government, was one of the most revolutionary steps in surface transport and changed the economy of rural areas.

The PMGSY roads were planned to be of good standard and gradient and have longer durability. There was a vast improvement in the planning, tendering and implementation of PMGSY roads vis-a-vis the Inter Village Roads (IVRs) constructed by state Public Works Departments (PWDs). Unlike the IVRs, once the road alignments under the PMGSY were firmed, it was not possible to change these at anybody's whim and fancy.

AN ENTHUSIASTIC MINISTRY OF RURAL DEVELOPMENT

In the year 2001-02, about Rs 3,500 crore was available with the Ministry of Rural Development to be given to states for implementation of PMGSY roads. I learnt that the Ministry had worked out that about Rs 55,000 crore would be needed to construct all roads under PMGSY in India. The Ministry under Mr Naidu, was actively considering finding ways and means of completing all PMGSY roads covered under the Core Networks by 2004, the time when the Vajpayee government would complete its term.

This was an excellent plan. It could have helped BJP in the next general elections to Lok Sabha but for a serious flaw. This pertained to the availability of about Rs 55,000 crore required to complete all PMGSY roads. This meant that on an average, the Ministry would have to release about Rs 20,000 crore annually to the state governments as against the availability of about Rs 3,500 crore to them from the cess on oil.

Another difficulty was to get the actual work done by the state governments and the state rural roads agencies, which had just been set up by the ministry. The process and preparation of tender papers, bidding, awarding the contracts and completion of roads were other serious challenges. It all depended on the capabilities and wherewithal of the contractors and the efficiency of the state rural roads agencies.

MEETING WITH THE PRIME MINISTER

The Ministry proposed to obtain about Rs 55,000 crore loan from banks over a period of three years and securitise the loan with the annual cash flows from the cess on oil. It appeared that the banks had agreed to the proposal of the Ministry and that was why Minister Venkaiah Naidu wanted to take the Prime Minister's blessings for the proposal. I was also sounded out by him about the proposal and he informally hinted that I should support the proposal in front of the PM.

The Ministry had done its homework properly. The meeting was held at 7 RCR, the PM's office, and I assisted the PM during the meeting with the Minister and officials of the Ministry of Rural Development. Venkaiah Naidu carefully explained the proposal to the PM. He spoke of the need to prepone the completion of roads under PMGSY, its impact on rural economy as also on the prospects of BJP in the general elections in October 2004. He also informed the PM that about Rs 55,000 crore would be available to the Ministry by securitisation of loan against annual cash inflows from the oil cess.

VAJPAYEE—A DEMOCRAT AT HEART

The PM did not fully grasp the proposal, so the Minister explained once again about the availability of Rs 55,000 crore during the next three years from banks against the securitisation of loan through the oil cess cash inflows. PM Vajpayee did not fully understand the securitisation concept and the availability of such a large sum as Rs 55,000 crore to the Ministry. He quietly thought for a while and then turned towards me. I explained to him in simple language that the Ministry of Rural Development wanted to avail of about Rs 55,000 crore loans by assuring banks and lenders that the Government of India would keep on imposing oil cess for about 20 years or so, till about the year 2022, and would keep repaying to banks and lenders about Rs 3,500 crore per annum as repayments of loan principal plus interest. This implied that the present government guarantees the banks that oil cess would remain in place till the loan of Rs 55,000 was fully paid. When the PM heard this, he again asked whether loan amount of Rs 55,000 crore from banks would be based on the commitment of the Government of India to pay annually loan principal plus interest repayments from one-third portion of the oil cess. I answered in affirmative and said that if there was no such commitment from Government of India, banks would not lend the amount over three years to the Ministry. PM Vajpayee understood the proposal.

He then spoke in a soft but firm tone, 'The term of my government is for three years more. I cannot give any commitment to banks that the next government would also impose oil cess. Whatever work the Ministry can do with the oil cess in three years, should be done. There is no need to take loan from banks.' After the PM spoke, the Minister looked at me with disappointment and thus the meeting ended. I saw the Minister and his officers walk out quietly, somewhat disappointed. This was a simple incident, which illustrated that PM Vajpayee was a democrat at heart. He did not want any legislative commitment to be passed on to the new government after his term ended in October 2004.

R.K. SINGH: BRINGING ENERGY INTO RAILWAY BOARD

In July 2003, Ravindra Kumar Singh, who was working as general manager in the Railway Board, was appointed as its chairman, superseding all six members of the Board. This was an unprecedented development. As per a 1987 decision of the government, a Railway Board member can be considered for the chairman's job if the aspirant has more than a year of service left. Or, if a person is one of the 17 general managers, then he or she can be elevated to the position if he/she has more than two years to go before retirement. In the past, as per convention, the senior most member of the Board was generally made the Chairman of the Railway Board.

The Railways have a complicated system to determine the seniority of officers as they come in from eight different services. The general manager posts being ex-cadre posts, seniority is determined by virtue of when an officer became a general manager. Whatever happened in the appointment of chairman, Railway Board, R.K. Singh was very good. He proved to be an energetic head and the railways performed well during his tenure. As and when the PMO needed any information or note from the railways, he was very prompt and always checked back later on the information for its accuracy. He always assured timely delivery of information. I had not seen any other Secretary in the Government of India who was so responsive, energetic, and took matters head on.

JAMMU-BARAMULLA RAILWAY LINE

The Jammu-Baramulla railway line was an important project where the work was going at a very slow pace. The work picked speed after the Prime Minister announced in 2002 that it would be funded as a national project. The PM also announced that the first train would enter Kashmir valley through Qazigund tunnel on 15 August 2007. The Jammu-Baramulla railway line crosses major earthquake zones, it is subjected to extreme temperatures of cold and heat and is in an inhospitable terrain, making it an extremely challenging engineering project. It was during R.K. Singh's tenure that work on the project started moving at a good pace.

A couple of times, an officer, who had handled Konkan railways matters after K. Sreedharan, met me in the PMO and suggested that the route alignment of the railway line was wrong and should be redone. He suggested that it should not go near the International Border or Line of Control (LoC). He also suggested more tunnels and a shorter distance from Jammu to Qazigund and Baramulla. I wondered why these suggestions were not being given to Chairman or others from the said ministry instead of me. I spoke to the Chairman about this and he said there was a forum and system available in Railway Board, and the officer should give his suggestions there. He mentioned that some of the senior officers were not behaving as they should.

TUNNEL BELOW ROHTANG PASS

There were discussions in the PMO about the need for an all-weather road to Leh from Himachal Pradesh. The necessity of such an alternative route to Ladakh region was felt more during the Kargil conflict as the Srinagar-Leh road fell in the firing range of Pakistan. The Army and the defence establishment, too, wanted such a road from Punjab and through Himachal Pradesh.

The Manali-Leh road, considered to be the highest road link on earth, remained operational only during the summer months of May-October. The rest of the year, the 3,978-metre-high Rohtang Pass, the gateway to Lahaul valley, remained blocked due to about 30 feet thick sheet of snow in many places. This could be made an all-weather road only if a tunnel was made at Rohtang Pass. Brajesh Mishra was quick to understand the strategic importance of building such a road. He pushed forward the decision to build a tunnel below Rohtang Pass. With completion of this tunnel, the road to Leh-Ladakh would become useable by defence forces throughout the year.

After considering the strategic importance of the route and keeping in view its impact on the socio-economic development of Lahaul-Spiti areas of Himachal Pradesh, PM announced that Manali-Leh road would be made an all-weather road and that funds would not be a problem. At that time, we were not aware that the environmental issues would delay the start of Rohtang tunnel for a long time as it happened later on.

A QUICK DECISION-MAKER

I found PM Vajpayee quick at decision-making. The presence of Brajesh Mishra expedited it further. I had experienced this in Srinagar when PM agreed to provide up to Rs 1,000 crore per annum for Jammu-Baramulla Railway line and complete it in a record five years. Similarly, the PM agreed to construct the Rohtang Pass tunnel very quickly. My observation was that governments take years to take such decisions. But the PM gave his approval immediately and the foundation stone for Rohtang Pass tunnel was laid by him on 3 June 2002. The Border Roads Organisation (BRO), a tri-service organisation of the Defence Ministry, specialising in road and bridge construction in difficult terrains, was made overall in charge of the project.

The project work, however, could not start because of delays in getting environmental clearance. Some of the objections raised by environmentalists were very strange. One point raised pertained to the location where the dug-out earth from the tunnel would be dumped. If those interested in moving forward were quick in decision-making, some of these objections could have been removed early. In the meantime, the work on the horseshoe shaped nine-kilometre-long Rohtang tunnel got further delayed and the project cost kept going up.

In June 2012, UPA chairperson Sonia Gandhi declared open the tunnel drilling at South Portal, 30 km north of Manali, in the presence of the then Defence Minister, the Himachal Pradesh Chief Minister, and the Union Minister for Steel, Virbhadra Singh. Speaking on the occasion, she spoke of former PM Vajpayee's dream to get the Rohtang Tunnel constructed in 2002. She referred to the complicated nature of the project and expected the work to be completed. The tunnel project, also affected by geological surprises, is now expected to be completed by 2020 at a cost of about Rs 4,850 crore. On completion, this would be one of the most strategically important projects initiated by PM Vajpayee.

EXPRESSWAY TO TEZU

The Chief Minister of Assam repeatedly requested the PMO to connect the Eastern leg of the East-West Expressway to Tezu, an old trading point of North-East with Myanmar. In the PMO, we took up this matter with the Ministry of the Road Transport and Highways. For some unexplained reasons, the Ministry kept refusing the proposal. It was quite surprising as the people pursuing the proposal could not get a rational answer for denial of their request. Since I attended meetings of CMs of the north-eastern states with the PM, many times I cut a sorry figure as no satisfactory answers could be given to them for not sanctioning expressway up to Tezu at that time. As the proposal fizzled out at the Ministry-level, the eastern leg of the East-West Expressway did not connect toTezu.

13

STRATEGIC ISSUES OF PETROLEUM SECTOR

In 1997-98, petroleum and natural gas constituted about 42 per cent of the energy consumption in India whereas the share of coal was 55 per cent, hydel power 2 per cent and the nuclear 1 per cent. I may clarify here that coal used for power generation is taken in the share of coal. Petroleum and natural gas has been the most important sector, which determined the growth of Indian economy as well as its trade balance. India has been heavily dependent on imports of crude oil and petroleum products in the 1980s and 1990s. Whenever the price of crude oil in international market increased, it created serious issues of trade imbalance. The dependence of Indian economy on the international price of crude oil had been engaging the attention of the government for many years. Moreover, India did not have any control or influence on the prices of crude oil.

The levels of per capita energy consumption in India in the 1980s and 1990s were extremely low as compared to the rest of the world. In terms of comparison with developed countries, the differentials had been even more marked. In 1997, the per capita energy consumption for

India was 285 kilogrammes of oil equivalent (kgoe) of primary energy and 113 kgoe of hydrocarbons as compared to 1454 kgoe of primary energy and 927 kgoe of hydrocarbons for rest of the world, 688 kgoe of primary energy and 169 kgoe hydrocarbons for China, 3962 kgoe of primary energy and 2520 kgoe of hydrocarbons for Japan, and 4102 kgoe of primary energy and 2539 kgoe of hydrocarbons for Germany. It is a well-known economic hypothesis that the growth of the economy would automatically lead to a growth in energy consumption because of a direct correlation between the Gross Domestic Product (GDP) and energy consumption. To expedite the economic growth of the country and to provide energy security, it was desirable to have a stable growth of the hydrocarbon sector and reduce dependence on the external resources.

The Ministry of Petroleum and Natural Gas had identified its priority thrust areas for improving energy security and growth of the petroleum sector. The thrust areas included dismantling of administered price mechanism (APM) of petroleum products, expediting the setting up of refineries at Paradip in Orissa, Bina in MP, and Bathinda in Punjab, increasing indigenous crude oil production, putting in place an attractive New Exploration Licensing Policy for crude oil and natural gas, acquiring Equity Oil abroad and allocating petroleum product outlets in a transparent manner. The Ministry continued its efforts in all these areas from upstream (exploration and production of crude oil and natural gas) to the downstream side (marketing of products).

ADMINISTERED PRICE MECHANISM

From the early 1970s, the Government of India had developed and adopted APM in the petroleum and natural gas sector. Under the APM regime, the sector was controlled by government in all stages: from production to refining, distribution and marketing. The supply of crude oil to the refineries at point of refining was done at a predetermined price called 'delivered cost of crude'. The finished products were also made available at predetermined price called 'ex-refinery price'.

The government-controlled prices were based on the principle of compensating normative cost and allowing a pre-determined return on investments to the oil companies. In the case of crude oil production in India, primarily done by Oil and Natural Gas Commission (ONGC) and Oil India Limited (OIL), both PSUs were compensated for their operating expenses and allowed a 15 per cent post-tax return on the capital employed by them. Both ONGC and OIL sold crude to refineries in the country.

As far as the refineries were concerned, the pricing was based on the concept of retention price, by which refiners were allowed to retain out of their sale proceeds the cost of crude, refining cost and a reasonable return on investment employed. The same mechanism was extended to marketing and distribution companies, which government sector PSUs such as Indian Oil Company Limited (IOCL), Hindustan Petroleum Corporation Limited (HPCL), and Bharat Petroleum Corporation Limited (BPCL), and Assam Oil were compensated for operating costs along with an assured return. In addition, the prices at which the finished products such as HSD, petrol, kerosene and LPG were finally sold were set by the government.

The APM insulated oil producers, refiners and marketing companies from global oil price fluctuations, and fulfilled the socio-economic objectives of the government considerably. But it failed to generate adequate incentives for investment in petroleum and natural gas, which hindered the creation of a vibrant, and globally competitive oil sector in India. During the 1980s, there was an upward swing in the crude oil prices and this increased prices and increased demand of petroleum products overburdened the PSUs. At the same time the PSUs had started additional imports of crude oil at high costs.

DISMANTLING OF APM AND INTRODUCTION OF A NEW SYSTEM

In April 2002, the Government of India decided to dismantle the administered price mechanism (APM) due to various reasons. The cost-plus formula for refineries and crude oil production was not encouraging efficiency in production. As long as PSUs were the only players in the oil sector, the government was able to effectively control the investments and costs. However, when private players entered, the inflated costs of private sector could be a drain on the government finances. Further, no large private investments were coming to the oil sector as private players were wary of government decisions, which could affect their profits sharply.

Under the new system, the oil marketing companies (OMCs) were free to set retail product prices based on an import parity pricing formula. The domestic refining and retail sectors were opened to leading private players such as Reliance Industries Limited. Due to the importance of LPG and kerosene, the subsidies from the government's budget were maintained on LPG and on a fixed proportion of kerosene.

This system continued till mid 2004 after Dr Manmohan Singh took over. At that time, the new system was abandoned and the Central government once again controlled upward price revisions. The government increased or decreased the price of petrol and diesel, while the prices of LPG and kerosene prices remained effectively fixed due to the heavy government subsidy. The prices of petrol and diesel were protected because of the importance of these products as transport fuels (especially as these are widely used in public transport, food freight). Diesel, in particular, has uses outside transport, for e.g.. as an input into agricultural production.

In 2003-04, the dismantling of APM led the private-sector to rapidly set up retail operations and all of a sudden, many new petrol pumps belonging to RIL, Shell and Essar came up. But when the prices again came under de facto control of the government in mid-2004, the three private firms, which had retail license in India, were forced to close their retail outlets across the country because of uneconomical business of retail trading of petrol and diesel. Many petrol pumps of these private companies could be seen closed or lying idle.

INDIA'S HYDROCARBON VISION 2025

Realising that the hydrocarbons sector plays a vital role in the economic growth of the country, the PM constituted a 'Group on India Hydrocarbon Vision 2025' on 31 March 1999, to work out a specific framework for creating a vision for India to become a major hydrocarbon world power in the future. The Group was headed by the then finance minister. The India Hydrocarbon Vision 2025 was among the many good initiatives taken by PM Vajpayee. The person behind this initiative was N.K. Singh. He had worked in the Union Finance Ministry and knew the implications of having short- and long-term hydrocarbon policies and its impact on the economic development as well as trade balance of India. To a large extent PM and the Principal Secretary had given Mr Singh adequate freedom to work out the policy initiatives.

This Group set up six sub groups with specific terms of references for each. These were Exploration and Production Sector, External Policy and Oil Security, Natural Gas, Refining and Marketing, Tariff and Pricing, and Restructuring and Disinvestment headed by experts in the respective fields. The sub group on Natural Gas was headed by R.K. Pachauri, Chairman of Tata Energy Research Institute, and I was the convener. The groups submitted their reports after six months, suggesting short- (three-five years) and long-term (beyond five years) measures to increase production and use of hydrocarbons in India.

HYDROCARBON VISION REPORT[1]

The reports were consolidated into one. The final report put together a framework to guide policies concerning the hydrocarbons sector for the next two and a half decades. The report admitted that issues such as 'energy security, use of alternative fuels, and interchangeability of technology were vital to ensure that the mix of energy sources used in the economy was optimal and sustainable'. It also suggested that 'adequate quantities of economically priced clean and green fuels be made available to Indian consumers'. The estimated energy supply mix in India for a period up to 2025, was also estimated.

The report also said that oil and gas would continue to play a prominent role in fulfilling the energy requirements of India. About 45 per cent of the total energy needs would be met by the oil and gas sector, though some amount of interchange between oil and gas was foreseen. The report aimed at achieving the following:

- Energy security by achieving self-reliance through increased indigenous production and investment in equity oil abroad
- Enhance quality of life by progressively improving product standards to ensure cleaner and greener India
- Develop hydrocarbon sector as a globally competitive industry and benchmarked against the best in the world through technology upgradation and capacity building in all facets of the industry
- Have a free market and promote healthy competition among players and improve customer service
- Ensure oil security for the country keeping in view strategic and defence considerations

EMPHASIS ON EQUITY OIL ABROAD

The Group suggested that India's energy policy should have a focused approach to get equity oil and gas abroad besides building relationships with international oil companies. The policy for acquisition of overseas assets was launched in the 1990s. It was a bid to minimise India's burgeoning oil imports even as domestic crude production continued to stagnate at around 33 million tonnes per annum against a demand of 108 million tonnes. Thus domestic production met only 30 per cent of the demand at that time.

As per estimates of the Ministry of Petroleum and Natural Gas and the Planning Commission by 2025, the demand for petroleum products would touch 370 million tonnes. It has been suggested that India should produce about 110 million tonnes of crude oil per year domestically, so as to maintain 30 per cent share of domestic production in the total demand. Therefore, to maintain this 30 per cent level, India needed to add 60 million tonnes of oil from its equity oil abroad.

ONGC VIDESH LIMITED – ENCOURAGEMENT BY BRAJESH MISHRA

To acquire equity oil abroad, the Government of India set up ONGC Videsh Limited (OVL) in the late 1990s. The sole aim of OVL was to scout for oil resources in countries with whom India could have strategic relations, and where the commercial deals for explorations of oil and gas could be done properly. The MEA provided inputs about the possible sources of equity oil in different countries as well as perceptions of country-specific risks. During the years when I was in the PMO, OVL had become quite active in the sea near Vietnam, in Sakhalin project in Russia, and Sudan. Since these were initial days, the capacity of OVL to take risks for acquiring was also limited.

During PMO meetings on issues relating to acquisition of new oil equities abroad, I found that the OVL officials were hesitant to take quick decisions even for those areas where there was a very strong prospect of oil and gas. I found the presence of Brajesh Mishra very helpful in pushing decisions. He was able to comprehend the security and foreign relations angles as well as the international security environment aspects vis-a-vis Indian energy security environment in the short and long term. On a few occasions, I found the officials of the Ministry of Petroleum and Natural Gas also uncertain, and depended on the advice and support of Brajesh Mishra.

Over the years, the efforts, encouragement and the initiatives taken during the Vajpayee government's tenure helped OVL develop a large portfolio of oil equity in different parts of the world. I remember the note written by T.R. Satish Chandran, Principal Secretary to PM Deve Gowda in 1996-97, it too had suggested to look beyond India to secure energy security for the country. It was Satish Chandran who had supported the idea of Iran-India Gas Pipeline through Pakistan despite the contrary views of MEA officials.

During 2016-17, the OVL had a stake in 38 oil and gas projects in

17 countries, including Vietnam, Russia, Sudan, South Sudan, Iran, Iraq, Libya, Myanmar, Syria, Brazil, Colombia, Venezuela, Kazakhstan, Azerbaijan, Mozambique, Bangladesh and New Zealand. ONGC Videsh had ventured into midstream and successfully completed a 741-km product pipeline project in Sudan in 2005, and is a partner in the Baku-Tbilisi-Ceyhan (BTC) pipeline in the Mediterranean. OVL produced about 26.20 per cent of India's domestic oil and 20.70 per cent of India's domestic oil and natural gas production put together in 2017-18. In terms of reserves and production, OVL is the second largest petroleum company in India, next only to its parent ONGC.

NEED FOR STRATEGIC OIL RESERVE

Oil is required for running the economy as well as for maintaining internal and external security. Currently, India depends on oil imports for more than 80 per cent of its crude oil needs. India experienced the need for strategic security for petroleum products during the 1965 and 1971 wars with Pakistan. Whether India could conduct war for a month or two, or even three, depended on availability of adequate petroleum products for security and basic economic needs. The demand for crude oil is unlikely to go down in near future. Since India is also a regional refining hub, India imports more crude than its own domestic requirements to refine and re-export the petroleum products.

Strategic oil reserve is not only an important element of our nation's energy security but also to maximise long-term protection against oil supply disruptions. Oil imports are always vulnerable to risks of supply disruptions as well as changes in the prices of crude oil. Any price aberration in crude has a direct impact on the current account and inflation in the country. These risks amount to strategic risks. In 1997-98, the Ministry of Petroleum and Natural Gas started to seriously think about building strategic oil reserves similar to the USA and other countries. This was specifically because of our heavy dependence on oil imports, and the fact that we did not have our own large oil reserves like the USA. In 1997-98, the USA had about 90 days strategic oil reserves in four different locations, mostly in underground storage facilities. India at that time had less than 10 days of such reserves in addition to the reserves available with oil companies.

A PLAN FOR STRATEGIC OIL STORAGE

Under the Vajpayee government, it was decided to go ahead with the development of strategic oil reserves in phases. Brajesh Mishra pushed for the creation of such reserves. Different strategies were explored for its development. The well-protected storage facilities could be either underground or over ground. Underground storage facilities required heavy investment and the oil kept in these storages also cost the exchequer heavily. In a country like India, it is costly to suddenly build large strategic oil reserves. The initial plan was to build storage for 10 days first, and then create one for 30 days over the next 10 to 15 years.

In 2002-03, the cost to build storage of a capacity of about five million tonnes for 10 days oil consumption was more than Rs 10,000 crore, including the cost of construction and the stored oil. This was based on the crude oil price of US$50 per barrel. With the consumption of petroleum products going up, the requirement of building storage capacities too increased. It was decided to build the storage in two phases. In the first phase, for about 5 million tonnes at three locations and in the second phase, to create 12.5 million tonnes storage capacity at Padur, Chandikhol (Odisha), Bikaner (Rajasthan) and Rajkot (Gujarat).

INDIAN STRATEGIC PETROLEUM RESERVES LIMITED

In 2005, based on the work done during the NDA regime in 2003-04, the construction and maintenance of the Strategic Petroleum Reserves (SPR) was given to the Indian Strategic Petroleum Reserves Ltd (ISPRL). ISPRL is a special purpose vehicle of the Oil Industry Development Board, a statutory body created for India's energy security. It was building the underground rock caverns at Visakhapatnam with capacity of 1.33 million tonnes of oil, at Mangalore of 1.5 million tonnes, and at Padur of 2.5 million tonnes. While Visakhapatnam is located on the eastern coast, the other two locations of Mangalore and Padur (near Mangalore), are located in the western coast in Karnataka.

The three strategic reserves would have a combined capacity of 5.33 million tonnes and would store crude oil for about 10 days. The construction of these storage spaces was expected to cost around Rs 4,100 crore. The main expense to be incurred was on the filling of the reservoirs with crude oil, and was expected to cost over Rs 8,000 crore based on average crude prices of US$55 a barrel. However, after the UPA government came to power, the second phase for building of 12.5 million tonnes strategic oil storage got delayed. The government decided to review the strategic storage plan and precious time was wasted in studies by the Planning Commission. It appeared that the government was going slow on building strategic reserves as policy planners, and decision-makers in the UPA government were seeing the huge investments in strategic reserves as idle investment. The 'strategic' nature of these reserves slowly lost its significance as there was more emphasis on economic development and less on being ready for a war or conflict.

NOTE

1. India Hydrocarbon Vision-2025; http://petroleum.nic.in/sites/default/files/vision.pdf

14

PETROLEUM AND NATURAL GAS: CHALLENGES AND SOLUTIONS

NEW REFINERIES: DEPENDENCY ON TAX SOPS

By 1996, three refineries were planned in the public sector. Hectic discussions were going on to achieve financial closure and to start work on the construction of refineries. These were Paradip Refinery (15 million tonnes per annum [MTPA]) of Indian Oil Company Limited (IOCL), Guru Gobind Singh Refinery (9 MTPA) of Hindustan Petroleum Corporation Limited (HPCL) and Bina Refinery (6 MTPA) of Bharat Petroleum Corporation Limited (BPCL). I often handled issues relating to these refineries, particularly those relating to coordination and arranging meetings. In the administered pricing regime of the petroleum products existing at that time, the setting up of refineries and their viabilities depended on the sops and tax incentives provided by the state and Central governments.

The private investors in these refineries too were looking at government policies, especially those relating to APM of petroleum products. Paradip refinery was planned by IOCL, thus, there was no private sector involved because of its strong financial standing. For the Guru Gobind Singh refinery at Bathinda, HPCL had planned a tie-up with Saudi Aramco of Saudi Arabia, and the refinery was being planned as a joint venture. The Bina refinery was being set up as a joint venture project with Oman Oil Company. The presence of Saudi Aramco and Oman Oil Company were to give financial strength to HPCL and BPCL, respectively, for setting the refineries.

OBJECTIONS FROM STATE BUREAUCRACY

The viability of the refineries was being worked out and high tax exemption sops were being given to these refineries; some to continue up to even fifteen years. For the states, a 15-year tax exemption was too long, and the complete exemption of taxes on refineries deprived them of their tax revenues. When I met Dr U. Sarat Chandran, Principal Secretary Finance, Odisha where the Paradip refinery was being set up, he was quite reluctant to agree to the 15-year tax exemptions. A doctorate in economics from the University of Wisconsin, USA, Dr Chandran had been Joint Secretary in the Department of Economic Affairs, Ministry of Finance, Government of India and in charge of capital markets for five years before going back to his cadre Odisha.

He calculated the present value of all the tax sops proposed to be given to Paradip refinery and the numbers were baffling. His counter offer was to let IOCL treat the present value of tax sops as equity of Odisha government, which IOCL and the Ministry of Petroleum and Natural Gas were not willing to do. I had heard similar opinions from senior bureaucrats in Punjab and Madhya Pradesh too. The states wanted the oil companies to set up refineries but were not willing to give large tax sops requested by the promoters of the refineries.

The tax sops appeared too large and the benefits from refineries to states were back loaded, which were neither visible nor could be quantified properly. There were a number of meetings to discuss the quantum of tax sops as well as the time period over which it should be given. These discussions were time consuming as no quantified figure of benefits to states was given that could be used as an argument for such tax sops.

RELUCTANT FOREIGN PARTNERS AND LENDERS

While the agreements for the finalisation of tax sops were taking time, it was also making the foreign partners and financial institutions jittery about funding the refineries. Saudi Aramco had a sound financial standing but began to show a lot of reluctance to continue. When large investments by a company like Saudi Aramco are planned, serious due diligence is done through a rigorous mechanism. Eventually, Saudi Aramco did not participate in the Guru Gobind Singh Refinery joint venture with HPCL. A new partner, Mittal Energy Investment Pte Ltd of Lakshmi N. Mittal, Chairman and CEO of ArcelorMittal, joined.

This arrangement to change the joint venture partner took time and delayed the financial closure further. The refinery was finally completed in April 2012. Similarly, Bina refinery, initially conceived with an equal partnership between BPCL and the Oman Oil Company, faced significant delays on account of environmental clearances and poor infrastructure. It suffered from severe cost overruns as a result. Following these, the Oman Oil Company initially dropped out of the refinery, but subsequently, decided to be a minority stakeholder in the project, holding 26 per cent equity. The refinery, which was to be commissioned in 2009, was finally completed in May 2011.

LAND ACQUISITION AND ENVIRONMENTAL CLEARANCES

Land acquisition and environmental clearance were some of the factors delaying these refinery projects. The Paradip refinery faced problems as it required more land due to its larger size. Whenever we reviewed the progress of the Paradip refinery in PMO, there was no progress in land acquisition. To acquire land for public purpose, the state government issues a notification to notify the land parcels that it is going to acquire, in the state Gazette and newspapers. In each meeting in the PMO, the IOCL officials said that the state revenue department in Orissa had not prepared the schedules for land parcels. When these reasons were repeated many times, it became apparent that the revenue department did not have adequate staff to prepare schedules and maps of the area to be included in the land acquisition notification, and hence would take a longer time. So, I suggested that either the IOCL hire some retired revenue officers who could help the state revenue department in this work, or additional manpower be augmented by the Odisha state government themselves. After this the matter moved forward. Then it became apparent that the paperwork involved in land acquisition was huge. Moreover, this was extra work required to be handled by the staff. Hence there was reluctance on their part, leading to delays.

OPENING TO PRIVATE PLAYERS: NEW EXPLORATION LICENSING POLICY

India wanted to increase acreage under oil explorations. The country has an estimated sedimentary area of 3.14 million sq km, consisting of 26 sedimentary basins, of which 57 per cent is in deep waters and remaining 43 per cent is in land and shallow offshore. About 1.06 million sq km area is held under Petroleum Exploration Licenses in 18 basins by national oil companies, namely ONGC, OIL, and private-JV companies. There were some good prospecting areas and some not so good for the prospective players in oil exploration. To increase the domestic production of crude oil and gas in India, the government was considering giving equal opportunities to public and private sector companies.

In 1997-98, the government prepared a New Exploration Licensing Policy (NELP). It aimed to boost the production of oil and natural gas, and provide an equal platform to both public and private sector companies in exploration and production of hydrocarbons. The Directorate General of Hydrocarbons (DGH) was designated as a nodal agency for implementation of the NELP. Of the 26 sedimentary basins identified in India, only 20 per cent of the total area had been well explored. The remaining areas needed to be extensively explored with the best of technologies, with special emphasis on the frontier basins. NELP made possible the much-needed capital and state-of-the-art technology in exploration.

NELP policies and regulations were among the most transparent in the world and meant to revive a healthy spirit of competition between national oil companies, private as well as multinational companies. The development of the exploration sector received a significant boost through this. It brought liberalisation in the sector and created avenues for private and foreign investment (100 per cent Foreign Direct Investment). Under NELP, which became effective from February 1999, the process of competitive bidding was followed, wherein acreages were offered to the participating companies.

ISSUES OF BID EVALUATIONS

There were many versions of the NELP labelled as NELP I, NELP II, NELP III and so on. The bids were invited under these and sent to the Cabinet for approval. I used to see the proposals at the stage when these were placed before the Cabinet and the PM was briefed about them. My stint at Harvard University, had made me quite good at investment appraisal. As and when I got the Cabinet notes, I would check these calculations. Since the proposals were related to exploration, they were based on 3D and other surveys and data. Different bidders would give different options of yield and the availability of crude oil to the government. However, when I used to check these calculations, I used to find many variables and there was no surety that the selected bidder would provide the highest amount of crude oil to the government. With one or two assumptions changing, the higher bidder positions too changed.

I was quite perplexed about why there were no firm evaluation procedures. It appeared to me that the data available was not accurate and the firms were not able to assess the available and extractable oil. All through my stay in the PMO I had reservations about these evaluations. This could be partly because of my lack of knowledge, or partly because of something wrong in these evaluations. I could not be certain about this. Data uncertainties and too many variables made the bid evaluations uncertain and nothing could be done about that.

IOCL–RELIANCE TIE-UP TO MARKET PETROLEUM PRODUCTS

Private oil refineries such as Reliance Refinery of Reliance Industries at Jamnagar could not market their petroleum products at retail outlets themselves. The hidden subsidies available to government sector oil companies such as IOCL, BPCL and HPCL, were not available to private refineries. In a way, it was financially impossible for private sector refineries to sell their petroleum products at the prevailing market price.

The IOCL was a Navratna company and had powers to take decisions in respect of capital expenditure, investment in joint ventures, subsidiaries, signing of marketing agreements, mergers and acquisitions, and human resource management. As a Navratna, it could sign an agreement with Reliance Refinery for marketing their petroleum products in the country. The IOCL board was competent to approve the agreement after getting this vetted by their legal, finance and other wings. Despite this, a senior official of Ministry of Petroleum and Natural Gas prepared a file on this proposed agreement and sent it to the office of the OSD to the PM for obtaining approval on priority basis. From there the file was sent to the Director in charge of handling matters relating to petroleum and natural gas in the PMO. In the evening when I came back from 7 RCR after attending meetings, the Director informed me that he had been advised to process the file and obtain the PM's approval to the proposed agreement between IOCL and Reliance Refinery on urgent basis.

The PM does not have more power than the Minister of Petroleum and Natural Gas in respect to subjects relating to them as well as the PSUs working under the Ministry. I wondered why the file had been sent to the PMO. If the officials in the Ministry had read the *Government of India (Allocation of Business) Rules* and the *Government of India (Transaction of Business) Rules* this would not have happened. Ordinarily, the proposals or files of all ministries of the Government of India, under these Rules, do not require approval of PM. Anything beyond the power of the Minister would go to the Cabinet or the concerned Cabinet Committee for approval. For sending a proposal to the Cabinet or a Cabinet Committee, the Ministry had to prepare a Cabinet note, take comments of concerned ministries such as Finance Ministry etc., and then send the note to the Cabinet Secretariat where the officers would decide the correctness or otherwise of the subject for placing before the Cabinet. In this case, it appeared to me that someone had sent this proposal without proper application of mind or it could be a mischief also to involve the PMO in this. I was quite stickler for rules and returned the file to the same officer who had sent the file to the PMO. I was surprised that even the Secretary Petroleum and Natural Gas too failed to see the incorrectness of the process.

15

POWER SECTOR: OLD LEGACIES, NEW PATHS

INDEPENDENT POWER PRODUCERS

During the early 1990s, there were serious power supply shortages in the country. Power being the most important input for all industrial and commercial activities, the shortages hampered economic growth. There was a rising demand for power in northern, eastern, western, southern and north-eastern regions of the country. The targets fixed for addition of power generation capacities for each year and the Five-Year Plans had been slipping regularly. The state electricity boards did not have adequate resources to fund additions in power generation capacities as they were incurring heavy financial losses in distributing power to rural and agriculture sectors.

The Narasimha Rao government initiated a move to allow standalone private sector power-generation projects called Independent Power Producers (IPPs). By definition, an IPP is an entity that is not a public utility but owns facilities to generate electric power for sale to utilities and end users. The IPPs could set up power generating stations and were required to sign commercial power supply agreements with power utilities such as the state electricity boards, which distributed power to consumers in their licensed areas.

These entities required assurances and guarantees from the Government of India so that they could in turn raise resources from their lenders and banks for setting up power generating units. The comfort letters from the state governments or the Government of India were all the more necessary if these were foreign lenders. They were very well aware of the financial positions of the state electricity boards and their inability to pay IPPs in a timely manner for the energy consumed.

MOU ROUTE PROJECTS

The quickest method to set up an independent power generating unit was through an MoU between the government, power purchasers and the intended promoters of the power project. During early 1990s, the government signed MoUs for six projects including Enron's Dabhol Power project, Hinduja's Visakhapatnam Thermal Power project, 1,000 MW plant of the Mangalore Power Company (MPC) funded by Cogentrix of the USA, etc. Numerous meetings were held to resolve all issues which could lead to their financial closures. However, resolutions of various parameters such as power tariffs, conditions of power and fuel supply, etc., were becoming difficult as the discussions held were based on data discovered without call of open tenders.

In such projects, where there were more than a few hundred parameters, it was very difficult to negotiate and settle optimum prices, costs or performance levels for each of these projects. Many meetings were held and discussions continued in the PMO before and during my tenure. As per the understanding reached between the government and each proposed IPP under the MoU, the Ministry of Finance was required to give a counter guarantee to repay loans to foreign banks or lenders, in case the state electricity boards or the concerned state governments were not able to repay the energy charges to IPPs. Except for one project relating to gas turbines in Andhra Pradesh, all other IPPs had problems. Enron's Dabhol Power Project was set up quickly, but there was a hue and cry about its high power tariff. Despite many meetings there was little forward movement in the financial closure of the projects.

TEHRI HYDROELECTRIC PROJECT

In 1988, the Tehri Hydro Development Corporation (THDC) was formed to manage the Tehri dam. About 75 per cent of the funding was provided by the Central government and 25 per cent by the Uttar Pradesh government. In addition, the state government was required to finance the entire irrigation portion of the project. The total installed capacity of Tehri Dam Hydro Power Complex was to be 2,400 MW. Of this, the Tehri dam installed hydroelectricity generation capacity was to be 1,000 MW, along with a 1,000 MW capacity at pumped storage as well as 400 MW at Koteshwar dam.

Tehri Dam Hydro Power Complex was the only hydro power project of this size under construction in India at that time, and matters relating to it quite often reached the PMO. I noticed that the PMO too was very receptive to the concerns of the people near Tehri dam. This was primarily because of Sunderlal Bahuguna who brought these concerns to the government's attention. Sunderlal Bahuguna, well-known for his simple lifestyle and honest approach to environmental issues of the country had successfully launched many movements in the country to save forests, Chipko movement being one of them. Whenever he came to meet the PM, he was welcomed by all, his concerns heard carefully, and necessary action taken. It had been already agreed by the government to address all matters relating to environment, safety of dams, and rehabilitation of the affected people before implementing the big projects.

Strangely, in the case of Tehri Dam Hydro Power Complex different issues were projected one after another, which not only took time to resolve but also delayed the project leading to cost escalation. I mention here the different issues raised regarding the Tehri Project and to some extent, these show the tendency among people, including important public figures, to derail and delay big projects.

DAM SAFETY CONCERNS AND REHABILITATION

Located about 7.5 km above the Central Himalayan Seismic Gap, which is vulnerable to high magnitude earthquakes, Tehri dam project had initially fuelled concerns regarding its geological stability. In 1991, this region witnessed an earthquake of a magnitude of 6.8 on the Richter scale with its epicentre five kilometres from the location of the dam. There were some opinions that construction of the dam would put further pressure on the seismic gap and increase the chance of another earthquake in the area. Even though the Tehri dam was designed to withstand an 8.4-magnitude earthquake, some seismologists said that earthquakes with a magnitude of 8.5 or more could occur in this region. It could damage the dam and the flood waters could submerge numerous towns on the downstream side.

Another concern was about relief and rehabilitation (R&R) of affected persons and environmental clearances of the Tehri dam. Due to these issues, environment activists and local people of the region actively agitated against the dam. Some environmentalists believed the Tehri dam project had brought onto the centrestage the problems of constructing large dams in the delicate ecosystem of the Himalayan foothills.

HANUMANTHA RAO COMMITTEE

To address the safety, environment, and R &R issues the government set up a committee under the chairmanship of Dr C. H. Hanumantha Rao, a former member of the Planning Commission, in September 1996. The Hanumantha Rao Committee (HRC) studied all issues relating to the Tehri dam and submitted its report in 1997. University of Roorkee, which had one of the best available expertise in dam safety and civil engineering in the country, aided the Committee. The Report was comprehensive and dealt with all aspects of rehabilitation and environmental clearance of the Tehri project.

It appeared that most of its recommendations were acceptable to the people of Tehri and surrounding areas. These were also accepted and implemented by the Central government, the state government and the project authorities. The government after examining the recommendations approved additional benefits and measures, which were incorporated in the Rehabilitation Policy issued in 1998.

One of the recommendations approved by the government, regarding rehabilitation, was the definition of family to include all major sons and daughters, who attained the age of 21 years, and dependent parent (Mother-Father) of the fully affected entitled land owner eligible for ex-gratia payment. This ex-gratia payment was equal to 750 days minimum agricultural wage. In addition to this, the grant of house-construction assistance to the urban landowner families was linked with the progress of construction and shifting, and allotment of a constructed shop was also approved. The government recognised the rights of people living in the villages upstream of Tehri reservoir over the water from Bhagirathi and Bhilangna rivers and tributaries for drinking and irrigation purposes. Once this liberal assistance was approved, it was expected that people of this area would not agitate, and the work on project would go on smoothly and completed in time.

ALLEGATIONS AGAINST CMD OF THDCIL

Even after all the concerns in respect of Dam safety, environmental issues and R & R matters were settled satisfactorily, a delegation met the PM and levelled allegations against the Chairman and Managing Director (CMD) of Tehri Hydro Development Corporation India Limited (THDCIL). They requested PMO for an investigation into the allegations. This appeared to be a way to put pressure on the CMD so that he would become pliable to their demands. We did not know the demand of the local population, but guessed that some local contractors were asking favours for contracts from him. However, since a complaint had been made against the CMD and irregularities alleged in the award of various contracts and implementation of R&R works, we got the issues verified from different agencies.

All allegations were found to be baseless. The CMD was found to be doing a commendable job despite public pressure against continuing work on the dam and its associated works. The demand of the local people to stop work on this ground was again ignored by the government.

TEHRI DAM vs GANGA WATER

When all issues seemed to have been resolved, a letter came from the Vishwa Hindu Parishad (VHP) claiming that the Tehri Dam would destroy the self-purifying qualities of Ganga water, and hence the project should not be implemented. This was strange indeed. Immediately, a Committee was set up by the PM under M. M. Joshi, the HRD Minister, to examine the issues raised, and identify the self-purifying qualities of Ganga water as well as suggest remedial measures.

Setting up of a committee under Joshi seemed a master stroke by the PM. It seemed he knew the people from the VHP who were behind this letter. Moreover, Joshi, a Doctorate in Physics, would have been the best person in the government to chair such a committee and advise the government on this issue. Surprisingly, no meeting of this committee was held for about six months. We issued reminders to the office of the chairman but did not receive any reply to the suggestions to hold early meeting of the committee. Neither were any remedial actions given for preserving the self-purifying qualities of Ganga water for about a year. VHP too did not press for an early resolution of the issues raised by them. It seemed they developed cold feet and did not have solid data to support their contentions before the committee set up for that purpose. In the meanwhile, the work on the Tehri dam continued.

While handling matters relating to the Tehri project I used to feel that the Ministry of Power was not pushing hard to expedite the work. May be the Minister was going slow for fear of antagonising the VHP, or others as there was no other reasons not to speed up the work. The Ministry knew very well that delay in project completion would increase the project cost and its power tariff.

TAKING QUICK DECISIONS – BRAJESH MISHRA SHOWS THE WAY

While the dam was being built, water was diverted through tunnels T3 and T4 bypassing the dam site. As soon as the work was completed there was a need to close these tunnels so that water did not go downstream, instead filled the Tehri reservoir. For some time, there was hesitation within the Ministry of Power to order the closure of tunnels T3 and T4. Closure would have meant that reservoir surrounding the old Tehri town would get filled and the residents would have to be shifted out. If the tunnels were closed in December, the residents from the reservoir areas would have to be shifted prior to that, so that the reservoir would be filled the following monsoon season.

THDCIL had already completed the alternate complex for housing the affected families. Keeping in view the somewhat timid response from Ministry of Power, PMO received calls from the THDCIL and from the Ministry for orders on closures of Tunnels T3 and T4. I informed Principal Secretary Brajesh Mishra about the immediate need to do so. After about an hour he informed me to advise both the Ministry and the THDCIL officials to close these two tunnels.

I remember the day clearly. The landline was not working properly, and I had to speak very loud to someone at Tehri dam for the closure of T3 Tunnel. I mention this here to explain that but for the push from the PMO, particularly Brajesh Mishra and the PM, I cannot imagine the Minister of Power giving orders to close the tunnels. The Minister seemed overawed by the representations of the VHP with respect to the dam and did not want to take any action to antagonise them. This seemed incorrect for the complaints were found frivolous, and on his part, he should have actively worked for the early completion of the dam.

THE SUDDEN CALL

It was a Saturday, and I left the PM office at about 1.30 p.m. I had just reached home and was in the process of unwinding when the

RAX telephone rang. It was from the Principal Secretary's office. I was informed that he wanted to speak to me immediately. Since he rarely rang us at our residence, I thought something urgent must have come up in the PMO.

Within a few seconds he was on the line speaking to me. He said, 'Jarnail Singh, I have two union Cabinet Ministers sitting in front of me. They are suggesting the deletion of a line by the PMO from the Cabinet note of the Ministry of Power relating to Visakhapatnam Thermal Power plant promoted by Hindujas. The line they want to be removed relates to competitive bidding for EPC (Engineering Procurement and Construction) of the project. They say that this project is a state sector project, and if Andhra Pradesh government wants to adopt competitive bidding then let them do that. Why should the Government of India insist on competitive bidding for EPC, which is only giving counter guarantee for repayment of foreign loans?'

After listening to him I informed him that if the Ministry of Power wanted to revise their own Cabinet note, they should request the Cabinet Secretary and withdraw it. No line can be added or deleted in any of the Cabinet notes signed by Secretary or Joint Secretary of the ministries concerned, in the PMO. More importantly, EPC constitutes about 95 per cent of the total cost of the project. For a project, which had a total cost of out about Rs 5,000 crore, EPC would be about Rs 4,750 crore. If EPC was not tendered, then the completion cost of the project could be very high and arbitrary. I told him that EPC should be discovered through competitive bidding alone.

I also said that because of the foreign exchange crisis of East Asian countries, the prices of power projects had reduced by about 25 per cent to 50 per cent as compared to their prices a couple of years back. The reduction in prices of EPC of power projects, I pointed out, had been discussed quite often in meetings in PMO relating to MoU route projects. After hearing me out he realised that it was a very serious issue, and he was aware that PMO had always insisted on competitive bids to discover prices. Immediately, he asked me to come back to office and brief the PM on this.

I rushed back to the PMO. On my way I wondered why the Ministry of Power did not request the Cabinet Secretary to return their Cabinet note and revise it the way they wanted it. Did the Secretary Power refuse to omit that line? Even if the Ministry of Power had proposed deletion of that line, was the Ministry of Finance against the move? As soon as I reached office, I met the Principal Secretary and we went into the PM's office. The PM was working on the main table. He finished his work within a few minutes, and I sat down and explained the position of Visakhapatnam Thermal Power project. It seemed the PM had been already briefed by somebody on this.

I explained that EPC, which constituted about 95 per cent of the total project cost, must be tendered as prices had come down in recent years due to the foreign exchange crisis in East Asian countries. If this was not done, it was likely that the EPC price of the project would be higher by about Rs 1,000 crore than competitive bid price. In addition, the power tariff of the project would also be higher by about 20 per cent or so as the project promoters would fix it based on higher project costs. In that process, the project promoters would get twin benefits from higher EPC price as well as higher power tariff.

I was just finishing explaining to the PM when Jaswant Singh entered the room. He too heard my explanations. As soon as I finished speaking, he said that he had chaired a Parliamentary Committee on Energy some years back in which the committee had recommended that in all MoU route projects, the EPC prices should be only decided through open and competitive bidding. He also quoted a paragraph from the Committee's report where the need for competitive bidding for EPC of all MoU route projects was mentioned.

After listening to us, the PM understood the seriousness of the issue and also realised that some persons were up to mischief. I was asked to wait outside. The two Union Cabinet ministers, who were waiting outside, were called in by the PM. It seemed the PM gave a piece of his mind to both ministers. I learnt that he did not like the brazenness with which the two ministers approached PMO to not only suggest the deletion of a line from a Cabinet note in PMO but approach the subject contrary to the established principles of fairness and competitive bidding being emphasised by his government.

It may be mentioned here that as per the *Government of India (Transaction of Business) Rules* and the *Government of India (Allocation of Business) Rules* the Ministry concerned prepares the Cabinet notes. The Cabinet Secretariat vets each note and checks whether the procedure had been followed by the Ministry for preparing it. The Cabinet Secretariat checks whether the relevant ministries had been consulted and their comments incorporated in the note. Only after all stipulations have been found in order, does the Cabinet Secretary deem the note ready for consideration of the Cabinet.

Later on, the Cabinet and government approved the Visakhapatnam Thermal Power project wherein it was decided that the EPC of the project would be discovered through competitive bidding route as had been proposed by the Ministry of Power in their Cabinet note. I was very happy that Jaswant Singh, who spoke clearly and effectively, drove the point home to the Prime Minister that day.

16

CHALLENGES TO POWER INITIATIVES

50,000 MW HYDROELECTRIC POWER INITIATIVE

In 2002, R.V. Shahi joined as Secretary (Power). He had earlier worked as General Manager in National Thermal Power Corporation Ltd (NTPC) when I was Deputy Secretary in Department of Power, Ministry of Energy in 1983. He was a technocrat appointed to a post where generally, IAS officers are posted. Even though Secretary Shahi was a very competent person, yet there were rumours that Shiv Sena, a coalition partner in the NDA government had thrown their weight behind him for this posting.

After he took over, Secretary Shahi took a number of initiatives to give push to the power sector. An important initiative taken in 2003 was the identification of the 50,000 MW hydroelectric potential. The Central Electricity Authority (CEA), scrutinised all the basins, river falls and the potential sites and prepared a list of locations where the hydroelectric stations could be built. However, since these locations were primarily identified from contour maps, there was a need to do complete survey and investigation for each site.

On 24 May 2003, PM Vajpayee launched the 50,000 MW hydroelectric initiative, which included 162 new hydroelectric schemes in sixteen states. The CEA was entrusted with the overall responsibility for acting on this initiative. It was also decided that the CEA would be responsible for preparation of Preliminary Feasibility Reports (PFRs) of all schemes by September 2004. Even though the initiative started with a lot of fanfare and enthusiasm, the preparation of PFRs was very slow. Most of the 162 project sites were in remote areas and required detailed investigations that generally take over five to six years. These included soil investigations for the tunnels, dam sites and other important components, drillings by Geological Survey of India (GSI), collection and availability of hydrological data, etc. These required adequate time and a lot of resources in terms of money and manpower. CEA lacked both resources and were not expected to spare many people for this work. Some projects moved forward, but work relating to preparation of PFRs of majority of the projects did not take off for lack of clarity on availability of resources. Moreover, the requirement and the delays in obtaining environment and forest clearances, even for investigation work of projects, virtually stalled the work. It is a pity that this 50,000 MW hydroelectric initiative, which could have generated a huge amount of renewable energy and provided huge employment was lost out.

Along with the hydroelectric initiative, other steps such as simplification of procedures for environment and forest clearances for investigation work, etc., should also have been taken up simultaneously. It was possible to do it and the PMO was fully behind the initiative. But the procedures for obtaining clearances were not simplified and this impacted the implementation of the 50,000 MW hydroelectric power initiative.

RESTART OF WORK ON DULHASTI PROJECT

The NHPC had started work on 390 MW Dulhasti Hydroelectric

Project in 1985. A French consortium had been awarded work at a cost of Rs 150 crore. A run of the river project on Chandra River, a tributary of Chenab, it had been designed to supply peaking power to the northern region. The project was located hundreds of kilometres away from town areas in a most inhospitable terrain of Jammu and Kashmir where it was very difficult to provide logistic support for construction of the project. The project area was almost totally devoid of supporting infrastructure, including adequate logistics network of roads and rail lines. All supplies and raw materials to the project site, including cement, wood, stones and steel were transported by helicopters for miles through snowbound areas at exorbitant costs.

Added to the difficult terrain were the problems of Kashmir militancy, as Kishtwar was a hot bed of militancy. There had been several incidents where the militants killed engineers and workers of the projects.

Moreover, about 10.5-km-long tunnel of the project passed through a major geological fault zone termed as fossil valley. It proved to be the most challenging task for the engineers and contractors. The tunnel experienced many geological surprises too, and it collapsed several times during the construction killing workers and damaging equipment. The French consortium which was implementing the project abandoned the work in 1992, after the collapse of the tunnel when tunneling machines were buried under the debris.

The project lay almost abandoned and the cost estimates kept increasing, finally reaching Rs 2,400 crore in the year 2000. The Minister of Power, P.R. Kumaramangalam, quickly took steps to restart work on the project. A note for the government to approve the restarting of work on the project was quickly prepared. Many departments were flabbergasted at the high cost of power generation at Rs 6-7 per KWH of power. However, most of them seemed to ignore key issues such as even if the cost of power generation in 1998-99 appeared very high the fact that the Dulhasti project would produce peaking power, to some extent, justified the higher cost of power generation. In addition to this, the location of the project and the utilisation of the waters of Chenab would improve country's strategic issues vis-à-vis Pakistan as India would start using water from Chenab basin.

Despite opposition from many quarters, Kumaramangalam pushed to restart work on the Dulhasti project and the Cabinet approved it. Due to his efforts, the project was completed in 2007 and it is supplying peaking power to the northern power grid consisting of Jammu and Kashmir, Punjab, Haryana, Uttar Pradesh, Uttarakhand, Rajasthan, Delhi and Union Territory of Chandigarh. I found Kumaramangalam to be a man of action.

INDIAN ELECTRICITY ACT 2003

Before independence, the electricity systems were managed and constructed under the provisions of the India Electricity Act 1910. Immediately after independence, with a view to consolidate the electricity supply systems, the Electricity (Supply) Act 1948 was enacted and state electricity Boards were constituted in almost all the states. These Boards were the licensees responsible for generation, transmission and distribution of electricity in their states. Due to political compulsions in the states, the subsidies, particularly in the agriculture sector, reached an unsustainable level and Boards did not have many resources to upgrade the electricity supply systems. This led to electricity shortages and cuts in the power supply. There was a serious need of increased investments in the power sector which could easily come from private sector. But private sector could only invest in electricity sector if the viability of the electricity supply systems improved.

In 1998, to encourage private sector participation and to provide a level-playing field to different players, the Electricity Regulatory Commissions Act 1998 was enacted, and regulatory commissions were set up in the states as well as at the national level. These commissions were given the power to fix power tariffs, and specify performance parameters to be followed by each electricity supplier for fixing of tariffs. This led to transparency in the fixing of electricity tariffs, and to a large extent the power to fix electricity tariffs became non-political. It also specified that if any state wanted to give electricity subsidy to a particular section of consumers, then it should provide the subsidy from its sources.

The Indian Electricity Act 2003 was enacted to spur the growth of electricity sector, encourage private sector investment in this sector and to provide reliable power supply to the consumers. The work on new electricity legislation was initiated by the Ministry of Power and the Planning Commission. The first step was to consolidate all the old Acts, namely, Indian Electricity Act 1910, Electricity Supply Act 1948, and Electricity Regulatory Commissions Act 1998, and include the provisions to allow the development of electricity sector without least political interference. The whole process took more than a year, and a number of meetings were held in the Ministry of Power, the Planning Commission and the PMO with experts and stakeholders.

The Indian Electricity Act 2003, addressed issues that had slowed electricity reform process in the country and generated new hope for the electricity industry. It consolidated laws relating to generation, transmission, distribution, trading and use of electricity. It promoted competition among different players in public and private sector, protected the interest of consumers, ensured supply of electricity to all areas, rationalised electricity tariffs, ensured transparent policies regarding subsidies, promoted efficient and environmentally benign policies, etc.

The issues related to open access were discussed in detail. There were a number of opinions on allowing the consumers to choose electricity suppliers of their choice. While some experts thought this would encourage efficiency in the electricity supply system, others felt that the step was too revolutionary to be handled by the existing electricity supply systems. No doubt, such a step, wherein the choice was given to consumer to choose its electricity supplier was the ultimate requirement; the time seemed not ripe enough for this revolutionary step. Further, the electricity distribution system required non-discriminatory policies to fix wheeling charges for different electricity suppliers. This was expected to be difficult in many electricity supply systems where some areas and components were still using a mix of old and new accounting methods.

Another factor, seen to possibly hinder free and fair competition among different players, was the dominance of a few big players in the electricity sector. It was expected that with the passage of time, depending on the requirements of the situations, and with amendment and changes in the Act and Rules, there would be a way for the growth and development of the electricity sector. The Indian Electricity Act 2003, was a major step for encouraging more investments and making the electricity sector sustainable.

PRIVATE SECTOR IN POWER TRANSMISSION

The 2003 Act allowed installation of dedicated transmission lines by private power generating companies or captive power generating plants. This helped the generating companies and captive units to establish connectivity with sub-stations and load centres by laying dedicated transmission lines. A joint venture between the Tata Power Company Limited and Power Grid Corporation of India Limited set up a transmission line between Siliguri in West Bengal to Mandola in Uttar Pradesh, covering a distance of 1166 km. The project was completed within the scheduled time and successful commercial operations started in 2006. This was an important event as it was expected that additional private investment might flow into the transmission sector.

POWER TARIFF FOR BHUTANESE PROJECTS

India had been helping Bhutan in setting up several hydroelectric projects. These projects produced more electricity than was required by Bhutan. Most of the electricity produced by these power stations in Bhutan was being sold to India under existing arrangements. Initially, the power tariff was Rs 0.25 per KWH. I attended a few discussions where Bhutanese government proposals to increase the power tariff to rupee one or more was discussed. All investment cost of these power stations and associated transmissions were provided as grant to Bhutanese government, hence, the power tariffs were low. Since no established methods or principles were followed to calculate the tariff for sale of power from Bhutanese power stations to India, the decisions were taken to fix the tariff at a political level in consultation with the MEA.

After some meetings and discussions, a decision was taken to fix power tariff at 50 paise, which was subsequently raised. Indian government did not want any irritants in the power purchase from the Bhutanese projects. This was the case with projects which were set up with financial grants from the Government of India. However, if there were any power projects set up with private sector investment, the tariffs from such projects would be based on established financial principles and acceptable to the private investor.

PRIVATISATION OF ELECTRICITY DISTRIBUTION IN DELHI

In 2002, the electricity supply system in the national capital territory of Delhi was in very poor shape. There was massive power theft and the system was not at all sustainable. The power loss in distribution was as high as 57 per cent in some areas with average loss being around 45 per cent. Due to faulty meters and theft of power, the distribution lines and transformers were overloaded leading to frequent breakdowns. There were reports of large-scale collusion of lower level staff with unscrupulous consumers. The Government of Delhi decided to go for privatisation and the Central government fully backed the move.

There were initial hiccups in preparing the Request for Proposal (RFP) for inviting private players to participate in the bid. An issue that came up for repeated discussion in the PMO was that of the decision parameter in the RFP. This was a tricky question since this could make a lot of difference for the selection of successful bidders. Since power loss in Delhi was the most important issue in Delhi Electricity Supply Undertaking (DESU), it was decided to use reduction of loss as the decision parameter.

Despite contrary opinions, the management of DESU and senior officials in Delhi knew that even a one per cent reduction in power loss would bring massive relief to the state exchequer. Having decided thus, the RFPs were floated. Reliance Infrastructure and Tata Power were the two successful bidders for different parts of Delhi. There has been tremendous improvement in the electricity supply in Delhi NCR. The privatisation of electricity in Delhi proved to be a success despite objections raised against Sheila Dixit's Congress government for taking the step. However, the Vajpayee-led NDA government at the Centre gave full support to the Delhi government.

POWER REFORMS IN ODISHA[1]

The Odisha government was among the first states to unbundle the Odisha State Electricity Board in 1996, and convert it into different corporations for generation, transmission and distribution. The electricity distribution was then divided into corporations and privatised. The state government implemented the model of power-sector restructuring conceived by the World Bank. It was expected that the electricity reforms of the Odisha government would turn around the sector. The reform, however, belied all expectations and calculations. The privatised distribution companies, started with a clean balance sheet but were not able to make any significant dent in the commercial or technical losses. Distribution losses remained well over 40 per cent in all four distribution companies even after some marginal reductions were achieved.

Despite the collective wisdom of the bank professionals and numerous international consultants, the reform roadmap contained too many assumptions and fallacies which doomed it right from the start. The privatized distribution companies found it difficult to achieve any significant reduction in losses. Saddled with the baggage of the earlier set up, these distribution companies were either unwilling or unable to take the steps necessary to check the losses. In the PMO we kept a watch and tried to help the Odisha government, but it was not of much use.

HYDROELECTRIC PROJECTS IN NEPAL

Nepal has excellent potential for hydroelectric power generation. However, the country does not have the financial resources to exploit the potential. For private investors to come and develop hydroelectric sites, there had to be buyers of power and agreements for sale or purchase of power in place. Until the agreements for sale of power are in place for any hydroelectric project, the investors would not be willing. I was Deputy Secretary in the Ministry of Power in 1984, and my colleague used to handle hydroelectric projects with Nepal. He used to refer to projects such as Pancheshwar, Karnali, etc. in Nepal, and how these could be jointly developed by Nepal and India.

The Pancheshwar Multipurpose Project (PMP) is a bi-national hydroelectric project to be developed on the Mahakali River bordering Nepal and India. It is a mutual interest project and is covered under the integrated Mahakali Treaty signed between Nepal and India. According to this Treaty, equal sizes of underground power house, i.e. of 3240 MW, will be constructed on either side of Mahakali River. The PMP also offers the benefit of regulated water for irrigation to a vast area of agricultural land in both countries, and flood control at downstream.

I was surprised that the same projects were still under discussion between the two countries in 2002, when I was Joint Secretary in the PMO. A delegation from Nepal came to meet the Principal Secretary and discussed about joint ventures in hydroelectric projects with India. They were more interested in increasing dam heights and producing peaking power. Increasing of dam heights would lead to increased cost of projects, which was not in Indian interests. That was why India was uncomfortable with an increase in installed capacity, which would also give a low plant load factor.

The Nepal government's position on these hydroelectric projects had been changing frequently and this did not help in taking any decision on big investments in these projects. By the time I left the PMO in August 2004, there was still no firm view from Nepal on these projects. As compared to Nepal, the construction of projects in Bhutan had been going on at full speed and it has become a big exporter of power in the region.

CAPITAL BASE

After the unbundling of the state electricity Boards, the privatisation of the electricity distribution companies was one of the logical next steps. It was expected that privatisation would improve the management of the distribution companies and their efficiencies, reduce pilferage of electricity and introduce quick decision-making. However, to form distribution companies, the government had to prepare balance sheets of assets and liabilities of the companies. The state electricity boards had been following an accounting system from which it was difficult to work out the capital base of any distribution company. The materials such as poles, transformers, conductors, etc. had been purchased over the years, and the accounting had neither been correct nor updated. The calculation of the depreciated values of all works implemented and materials installed, was a mammoth task. It was unworkable and some approximation was necessary to move forward.

During a discussion on this subject in PMO, a senior officer of Uttar Pradesh government suggested a better method to work out the capital base of such a distribution company. According to him, if it was assumed that the distribution company would get 10 per cent return on investment, which was its capital base, then reverse calculations could be done to find out the capital base. For example, if the profit generated was Rs 150 crore in any distribution company, then the capital base of that company could be taken as Rs 1,500 crore. This was simple and also made financial sense. This could be then compared with whatever capital base had been worked out, by adding the depreciated values of all the equipment and materials used in the distribution company. It seemed workable in the prevailing system.

NOTE

1. Odisha was formerly known as Orissa till it was renamed in 2011.

The author with wife Seraphina Singh and sons Paramjit and Vikramjit at the India Gate lawns in 1983.

The author receiving Master's degree in Public Administration (Public Policy and Management) under the Edward S. Mason Program from John F. Kennedy School of Government, Harvard University, USA, in 1989.

The author (first, second row from left) with Prime Minister H.D. Deve Gowda and other senior PMO officers at the then 7 Race Course Road (now 7 Lok Kalyan Marg), PM's Office, New Delhi on 1 January, 1997.

The author (second from left) with Prime Minister Inder Kumar Gujral and senior PMO officers at the then 7 Race Course Road (now 7 Lok Kalyan Marg), PM's Office, New Delhi on 1 January, 1998.

The author (to PM's right) with Prime Minister Atal Bihari Vajpayee and senior PMO officers at the then 7 Race Course Road (now 7 Lok Kalyan Marg), PM's Office, New Delhi on 1 January, 1999.

The author wishing Prime Minister Atal Bihari Vajpayee on his birthday at the then 7 Race Course Road (now 7 Lok Kalyan Marg), PM's Office, New Delhi on 25 December 2001.

The author (extreme left) visiting the Ropar Thermal Power Station of Punjab in 2001.

The author and his wife Seraphina Singh with Prime Minister A.B. Vajpayee at a dinner hosted by the PM at the PM's residence in the then 5 Race Course Road (now 5 Lok Kalyan Marg), New Delhi in 2002.

The author (behind the PM) and other senior PMO officers with Prime Minister Atal Bihari Vajpayee on his birthday at the then 7 Race Course Road (now 7 Lok Kalyan Marg), PM's Office, New Delhi on 25 December 2002.

The author (5th from right) and his PMO colleagues pose with Prime Minister Atal Bihari Vajpayee on his birthday at the then 7 Race Course Road (now 7 Lok Kalyan Marg), PM's Office, New Delhi on 25 December 2003.

The author (second from left) with his colleagues in Panchavati of the then 7 Race Course Road (now 7 Lok Kalyan Marg), PM's Office, New Delhi on 17 May 2004 during the farewell to PM A.B. Vajpayee.

The author receiving the Prime Minister's Award for Excellence in Public Administration for the year 2007-08 from Vice President M. Hamid Ansari at Vigyan Bhavan, New Delhi, on 21 April 2009. Union Cabinet Secretary K.M. Chandrasekhar is also seen.

The author, along with his team, posing after receiving the Prime Minister's Award for Excellence in Public Administration for the year 2007-08 at Vigyan Bhavan, New Delhi, on 21 April 2009.

17

FOCUS ON NORTH-EAST

AN AGENDA FOR DEVELOPMENT

The north-eastern region of India has about 8 per cent of the area and 4 per cent of the population of the entire country. This region lags far behind others in terms of infrastructure development, and other indices (electricity, telecommunication services, health and education facilities) used for measuring economic development of any area. Surface communication in the hill areas is difficult, making infrastructure development and conduct of business activities costly and challenging.

It was primarily to address this lag that Prime Minster Deve Gowda launched the 'New Initiatives for North Eastern Region'. The extent of remoteness and difficulties experienced by the people of this region do not get reflected in the national media as regularly as it should. As a result, people in other parts of India are not fully aware of the issues of the North-East, even though they are aware of the low level of development. Prime Ministers Deve Gowda and Vajpayee brought focus to the region. They emphasised on expediting the infrastructure and economic development of the region during their tenures in comparison to the Narasimha Rao period.

G. K. PILLAI: THE FULCRUM FOR DEVELOPMENT OF THE NORTH-EAST

The best thing that happened for the North-East was the appointment of G. K. Pillai as Joint Secretary (North-East) in the MHA from 1996 to 2001. He literally gave life to the NE Division and galvanised it. He had an aggressive working style and quick decision-making capability. During his five-year tenure in MHA, he was touring almost every fortnight and visited all remote areas of the North-East.

The officials in the NE Division of MHA often pointed out that as compared to Mr Pillai's visits to the North-East, his predecessor visited the region only once in his five-year stint and that too up to Guwahati. Mr Pillai was forthright in his views. A one-man walking encyclopaedia about all issues relating to the region, he almost singlehandedly prepared papers and notes used by the PMO for the PM's visits to the North-East. It would not be wrong to say that but for his proactive and constructive approach, the North-East would not have got as much attention during the tenure of the two prime ministers.

DEVELOPMENT SEMINARS: ASSESSING NEEDS

One thing Mr Pillai started during his tenure was the holding of development seminars in different district headquarters, preferably in the most remote districts of the region. Villagers, public leaders, NGOs, government officials and other stakeholders in development were invited, and new initiatives as well as the progress of on-going schemes were discussed threadbare. The need for new development projects and performance of different government departments (both of Central and the concerned state government) were also discussed and documented. Specific recommendations based on the consensus in these development seminars were made for new projects, programmes and schemes or for improving the working of existing programmes. The proceedings of these seminars were then sent to concerned departments of both the Central and state governments. Based on these, the MHA took initiatives on major schemes and projects with the ministries.

In organising these seminars, Pillai's idea gave voice to the people in the development planning of their areas. Such was his personal involvement that when I visited these areas after his tenure, people still fondly remembered him. He had left such a solid mark on the development of the North-East that it would be difficult for another JS (NE) to match his energy and enthusiasm. This is a singular example of how one person in the Ministry could make a difference in the way a division functioned and enabled development of a region in our country.

MAKING VISITS POSSIBLE

When Prime Minister Deve Gowda visited North-East in October 1996, it was noticed that the officers from different ministries and departments of the government rarely visited the region. One reason often given was the unavailability of travel facilities from Guwahati to the interiors. As such, the officers neither formulated development schemes for the region nor advised state governments in formulating projects and preparing development plans. The unavailability of transport was thus, a major reason behind fewer Central schemes and projects in the North-East and the region not getting the attention it deserved at the national level.

After PM Deve Gowda's visit, it was decided that the Secretaries of the different ministries should visit North-Eastern states once in two-three months, and at least one senior officer of the Joint Secretary level would visit once a month. In order to make the travel beyond Guwahati easy, a helicopter was stationed at Guwahati by the MHA for the use of visiting officers. The helicopter could be booked by any ministry from the MHA. Even though it was an excellent facility, yet, only a few officers used it during the first year and travelled to the North-East. It thus became apparent that most miniseries did not take interest in the development of the region. Not all officers working for the government were like G. K.

Pillai. He too could have, like his predecessor, sat in the North Block but he chose to contribute his might for the development of the region. As for the helicopter not being used, there were critical audit observations about the idle helicopter standing parked at Guwahati.

While instructions were issued from time to time to the ministries and departments, it had some effect for a few months and then all was forgotten. So much can be said about the interest of most senior officers in the development of North-East. The same officer who would give a number of excuses against visiting North-East, would take a flight to Europe or the USA with a few hours' notice. This was one of the reasons of underutilization of plan funds in the region leading to the formation of NLCPR.

COMMUNITY INFORMATION CENTRES

Many development blocks and districts in the North-East did not have an adequate telecommunications system. As a result, people did not have access to the latest information on recruitment, education and other programmes of the government. It was thought that telecommunications and information technology revolution would not be able to penetrate the interior areas of the region. To bridge this gap, the government decided to set up Community Information Centers (CICs) in all rural development blocks.

In August 2002, the Government of India, through the Department of Information Technology, launched the CIC project in each rural development block in the North-East. This was one of the biggest initiatives in the information and communications technology sector in the North-East. At that time there were 487 development blocks in the eight states of Arunachal Pradesh, Assam, Manipur, Meghalaya, Mizoram, Nagaland, Sikkim and Tripura. The project implementation encountered several difficulties because of the tough terrain and other logistical issues in remote locations. The initial configuration of each CIC was to give computer systems, internet facilities through satellites, diesel power generator wherever power supply was not available or was erratic, and two trained persons to man the CIC. The deputy commissioners of each district were asked to provide space and furniture for the CICs and recruit two people on a contract basis.

With time, due to the increase in the number of rural development blocks, the number of CICs increased to 555. The services offered by CICs expanded to include Information Technology education and training, facilities of E-mail and internet access for the public, information dissemination for the people, citizen-centric applications and services, as well as regular training by trained operators on computer basics for the local community. This scheme was extended to Jammu and Kashmir later.

NORTH-EAST: GETTING CONNECTIVITY

There were restrictions and ban on the extension of internet and mobile services in Jammu and Kashmir and the north-eastern states. Till September 2003, mobile telephones, as well as internet services, were available only in Greater Guwahati and Shillong areas. The main reason for non-extension of these services to the other areas of Assam, Meghalaya and to the states of Arunachal Pradesh, Nagaland, Mizoram, Tripura, and Manipur was the security concern of security forces. The MHA and Ministry of Defence were not in favour of extension of these services on the ground of high militant and terrorist activities and the fear that these services would increase subversive activities in the region. However, this also meant that an overwhelming number of peace-loving people of Jammu and Kashmir and the North-East would remain deprived of the benefits of the telecommunications technology which could improve business and trade as well as spur economic growth and create tremendous employment opportunities. What a pity it was!

In 2002-03, the discussion for extending mobile, internet and other value-added services of telecommunications in the North-East and Jammu and Kashmir began. The arguments of MHA and the security forces were ignoring the brighter side of internet and mobile. I was surprised at the extent to which the MHA and security agencies, including Intelligence agencies, were stretching their arguments to deprive the region of the benefits of telecommunications technology.

When Arun Shourie took over as Minister of Communications, he had a vastly different approach and suddenly, the move to extend these services to North-East gathered momentum. I also contributed my bit to this and was happy that Brajesh Mishra pushed this forward. In the meetings, the objections of security agencies were overruled and the government had realised that internet and mobile services would improve business, trade and working environment, and thus spur economic growth. It was also expected that improved business and trade would create tremendous employment opportunities, which would wean away the youth from militancy.

I remember a discussion in PMO where one of the arguments against these services was that militants could use mobiles to pass on information about the movements of security forces and plan subversive activities. To counter this, another participant pointed out that there were rumours that some militants were using satellite phones, which were better than mobiles. Eventually, the government decided to extend the services to all the states of the North-East, and to Jammu and Kashmir. It was also decided that the PM should launch these services for the North-East from Kohima in October 2003.

PREPARING FOR NAGALAND VISIT

Before going to Nagaland to launch mobile and Internet services, a meeting was held to discuss all important issues to be addressed during the visit. An important point for discussion in that meeting was about a possible reply to the Naga leaders about the demand of integration of Naga areas with Nagaland state. This question was expected from anyone or anywhere—the political leaders, a press conference or any other platform. Since peace talks were going on, the Government of India did not like to say much about the talks. I was present in that meeting when the Principal Secretary, fully aware of the discussions with NSCN (IM) wrote a note for the PM to use if a question is raised at any platform. I too kept a copy of the note.

PM LAUNCHES MOBILE SERVICES FROM KOHIMA

The Nagaland government was very eager to welcome the PM to Kohima. Accordingly, a tour programme was planned for him to first go to Dimapur, and then to Kohima by helicopter. The launch of the Bharat Sanchar Nigam Limited (BSNL) mobile and internet services for the North-East was on 27 October 2003. Along with the launch other meetings were also planned. The following day, PM was scheduled to address the convocation of Nagaland University and then a public meeting in the stadium in Kohima.

It had begun to rain when the PM's entourage landed at the Dimapur airport. The helicopters were unable to take off for Kohima, so we waited at the airport for the rain to stop. After a while, realising it would not stop raining, an alternate arrangement was made by road to Kohima. We travelled by National Highway 2 (the then National Highway 39), supposedly, one of the best roads in Nagaland. However, it was so poorly maintained that the PM commented about it in his public meeting the next day.

As soon as we reached Kohima, PM inaugurated the launch of mobile services from Kohima for the whole of North-East. It was a glorious day for the region as a major initiative was taken in the telecommunications sector that day. After the launch, he had short meetings with different delegations. When all meetings were over, I retired for the day. I was staying at the residence of Amarjit Singh Bhatia, Secretary to Governor of Nagaland.

AN URGENT CALL AND SOME IMPORTANT DISCUSSIONS

I had just gone to bed when I got a message to meet the PM urgently. I reached Raj Bhawan within fifteen minutes and found him in the lounge of the Raj Bhawan with the Chief Minister and his Cabinet colleagues. I assumed that they were discussing important issues in that late hour.

As soon as I arrived, the Prime Minister requested them to wait in the next room as he wanted to discuss some matters with me. When we were alone, he informed me that the CM and his council of ministers were requesting him to announce the integration of Naga areas of the neighbouring states with Nagaland in the public meeting the following day. I had a copy of Brajesh Mishra's note in my folder. I took it out and showed it to him. He read it a few times quietly, then he met the CM and his council of ministers again.

Despite the tremendous pressure from the CM of Nagaland, PM Vajpayee did not agree to make any such announcement the following day or thereafter. On the contrary, he informed them that the Government of India would not propose any change in boundaries of any state of the North-East, unless and until the states concerned, their political parties, and their people agreed to it on their own and requested the Central government to make such changes. This has been the stand of the government since then.

A CIVIC RECEPTION AND A PUBLIC MEETING

The Prime Minister was given a civic reception at the stadium ground in Kohima the next day, where he addressed a huge public meeting. It may be mentioned here that neither Indira Gandhi nor Rajiv Gandhi ever visited Kohima as prime ministers. On 30 March 1953, a visit by Jawaharlal Nehru saw an embarrassing spectacle when about 5,000 Nagas turned their backs on the PM after he had rejected their demand for a 'sovereign' Nagaland. Similarly, PM Morarji Desai who visited Kohima, too, is not remembered with fondness. Prime Minister Deve Gowda's visit in October 1996, however, struck a chord with the state government and its people for his down-to-earth approach, and for initiating long term development schemes for the state. It was during PM Vajpayee's time that the Government of India recognised the 'unique' history of the Nagas but admitted that mistakes had been committed and lamented the unnecessary spilling of blood in the state.

The Prime Minister began by speaking in Nagamese. In his opening remarks, he said that there was an overwhelming desire among Naga people for a permanent peace with honour and dignity. He spoke of his government's strong desire for permanent peace in Nagaland based on a lasting solution, and with honour and dignity for its people. He said this was the time for reconciliation and peace making. It was also the path that Mahatma Gandhi and Loknayak Jayaprakash Narayan, true friends of the Nagas, wanted all Indians to follow.

While referring to the 'unique' history of the Nagas, the PM pointed out that uniqueness had in no way diminished the spirit of patriotism among the Naga people, who were inspiring examples of patriots. He specially referred to the sacrifices of the jawans from Nagaland during the Kargil war. He announced assistance for roads, national highways, creation of employment opportunities and for development of IT sector. The PM's visit not only touched the hearts of the Naga people, it created a positive impact and was welcomed by all.

18

A PUSH FOR BIG PROJECTS

THE BRAHMAPUTRA BOARD

The Brahmaputra Board, set up under the Brahmaputra Board Act 1980, works under the Union Ministry of Water Resources. The jurisdiction of the Board includes both Brahmaputra and Barak valleys, and covers all the states of the North-East, Sikkim and parts of West Bengal which fall under Brahmaputra basin. The main objectives for the establishment of the Board were to prepare and implement Master Plans in association with the states for the flood management, bank erosion, drainage congestion, and development as well as utilisation of water resources of the Brahmaputra valley.

The focus of the Board was on survey and investigation, and the preparation of Detailed Project Reports (DPRs) of various schemes. After preparing the DPRs of projects, these were handed over to the states or PSUs for implementation. The Board did not have the power to raise funds from the open market for implementation of projects as could be done by other organisations such as National Hydroelectric

Power Corporation Limited (NHPC), and North Eastern Electric Power Corporation Limited (NEEPCO). Due to this, most people in Assam did not think that the present Board could serve much purpose.

When the Board was set up initially, people expected it would act as a fulcrum for projects relating to the development of water resources of Brahmaputra and Barak valleys. It did not fulfil their expectations and remained, primarily, a survey and investigation body. This led Chief Minister Prafulla Kumar Mahanta, in one of his meetings with the PM, to refer it as a 'board' (a sign board only). He was referring to its lack of power to raise resources and implement big projects for flood management and power generation. The satire was not lost on the PM, as he understood exactly what the Brahmaputra Board was all about.

G. K. Pillai emphasised a more active role for the Brahmaputra Board and the NEDFi in the development of North-East. From time to time, the need to entrust more projects to the Board was raised and discussed but since it was set up by an Act of Parliament, it was quite difficult to amend it. Creating the Brahmaputra Board like a PSU or a company could have given it a lot of flexibility to operate and raise funds.

One of the important projects given to the Board as a special case was the Pagladiya Dam project. The project was meant for flood moderation, benefit an area of 40,000 hectares and bring irrigation to 54,160 hectares. An incidental power generation of 3 MW was also proposed across Pagladiya River at Thalkuchi in Baksa District under Bodoland Territorial Autonomous Districts (BTAD) in Assam. The project envisaged the construction of a 25-metre-high and 21-km-long earthen dam with a concrete spillway. The Government of India sanctioned the project in January 2001, at an estimated cost of Rs 542.90 crore for construction by the Board. It was expected that after implementing this project, the Brahmaputra Board would start implementing other such projects too.

DIBANG MUTLIPURPOSE PROJECT

Dibang River is a tributary river of the Brahmaputra and flows through the states of Arunachal Pradesh and Assam. A Dibang Multipurpose

Project was initially investigated by Brahmaputra Board. I had reviewed the progress of the schemes implemented by the Brahmaputra Board a few times. During one such review, I noted that the cost of power generation of Dibang Project as per the project report was less than Rs 1.50 per KWH. Such low cost of power generation surprised me. As per the feasibility report, the project was to generate about 3,000 MW of power and moderate floods in Assam. I advised the Board to go ahead with the project but was told by the Board officials that they could not implement such a big project of Rs 10,000 crore. The Brahmaputra Board had virtually abandoned the Dibang project after investigation and preparation of its feasibility report.

Since this was one of the best projects I had ever seen with such a low cost of power generation and high Plant Load Factor (PLF)—as high as 53 per cent—I decided to take up the matter for the transfer of the project to National Hydroelectric Power Corporation Ltd. (NHPC). I felt NHPC was the best organisation in India to implement such big projects. NEEPCO was implementing medium-sized hydroelectric projects.

I talked to Yogendra Prasad, CMD NHPC, about this and asked him whether NHPC would like to take over the project. He was very enthusiastic to do so if the Government of India could ask Brahmaputra Board to transfer the project. I knew that Yogendra Prasad was a very good field engineer and had implemented projects for NHPC in difficult places and situations in India. I continued my discussions about transfer of the project with officials in the Ministry of Power, Ministry of Water Resources and Planning Commission. A few meetings were enough for everyone to realise what an excellent project this was. It was decided that NHPC should implement the project and the Brahmaputra Board was asked to hand over all project data and details to NHPC.

I advised the Central Water Commission (CWC) to do the scale/incremental analysis and revise the feasibility report by including all costs and benefits of the project. Initially, there was resistance in CWC for such analysis. I took a few meetings on this issue and when the benefits of this analysis was clear to all, the analysis was done. Other issues relating to the project too were resolved through meetings in the PMO. In addition, a transmission system was planned and designed to evacuate power of Dibang Project with interconnections at Misa.

It was an accepted fact that such a big project with high Plant Load Factor would add stability to the National Power Grid, which was an added advantage of the Dibang Multipurpose Project. It took time to design this dam, which according to experts, would be the highest straight gravity dam. Since the Dibang river floor was soft, the dam was planned with hollow concrete blocks. I heard that in 2008, PM Manmohan Singh laid the foundation stone for the Dibang Multipurpose Project. There were some objections raised by environmentalists, but those could be addressed by the project authorities.

AIRPORT UPGRADATION

The surface transport and communications were (and still is) difficult in the North-East. It takes a lot of time to reach Delhi and other cities in the country from the state capitals of the North-East. Railway connectivity is mostly limited to Guwahati and a few towns in the region. Air connectivity was easily the preferred mode of transportation. Improvement in air transportation required upgradation of infrastructure of all airports but the Airport Authority of India (AAI) did not have funds to upgrade all.

Keeping in view the fund shortage, Government of India started providing funds to AAI from the North Eastern Council (NEC) for improving the infrastructure of the airports. A formula was worked out under which NEC and AAI were to provide funds in the ratio of 60-40 per cent, respectively. This removed the main hurdle of fund scarcity which was delaying the upgradation of airports. The upgradation began once the new funding arrangement was worked out. When PM Vajpayee visited Manipur, the first comment he made after landing was that the Imphal airport was better than the Lucknow airport. I did not fully believe him and took it as a casual comment till he repeated it in the Imphal Raj Bhavan. I informed him then of the extra funds being provided to the AAI to improve infrastructure of airports in North-East.

NUMALIGARH REFINERY

The work on Numaligarh Refinery was going on for quite some time. At some stage, the work stopped because of non-availability of funds of about Rs 1,300 crore. Ranjit Dutta, the Managing Director, was making a lot of efforts to get funds to complete the refinery.

One of the arguments put forward against funding and completion of Numaligarh Refinery was that the consumption of petroleum products in the North-East was low and production of crude oil in the region had also slowed down. There was a need for a substantial amount of crude oil to be brought in from Bengal, then transport the refined petroleum products outside the North-East. This appeared to be a totally unfeasible project. It had put the viability of the project under a serious question mark. The financial viability of the Numaligarh Refinery would have become sound if either the production of crude oil in the North-East, or the demand of petroleum products in the North-East would have been enough to absorb all the refined products from the refinery. The apparent financial unviability of the project affected the funding and hence bringing work to a standstill.

The management of the refinery was not able to place orders for major equipments such as hydrocracker units, etc., for want of funds. Even though I was handling matters relating to the Ministry of Petroleum and Natural Gas, I was not fully involved in the detailed construction schedules and tying up funds for the refineries. Dutta knew Saikia well and he arranged a presentation on the Numaligarh Refinery. He also explained his failed efforts to get funds from Oil Industry Development Board (OIDB). I found Dutta to be a very persuasive and determined person who did not want to leave the project incomplete.

Even though it was mentioned in the 'New Initiatives' that adequate funds would be given for ongoing projects, and Numaligarh Refinery was specially mentioned, yet funds were not being provided. With pressure from the PMO, the Ministry of Petroleum and Natural Gas agreed to provide adequate funds by leaving aside the issue of immediate viability. When funds were made available, we found Dutta worked very hard to complete the project. On one occasion he came up to me to explain the difficulties faced to bring hydrocracker by a steamer through Bangladesh. Finally, with Saikia's assistance, the Refinery project was completed. If the PMO would not have pushed for this project, this too would have remained incomplete like the Assam Gas Cracker Project, which had been pending for decades without funding.

BOGIBEEL RAIL-CUM-ROAD BRIDGE: A FOURTH LINK OVER BRAHMAPUTRA

During PM Deve Gowda's visit to North-East in October 1996, the Assam Government had requested for a fourth bridge on the Brahmaputra between Dhemaji and Dibrugarh districts of Assam. In view of the serious bottlenecks of connectivity between the two sides of the river, the PM had approved the construction and agreed to provide Rs 1,000 crore during 1997-98 for this bridge. He had announced that the bridge would be completed during the Ninth Five Year Plan.

It was expected that once completed, the 4.94-km-long Bogibeel Bridge would be the longest bridge of its kind in India. There were initial hitches about the design and funding, and it took some time for the work to start. However, the construction started after PM Vajpayee laid the foundation stone on 21 April 2002. The bridge was planned to be completed within seven years of laying the foundation stone. But it has witnessed huge time and cost overruns due to delay in design, sanction and construction activities.

After several years of slow progress, the UPA government under Dr Manmohan Singh accorded national status to it in 2007. The Union Ministry of Finance then started funding 75 per cent of the project costs while the Ministry of Railways financed the remaining 25 per cent. Initially estimated at Rs 1,767 crore, the delay resulted in the project's overall cost escalating to around Rs 5,900 crore. Finally after 21 years of wait, the bridge was thrown open to traffic in 2018.

19

MINISTRY OF DEVELOPMENT OF NORTH EASTERN REGION

One of the most important initiatives of the Vajpayee government was the setting up of a separate Ministry of Development of North Eastern Region, also known as the Ministry of DoNER. This initiative had its origin in the setting up of the Non-Lapsable Central Pool of Resources (NLCPR), the credit for which goes to both Jaswant Singh and PM Vajpayee.

The NLCPR, as mentioned earlier, was based on the guidelines laid down by PM Deve Gowda in 1996. The Vajpayee government agreed with the guidelines to earmark 10 per cent fund for the North-East and pushed it forward and concretized it. The Department of DoNER was set up in 2001 to expedite the socio-economic development efforts in the region. In 2004, it was converted into the Ministry of DoNER (MDoNER).

The NLCPR was initially handled by the Planning Commission. After the establishment of the Department of DoNER, it was transferred to the Department of DoNER, and now the Ministry of DoNER is responsible for coordinating the planning, execution and monitoring of the development schemes and projects taken up with NLCPR. This is the only Ministry which has a territorial jurisdiction in the country.

NORTH EASTERN COUNCIL

The North Eastern Council (NEC) was set up in 1971 under direct administrative control of the MHA. The Joint Secretary, in charge of the North-East in MHA, was responsible for coordinating all matters of development, law and order and other affairs before the formation of MDoNER. I had been attending the meetings of NEC since 1979, when I was Joint Secretary (PWD) in Manipur.

In its initial years, the NEC set up several regional institutes for education, health, police training and other sectors, which the states of the region were finding difficult to set up on their own. The NEC also funded regional schemes such as interstate roads, regional power generating stations through NEEPCO, etc. A Governor from one of the eight states was nominated as chairman of NEC. The NEC Act has been amended from time to time based on the states' demands. Presently, the Home Minister is the ex-officio chairman of NEC, and Governors and Chief Ministers of constituent states are its members. In addition, there are two nominated members, and a person from NITI Aayog as member. NEC is now mandated to be an advisory body for regional planning of the North-East.

Our efforts to rejuvenate the NEC failed. We, in the PMO, were quite certain that the Governors need not be members of the NEC, as they were not directly involved in either planning or implementation of economic development programmes of the states. Hence, we were surprised that even after a strong opinion in the PMO, the Governors continued to be members even in the amended structure of the NEC.

I have attended over a dozen meetings of the NEC and heard all CMs criticising it for not giving adequate funds to their states. The CMs look at the NEC as a funding agency for additional schemes, and not as a regional planning body as it was originally envisaged. Many CMs openly stated that it would be better if funds came directly from the Government of India instead. The states have ceased to look at NEC for any advice on planning for the region. Perhaps, it is time to rethink the need, if any, of NEC today.

MANIPUR: A STATE CLOSE TO MY HEART

I belonged to the erstwhile Manipur-Tripura cadre (it has now been divided into two separate cadres of Manipur and Tripura) and had served for more than 15 years in Manipur. I worked primarily in the Naga dominated hill districts and visited most of the villages of Senapati, Ukhrul and Chandel districts. I knew the difficulties faced by the hill villagers and did not let go of any opportunity to make a difference. When the Government of India set up NLCPR and MDoNER, I took the initiative to propose the extension of 33 KV power grids to the hill areas of Manipur and provided funds for water supply schemes in a big way from the NLCPR. I talked to the state government officials and advised them to prepare schemes for power and water supply sectors for the hills.

The women in the hills walked far, and sometimes through steep places, to collect water. Much of their time was spent on fetching water. The state government prepared a project for 33 KV grid in all hill areas covering Thanlon (Pherzawl district); Tousem, Tamei (Tamenglong district); Phaibung, Lakhamai (Senapati district); Saikul (Kangpokpi district); Namrei (Ukhrul district); Kasom Khullen, Phungyar (Kamjong district); and Chandel and Chakpikarong (Chandel district). The important water supply schemes, which covered six to ten villages each, included Mao, Tadubi, Maram, Chakpikarong, and Motbung. These schemes were approved but the implementation took a long time. Once implemented, these schemes improved the infrastructure in the hills of Manipur substantially.

SENAPATI PHAIBUNG ROAD: WHEN POLITICS SPOILT THE PITCH

On 27 October 1996, G. K. Pillai and I were discussing and working on PM Deve Gowda's statement on 'New Initiatives', which he was scheduled to announce at the Guwahati airport. During our discussion, we included the Maram-Phaibung road (later changed to Senapati-Phaibung road) as one of the projects. This road was meant to provide connectivity between Senapati and the backward areas of Chilevai and Lepaona areas of the Poumai tribe of Manipur. This area had remained neglected for want of road communication and power supply system. For two weeks in 1976-77, I had toured these backward villages on foot as Sub Divisional Officer of Tadubi and knew the condition of the villagers.

The Chilevai and Lepaona villagers had treated me well and looked after me by carrying my luggage during my visits to these villages in February 1977. I felt sad when an old lady from the Sirong village carried my luggage with her daughter through 10 kilometre of hilly slopes. The only way this area could come out of its underdevelopment was good road communication and power supply system. It was keeping this in view that I included this road in the PM's statement. The road was handed over to BRO and the work started in right earnest. Our plan was to construct a direct road from Senapati to Phaibung and give connectivity to all villages on this route. This way, the road could be planned for upgradation as a state highway and later, converted into a two-lane road.

But the politics of different villages came in the way of having better alignment of the road. Each village wanted the road to pass through their village come what may. Many times, the villagers obstructed the construction of the road and forced changes in the alignment. Instead of becoming a good road with better alignment, the Senapati-Phaibung road became a circuitous inter-village road. I could not convince the villagers as they were more concerned with their village interests. In the end, the cost increased three-fold as did the road length. It marred the chance of the road being used by motorists travelling from Senapati to

Phaibung, as the time taken is more compared to an alternate road, part of which is NH 2.

NEIGRIHMS

The North Eastern Indira Gandhi Regional Institute of Health and Medical Sciences (NEIGRIHMS), designed as a postgraduate medical institute on the lines of All India Institute of Medical Sciences (AIIMS), New Delhi was established by the Government of India in 1987. It was planned as the first postgraduate medical institute in the north-eastern region under the Ministry of Health and Family Welfare. By October 1996, at the time of PM Deve Gowda's visit to the North-East, the progress of NEIGRIHMS was negligible.

Among the incomplete projects that G.K. Pillai had compiled before the PM's visit was the sad case of NEIGRIHMS. It seemed the Ministry of Health and Family Welfare had forgotten about NEIGRIHMS for 10 years after the laying of the foundation stone. The Government of India did not provide any funds and in 1996, Mr Pillai estimated that Rs 421 crore would be required to complete the project and this fund was allocated under the 'New Initiatives'.

Even after the tenure of the Deve Gowda government, the PMO continued to monitor all these programmes and schemes on a monthly basis. I was very particular about updating the progress on the PMO website so that the officials in the states could check and point out inaccuracies, if any. Regular meetings were held with the officials of the different ministries and officials to expedite work on projects announced by the PM. I closely monitored the progress of construction of the NEIGRIHMS.

During the meetings, I found the construction work of NEIGRIHMS was getting delayed. For quick completion and better management, the work was assigned to Hospital Services Consultancy Corporation Limited of India (HSCCL). The construction work was divided into four to five packages and awarded to different contractors. I found that HSCCL had been lax in monitoring the progress. It had not followed the provisions in the contracts for the cancellation of contracts of defaulting contractors. The work of defaulting contractors should have been got done by others at the risk and cost of defaulters. I was surprised that HSCCL, a premier organisation under the Ministry of Health and Family Welfare, had not handled the construction work as it should have. Primarily due to this mismanagement the construction work of some packages was lagging, so I escalated the matter. The senior management of HSCCL was pulled up and soon the Ministry took active interest in the completion of NEIGRIHMS. I wonder why there was a lack of interest in the Ministry regarding this project which had already been delayed by more than 10 years.

20

ANOMALIES AND SOME STRANGE CASES

The General Financial Rules (GFR) stipulate that no authority would split any estimate into two or more parts with the intention that the bifurcated portions would come under the sanctioning power of that authority. The primary intention of including such a provision in GFR was to prevent junior authorities from splitting the estimates so as to bring them in their sanctioning powers. If estimates are not split, these are sent to higher authorities where they are subjected to better scrutiny.

In spite of these provisions, the tendency among some officers is to split the estimates. But one case exceeded all limits. Generally, estimates could be split into two, three or four smaller estimates, but this case crossed all limits and made the provisions of GFR a laughing stock. It seemed there were other forces at play in this case.

A 120-KM ROAD AND 1,200 CONTRACTORS!

In one meeting of the NEC, it was informed that the earth work of a 120-km road in Arunachal Pradesh was allotted to 1,200 contractors at the rate of 100 metres to each. The state government wanted to please all 1,200 people and every one of them got a piece of the pie. All of these contractors were unskilled and did not have the required machinery to remove the earth and dump it as per the estimate. Not only was it difficult to monitor the progress of 1,200 contractors and the quality of work done, it was also a case of mismanaged contracting and gross violation of the GFR. The state had thrown the financial rules out of the window and the project implementation left much to be desired. With such examples of project implementation, good contractors do not come for big public works in the North-East. Poor quality contractors meant the quality of work was poor and the fund absorption capacity of the North-East remained low.

TUIRIAL HYDROELECTRIC PROJECT

NEEPCO planned to implement the 60 MW Tuirial Hydroelectric Project in Mizoram, which was expected to produce 250 million kWh of energy annually. At the time of planning, NEEPCO had been given a clear understanding by the state government that the land for the Tuirial project belonged to the state. If some land belonging to private individuals near the Bilkhawthlir village was to be acquired, it would be done at reasonable rates by the state government.

The Mizoram government had been requesting the Centre to implement the Tuirial Project at the earliest. The state was to get 12 per cent of the power generated as free power, which worked out to about 30 million kWh per annum. In October 1996, PM Deve Gowda announced that the Tuirial Project would be sanctioned in 1996-97, and funds would be arranged. Based on this, the NEEPCO went ahead and prepared the DPR. The Centre arranged funds through a Japanese loan and its own funds. The project started with a lot of fanfare in 1998 and was one of the biggest projects in Mizoram. In addition to creation of employment opportunities, the project was to supply the much-needed power to Mizoram and the North-Eastern region.

It was hence a surprise when after start of project construction many people came forward to claim ownership of the land where the project was being constructed. It seemed a well-planned strategy to milk the NEEPCO of funds. A news report said many influential people related to politicians had suddenly become owners of the land though they did not belong to the village or to the area. I wondered how could that be? There was complete disbelief, particularly in the MHA. One view was that some influential persons in the Mizoram government were trying to blackmail NEEPCO, and through it the Central government. This clique of influential politicians and bureaucrats put a spanner in the project and work stopped during the tenure of the Mizo National Front government led by Zoramthanga. The NEEPCO and the Japanese Overseas Economic Cooperation Fund Bank funding the project objected to these land compensation claims as these were never part of original project estimate. The controversy over the payment of suspicious claims compelled NEEPCO to suspend the construction of the project.

A CHANGE OF GUARD AND THE WORK RESTARTS

A PIL was filed by anti-corruption watchdog Society for Social Action (SOSA) in April 2010, and Guwahati High Court ordered investigation by CBI into the alleged compensation scam. The investigation revealed that compensation of more than Rs 20 crore was paid to fictitious landowners. In the elections that followed, Lalthanhawla came to power and became the Chief Minister of Mizoram. He took the initiative to revive the abandoned project. It was during his tenure that the work on the Tuirial Hydroelectric Project restarted on 12 September 2007. It was also due to his efforts that the Central government approved the revised project cost of Rs 913 crore due to delay in resumption of work.

AN AIRPORT AT ITANAGAR

One of the issues in the 'New Initiatives' that had not been resolved related to the construction of the airport at Itanagar. On 27 October 1996, the PM had assured that the new airport would be constructed and completed within the Ninth Plan period. The Arunachal Pradesh government was to give land free of cost for this airport. Unfortunately, this did not happen. I pursued the matter with the state government but there seemed to be a lot of pressure not to give land for the airport. One reason was the limited land available in Itanagar and the unwillingness of local villagers to part with it. There were also issues about location and resettlement of people affected by land acquisition. It was surprising to see a state government so enthusiastic about the airport but utterly helpless in allotting land for it. Even 20 years later the issue has not been resolved.

Sometime back, I read the statement by a Union Minister from Arunachal Pradesh about the inefficient functioning of the Manipur government. I wondered if he ever thought about the 20-year delay in providing land for the airport at Itanagar. May be he was not aware that the Manipur government had taken over about 550 acres of land for the expansion of Imphal airport and handed it over to the Airport Authority of India within 18 months of the request. Whereas for a project for his home state Arunachal Pradesh, it had taken more than 20 years. Only if he knew the facts!

A HOSPITAL FOR NAGALAND

Even though the restructuring of primary health care system in the states was not encouraged by the Government of India, yet, the Nagaland government initiated a proposal to restructure the primary health care system with the help of an Australian hospital and a middleman from Delhi. Following the 'New Initiatives', funds were approved for upgrading the hospital facilities at Kohima. Later, additional funds were also given. At the PMO, we assumed that the state government must have completed the work on upgradation of the hospital but that had not happened.

In February 2009, I took over as Secretary, MDoNER. We were reviewing the status of schemes and proposals of all incomplete projects. During one such meeting with officers from Nagaland, I was surprised to find that the Kohima hospital for which funds were given during 2000-01 was incomplete, and the officials had once again requested for funds. When I enquired further, I was informed that advance funds were released by the Nagaland government for this hospital through a middleman named Shakat Singh. A truck or two of prefabricated structures were dropped at the site on behalf of the Australian company, after that nothing happened, and the work remained standstill even after many years. It was a clear case of cheating and the Nagaland officers had been hoodwinked by the middleman possibly with the help of some state officials and political persons.

When I mentioned the name of Shakat Singh in my meeting with Nagaland officials in 2009, the officials were surprised to hear it from me. I told them that I had advised the Nagaland state officials at that time in 2000-01 to be careful about this middleman. It seemed they did not listen to my advice and continued with the proposal and had landed in this situation.

21

COAL CHALLENGES

With about 315 billion tonnes of coal reserves, India has the fifth-largest coal reserves in the world and is the fourth highest coal-producing country. Coal is the major source of energy in India as about 57 per cent of the primary commercial energy comes from it. Coal India Limited (CIL), the state-owned coal mining corporate, came into being in November 1975. With a modest production of 79 million tonnes (MT) at the year of its inception, CIL today is the single largest coal producer in the world. It has seven subsidiaries which mine coal in different regions of the country and meet the demand of the Indian industry and most of the coal requirements of the country.

If one looks at the steel and coal sectors, the differences between the functioning of the two ministries can be noticed immediately. While the Ministry of Steel handles all matters relating to the steel industry in India and not just concentrates all its efforts on Steel Authority of India Limited (SAIL) alone, the Ministry of Coal primarily focuses all its attention on CIL and its subsidiaries. There are several private producers of steel in the country, and the Ministry of Steel takes care of the interests of steel producers and consumers appropriately. On the other hand, the

Ministry of Coal pays very little attention to the coal industry as such. I have heard many senior officers in the Central government speak of the differences in the approaches of both ministries. While the Ministry of Coal broadly followed an incorrect approach, the Ministry of Steel is following the correct approach vis-a-vis steel and SAIL. There has been almost no attempt made to reform the coal sector in India.

PROBLEMS OF COAL MINING

The opening of new coal mines required environmental and forest clearances. This was quite cumbersome as there were several issues related to land compensation and rehabilitation of the affected families. Though the compensation per acre for forest land was raised to about Rs 16 lakh per acre, yet the resolution of these issues seemed insurmountable leaving CIL and its subsidiaries with plenty of work on their hands. The government too was worried that opening of new coal mines was becoming very difficult and time consuming due to these issues.

The ash content of coal mined in the country is generally 25-45 per cent whereas average ash content of imported coal varies from 10-20 per cent. Indian coal has comparatively higher ash content than imported coal due to the drift theory of formation of coal deposits in India. According to this theory, trees and plants which grew millions of years ago, drifted considerable distances from their original sites due to natural reasons or calamities, were redeposited in lakes, river valleys, etc. Over many million years it was covered by sediments of sand and earth. Due to this, there is more sand and other minerals in the Indian coal. Mainly because of the high ash content of Indian coal, some power-generating organisations started exploring the option of importing coal from Australia, Indonesia and other countries, during 2001–04. Some state governments also planned to import coal as it was cheaper in terms of cost per unit of heat contents. The difficulties in opening of new coal mines, non-availability of adequate transportation infrastructure and the low price of imported coal increased the import of coal over the years.

COAL REGULATOR

The Centre was interested in encouraging private investment in coal mining. It was expected that such investment could bring in better technology and improve the efficiency of the coal mining industry. This required a coal regulator to ensure a level playing field for both public and private players in the sector and encourage private investment. The Coal Ministry prepared a draft note on setting up of a coal regulator and the enactment of a Bill for the same and shared it with the PMO a couple of times. Some meetings were also held but all fizzled out. The labour unions in the different subsidiaries of CIL were apprehensive about such moves of the government. Since most of the coal was produced in India by CIL, the labour unions could hold the government to ransom if there was any attempt to allow the entry of the private players in the sector.

NO COMPETITIVE BIDDING

The entry of private players in coal mining would have allowed competitive bidding for the allotment of mines. However, the cumbersome procedures to obtain clearances before starting coal mines discouraged all private players. There was no system wherein the government would take all clearances for coal mines and then initiate competitive bidding for them. So, the private parties stayed away, and the Ministry kept following its old methods of allotment of mines and linking coal for different consumers.

PROBLEMS OF COAL TRANSPORTATION

During summer, the demand for power peaks in northern India. Consequently, the consumption of coal in the thermal power stations in the region also peaks. Most of the coal is transported through railway corridors between Delhi-Kolkata and Delhi-Central and southern India. The increased summer demand of coal in northern region chokes the railway transportation corridors as the number of coal transportation trains increase in these months. Hence, it becomes very essential that each thermal power station has a coal stock for at least a month to take care of any disruption in coal transportation. However, the higher the coal stock kept at any thermal power station, the higher would be its inventory and cost of power production.

COAL SAMPLING

The coal transported from the coal mines to thermal power projects suffers from a few problems related to its quality and quantity. These two issues of the coal supplied by CIL and its subsidiaries were very important for the power utilities. Not only did the high ash content coal create additional problems of ash disposal at the thermal power stations, but the heat content of coal per tonne with high ash contents was lower. This required the thermal power stations to design their boilers and ash handling plants bigger, and this increased the cost of projects.

I have seen frequent meetings held between officials of the Ministries of Power and Coal and the state power utilities for reaching agreements over the reasonableness of the quality of coal loaded at mines and transported. Teams were constituted for coal sampling at the loading and unloading points. This, to some extent, helped keep a watch on the quality of coal supplied to the thermal power stations.

Then there were issues of weight measurement. Weighing of coal at the loading sites and the receiving power stations was an impossible task. The coal wagons were loaded without weighing and it was assumed that if the wagons were filled up to a certain predetermined mark, the coal weight would be of correct quantity. But these were approximate methods and had a role to play in determining the cost of power generation. These issues made the power utilities wary and raise these concerns repeatedly at national platforms.

The quality and quantity of coal supplied posed real challenges to both the coal producers and consumers. As long as CIL had a monopoly in coal production, it worked well. However, when options of imported coal were available for coal consumers, CIL and its subsidiaries had to take steps to address the concerns of coal consumers, which started to happen in 2002.

THE ABSENCE OF REFORMS

There was virtually no reform in the coal industry in the eight years I was in the PMO. Attempts made by most officers failed either because of a fear of reaction from the labour unions of the CIL or because of the reluctance to take risks. There was a talk of allowing private sector coal washeries at the coal mines but that too was unsuccessful. This was a good step as washed coal would have higher heat value in one unit weight of coal. This would have also reduced the load on the transportation system.

I expected some reform to take place in the coal sector during Prime Minister Vajpayee's tenure, but the Ministry of Coal, CIL and its subsidiaries were reluctant. I must say that the two sectors, which did not see any reforms of the scale needed were railways and coal. Of course, there were some changes in their functioning with the introduction of information technology but those were not the reforms government wanted. The government wanted to improve efficiency of both these sectors by introducing some sort of privatisation in selected areas. That would have created competition between different players and would have been good for the consumers and the country.

22

A MATTER OF SECURITY

When Prime Minister Vajpayee planned his first visit to Assam, we were intimated by the office of the Assam CM that he would like to brief the PM about the law and order and other issues facing the state. Adequate time was scheduled for the meeting with the CM and his council of ministers. PM Vajpayee was received at the airport by the Governor, the Chief Minister, the Chief Secretary, the Director General of Police, the senior most Army Officer, the Deputy Commissioner and Superintendent of Police of the District as per protocol. From there he proceeded to the Raj Bhawan where he was staying. His meeting with the CM and his council of ministers was also scheduled there.

Generally, the host Governor is the first person to call on the PM in the Raj Bhawan. As soon as the PM was ready for the meetings, Governor Lt. General (Retd.) S. K. Sinha called on the PM and wanted to give him a presentation about his perspectives of the security environment and law and order situation in Assam and the north-eastern states. Ashok Saikia, who was with us, informed the secretary to the Governor that the presentation should not exceed 15-20 minutes as the PM was scheduled to meet the CM and the council of ministers immediately after this courtesy call. The secretary was also informed that the responsibility to brief the PM in detail about the security issues of the state rested with the CM and his council of ministers, as they are the elected representatives of the people. Ashok Saikia probably knew that Governor Sinha was fond of speaking and getting into details of security related issues. The Governor exceeded his time by an hour and busted our time allotments of other meetings.

START OF PEACE TALKS WITH NSCN (IM)

Insurgency in Nagaland has been the oldest in the country. Even though Shillong Accord was signed in 1975 between the Government of India and NNC, peace could not be sustained, and fresh violence started on 14 March 1981 in Ukhrul town in Manipur. A new organisation called National Socialist Council of Nagaland (NSCN) was formed (this later split into NSCN (IM) and NSCN (K), with the former being more powerful of the two). The Government of India had also realised that the NSCN (IM) was the mother of insurgency in North-East as it was able to encourage other ethnic groups in the north-eastern region. Hence, from the time of Narasimha Rao government, the efforts to contact NSCN (IM) leaders for settling the matter intensified.

In 1995, top NSCN (IM) leaders met PM Narasimha Rao in Europe and an initial understanding was reached to make efforts to settle the outstanding issues with the Nagas. Due to these efforts, primarily led by officers of Intelligence Bureau (IB), a ceasefire agreement was signed between Government of India and NSCN (IM) on 25 July 1997, which came into effect from 1 August 1997. At that time, I. K. Gujral was the PM and N.N. Vohra, the Principal Secretary. One of the important points discussed in 1995 was that the talks with NSCN (IM) would be at the highest level, which meant the PM in the Government of India. Due to this understanding, the Principal Secretary to the PM has a prominent role in the talks vis-à-vis the Home Minister of India.

Swaraj Kaushal, a well-known criminal lawyer, was appointed as interlocutor for the talks with NSCN (IM). He had played an important role in the talks between the government and the Mizo National Front (MNF) leadership, which led to the signing of the Mizoram Accord in 1986. The Government of India also announced the appointment of a full-time chairman of the ceasefire monitoring group in Nagaland. The Director IB, Arun Bhagat, played a crucial role in the initial years of signing of the ceasefire agreement with NSCN (IM).

Swaraj Kaushal was removed from the position of interlocutor after he gave a statement about the scope of the ceasefire between Government of India and the NSCN (IM). His reported statement mentioned that the ceasefire would exist everywhere in India and even abroad, wherever the NSCN (IM) persons were present. This implied that the ceasefire with NSCN (IM) was without any territorial boundaries, which was favoured by NSCN (IM). A large section within the government was uncomfortable with this and wanted the ceasefire restricted to some specified area.

The reasons for restricting the ceasefire within Nagaland boundaries were obvious as the government did not want the NSCN (IM) members roaming around freely. There were fears that some members of NSCN (IM) had links with members of other militant organisations of the North-East and could possibly create problems through other groups. After Swaraj Kaushal, K. Padmanabhaiah, former Union Home Secretary was appointed as interlocutor.

As soon as K. Padmanabhaiah took over, he wanted a full summary record of files which contained information relating to talks with NSCN (IM) right from the beginning. He wanted to know clearly the understanding reached with the top NSCN (IM) leaders. Since I oversaw MHA related matters, I asked the staff to search all papers related to informal or formal talks, and records of the 1995 meeting with PM Narasimha Rao in Europe. A list of papers was prepared, including the file cover on which the then Principal Secretary to the PM had in the 1995 meeting noted the points raised by NSCN (IM) leaders, and the reaction of the PM to the various issues. With the approval of the Principal Secretary, a set was sent to Mr Padmanabhaiah.

NSCN (IM) LEADERS AND PM RAO MEET IN EUROPE

The first meeting of NSCN (IM) leaders with PM Narasimha Rao was held in Europe and it seemed the Principal Secretary did not have a note pad or proper papers for recording or keeping notes of the discussions. I am assuming this as he recorded the main points of the discussion with a ball point pen on the back of the file cover. I prepared a proper file of this file cover with the handwritten notings typed for legibility. If I had not traced this and recoded it properly, it could have been easily overlooked as a cover and misplaced or possibly weeded out.

The record of the discussion had two very interesting points. First, that the discussions would be at the PM or PMO level and would not be handed over to the MHA to steer the talks. The second, was a reference to the comments of the former PM Morarji Desai about his meeting with A. Z. Phizo in London in June 1977, where the PM had reportedly stated that he would exterminate the Naga rebels and would show absolutely no leniency to the rebels. In his first meeting with NSCN (IM) leaders, PM Narasimha Rao reportedly stated that he did not agree with comments of Morarji Desai and that he had a different approach to the Naga insurgency and wanted to resolve it through discussions. His approach to resolve the issues through talks is reflected in a small record of the meeting. Whatever it was, it is correct to say that this meeting laid the foundation for finding a permanent solution to the Naga issues.

A CLEAR-HEADED GOVERNOR

Though I handled matters relating to MHA in the PMO, I did not manage issues relating to the talks. I do, however, recall a meeting between Governor of Manipur, O. N. Srivastva and the Principal Secretary to the PM to discuss the latter's views on matters relating to talks with NSCN (IM). Governor Srivastva had been the Governor of Nagaland, and the Principal Secretary wanted his views on some issues. The Governor explained his views and that of the Manipur state government. To the surprise of all, he was very clear about the stand of Manipur and the need for keeping its territorial integrity intact. Frankly speaking, I have not seen any politician or any other person from Manipur give such cogent arguments in favour of the territorial integrity of Manipur and its national security implications. His well-balanced arguments and approach to the talks was not only for the benefit of all communities of the North-East, but it also protected the interest of all states, communities and groups in the region. The discussions were very useful to the interlocutor. After listening to the Governor my respect for him increased.

ALL-PARTY MANIPUR TEAM CALLS ON THE PM

The neighbouring states, particularly Manipur had not favoured the extension of the ceasefire agreement 'without territorial limits'. The people of Manipur, particularly those in the valley areas were apprehensive about this. The general perception was that the ceasefire extension to Manipur would allow free movement of NSCN (IM) cadres into Manipur where the state police force would not be able to act against them. In addition, some in Manipur were apprehensive that the extension of ceasefire beyond Nagaland meant that areas of other states would also come under discussion for possible negotiations or discussion with NSCN (IM) for any possible solution.

In June 2001, when ceasefire agreement 'without territorial limits' was signed in Bangkok between the Government of India and NSCN (IM), there was widespread violence in Manipur, particularly in the valley areas. An all-party delegation from Manipur came to Delhi and met the PM at 7 RCR. By this time, the PMO had got a feedback from different security agencies about the states which were against the extension of ceasefire 'without territorial limits'. Some of the speakers in the delegation were quite vociferous but unfortunately, were not able to cogently list out the reasons in favour of their points of views.

Among the many agitated people who spoke against extension of ceasefire was a member of delegation from Manipur. He was sitting to the PM's right and thumped the table a few times, though some of his colleagues tried to stop him. The thumping alerted the SPG personnel guarding the PM. Two of them walked towards him to ensure that he did not throw any projectile at the PM. He also spoke against the interlocutor. This was the first time that I had seen such behaviour in a meeting with the PM. PM Vajpayee was also slightly irritated but kept his cool. I was sitting behind the PM and Principal Secretary Brajesh Mishra. When the latter asked me about the said person, I informed him that he had been a Minister in the state government and a politician of good standing. He seemed to have suddenly lost his cool and acted in that manner. I felt that such behaviour is not expected from anyone who meets the PM, least of all from a person who has been a Minister and an elected representative.

After consultations with NSCN (IM), the Government of India had already decided to remove the words 'without territorial limits'. I must appreciate the magnanimity of the NSCN (IM) leaders who agreed to delete these words from the Bangkok Agreement of June 2001. They had their long-term goal in mind and were right in going along with the views of the Government of India. They behaved like true statesmen in this case, whereas some politicians projected themselves in poor light.

The talks continued. Several people have made enormous efforts in the continuation of the talks and for its successful conclusion. Both sides have shown substantial patience and maturity. There are several issues and points which the government must consider in this process and it requires time and patience.

NAGAS FROM EAST NAGALAND

Some groups of Nagas from eastern Nagaland had been meeting officials in MHA. They did not want to be a part of Nagaland. The poor economic development of eastern Nagaland was the basis of their demand for a separate administrative unit, such as a Union Territory, under the administrative control of the Government of India. They referred to the eastern areas of Nagaland as Freeland. They were bitter about dominance of some major Nagaland tribes in political and administrative machinery of the state and felt left out of the state's mainstream.

Some of these groups wanted to meet PM and raise their demand for a Union Territory for eastern Nagaland. Though they visited New Delhi many times they were not able to move forward because of political reluctance on the part of the government. Moreover, with the talks with the NSCN (IM) going on, there was an understanding that the government would not enter into any discussions on Naga issues with any other group. The government was sincere in its commitment given to NSCN (IM) before the talks at the highest level and wanted to follow it in letter and spirit.

Two of these groups from eastern Nagaland were asked by MHA officials to meet me and give their memoranda. I offered them tea, listened to them, and kept their papers, which they had also given to MHA. I informed them that it was very difficult for the government to create a separate Union Territory for a small area. I pointed out that their development concerns could be addressed by keeping separate financial provisions in budgets and making proper administrative rules for the eastern areas under the existing Nagaland state. As regards their adequate representations in the state bureaucracy, the state government could design and develop a framework for improving education in these areas and reserve certain posts for people from these areas. After the cold response to their demands from the PMO, they never came back again on this issue during my tenure.

BRUS AND REANGS OF MIZORAM

The Brus also sometimes called as the Reangs are spread across the north-eastern states of Tripura, Assam and Mizoram. In Mizoram, they are mostly restricted to the districts of Mamit and Kolasib. The initial signs of tensions between the Brus and the Mizos emerged in 1995. There were demands from some Mizo NGOs that Brus be left out of the state's electoral rolls, contending that the tribe was not indigenous to Mizoram. The Bru leaders on the other hand wanted more delegation of administrative and financial powers.

During 1997, there was ethnic violence between Mizo and Brus tribesmen, which started due to the alleged shooting down of a Mizo forest person in Mamit district. The incident evoked a hostile reaction, and the Brus were at the receiving end of a violent backlash by the Mizos. It forced them to flee the state in large numbers to neighbouring Tripura. It was reported that more than 35,000 Brus left Mizoram and took shelter in seven camps in Tripura. When I was in the PMO, the MHA officials found it very difficult to facilitate the repatriation of Brus back to Mizoram.

MIZORAM GOVERNMENT'S RIGID STAND

As and when the Tripura Chief Minister met the PM, he raised the issue of an early resolution of the issue of Brus and their return to Mizoram. From the PMO, we used to request MHA to expedite the process by holding meetings with the Mizoram and Tripura state governments. I heard about several attempts made by MHA officials with the Mizoram government to facilitate the early return of Brus to Mizoram. It seemed the Mizoram government was not keen and was blocking the return of Brus on one pretext or the other.

There was fear among the Mizos that Brus could affect the electoral results in about 10 Legislative Assembly constituencies in Mizoram. As all attempts by MHA officials were bulldozed by the rigid Mizoram stand, I heard that the MHA was thinking of stopping a part of assistance given by MHA and other Central ministries to Mizoram. Though this strategy was talked of, it was not put into operation as it would have been inappropriate to do so. Even the Deputy PM L.K. Advani contended in 1999 that the Brus were being persecuted in Mizoram because many of them were Hindus. This was refuted by Mizoram Chief Minister Lalthanhawla. Whatever happened was bad, as about 35,000 people were living in sad conditions in Tripura camps. The attitudes of successive Mizoram governments were partisan and unfair to the Brus. It was partially dictated by the stand of Mizo NGOs. Otherwise, how could the Mizoram CM not take a proactive stand for an early return of the Brus? In this whole process, I found the attitude and stand of Tripura government sympathetic, and it was appreciated by the Centre.

EXTERNAL DIMENSIONS TO VIOLENCE IN ASSAM

The Bodos had been agitating for many years for a separate state. Their demand was followed by violence and many innocent people were massacred. In January 2002, the National Democratic Front of Bodoland (NDFB) suddenly increased its violent activities and massacred more than 30 people. After every strike, the NDFB militants used to quickly slip into Bhutan. The killings continued. The Indian security forces did not want to enter Bhutan to flush out the militants. The Government of India took up the matter with the Bhutanese government to flush out the militants. There were reports of many camps of NDFB militants and it seemed that the Bhutanese security forces could not overpower them. The discussion continued at various levels with the Bhutanese government and after every violent incident in Assam, the Government of India would pressurise the Bhutanese government to act against the militants hiding in Bhutan.

In December 2003, the Royal Bhutanese Army (RBA) launched a major offensive against the NDFB and ULFA militants holed up in about three dozen camps in Bhutan, for many years. It was reported that more than 5000 members of the RBA participated in the operation. More than 100 militants were reported to have been killed and many important persons were captured. The RBA busted more than two dozen camps of these militant groups. This was a successful operation by the Royal Bhutanese Army. Some leaders of the militants sneaked into Bangladesh. This operation broke the back of NDFB and ULFA.

BODO TERRITORIAL COUNCIL

A Memorandum of Settlement (MOS) was signed for the creation of the Bodo Territorial Council (BTC) on 10 February 2003, at a tripartite meeting held in New Delhi. This involved the representatives of the Centre, Assam government and a Bodo Liberation Tigers (BLT) delegation. The main provisions of the MOS was related 'to the creation of the BTC, an autonomous self-governing body within the State of Assam and under the provisions of the Sixth Schedule of the Constitution of India to fulfil economic, educational and linguistic aspirations, socio-cultural and ethnic identity of the Bodos; and to speed up the infrastructure development in BTC area'.

The BTC has 3,082 villages in four districts and 40 elected representatives, and the Assam government nominates six more. Of the elected representatives, 30 seats are reserved for tribals, five for non-tribals and the remaining five are open for general contest.

It was expected that the constitution of BTC under the sixth schedule of the Constitution would bring peace to the area. More than Rs 500 crores was given by the PM for infrastructure development work by the BTC. Since the organisational structure of the BTC was weak, the implementation of the projects was unsatisfactory, and these remained incomplete for a long time.

In 2009, when I was Secretary, MDoNER, I was asked by the PMO to visit Assam and review the progress of schemes covered under PM's Rs-500-crore package. I reviewed the schemes and was surprised to find that only one out of the 40-plus schemes was completed. There was no timeframe to complete the other schemes. The main reason for this was that the works for big water supply schemes were not given on a turnkey basis. While pipes and cement had been procured by the concerned BTC executive member, no contractor was willing to lay pipes on the ground and construct water tanks. Other schemes also faced similar fate. The only scheme which was completed related to the purchase of vehicles by the BTC. Surprisingly, the Assam government was least bothered with the poor implementation of the BTC schemes. It seemed that they did not want to be seen as interfering in the working of BTC.

23

WORKING WITH GOVERNORS

APPOINTMENT AND RESPONSIBILITIES

The President of India appoints the Governor of a state on the advice of the Prime Minister. There is no set selection procedure for the Governor, except that the person appointed should be at least 35 years of age, an Indian citizen, should not hold any office of profit, or be a Member of Parliament or of any state legislature at the time of appointment. The Governor holds the office at the pleasure of the President of India. He can resign on his own or the President of India can remove a Governor on the advice of the Prime Minister.

The Governor has certain executive, legislative and judicial powers. The executive power primarily consists of the appointment of the Chief Minister and council of ministers, Advocate General, chairmen and the members of state commissions such as State Public Service Commissions, State Human Rights Commissions, etc. The Governor appoints judges at district levels and is consulted by the President of India on the appointment of High Court judges. The business of the state government is run in the name of the Governor, as are the government orders issued, even though the Governor is not involved in these decisions.

Similar to President's powers with respect to Parliament, the Governor has the right and power to address and send messages, summon, defer, and dissolve the state Legislature. Even though these are formal powers, in reality, the Governor must be guided by the Chief Minister and his Council of Ministers before making decisions in these matters. The bills passed by the state Legislature become laws only after the Governor's assent. All money bills can be introduced in Legislative Assembly only after the Governor's approval. When the Legislative Assembly is not in session, and a law has to be brought into effect immediately because of any reason, the Governor can promulgate an ordinance. Such ordinance has to become a law in the next session of Legislative Assembly.

The Governor sends monthly reports to the President and the Government of India. These reports are about various aspects of the working of the state government, and other related matters which are of concern to the Government of India. The President's Rule can be imposed in a state based on the Governor's report about a failure of constitutional machinery in the state. In such an exceptional circumstance when President's Rule is imposed in a state, the Governor administers the state government with the assistance of advisers appointed for this purpose. He can also remit jail sentences and grant pardons.

Even though the Governor appears all powerful when looking at the legislative, executive and the judicial powers, in reality he is the nominal head of state, whereas the real executive head of the state is the Chief Minister. This becomes clear when one observes the functioning of the state government minutely and carefully.

During my eight years as Joint Secretary in the PMO, I handled matters relating to MHA and was the coordinating officer of the north-eastern states. Many outside the PMO thought that I might have had some say in the appointment of Governors, which was processed by the MHA. The fact was that I had no say whatsoever in the selection, even though I was involved in processing proposals for their appointments and other related matters.

The selection and appointment of Governors and Lieutenant Governors is done by the Prime Minister in consultation with the Home Minister or his other senior colleagues. The proposals are initiated by MHA and sent to the PMO. I used to process the proposals to obtain the approval of the PM, and then forward it to the President's Secretariat for approval by the President of India. That was enough for some to think that maybe I could swing something in their favour.

A couple of times some retired bureaucrats and army officers met me to give me their biodata and explain how suited they were for the post of Governor or Lieutenant Governor. I kept their biodata and did not do anything as I had no power. There is no list of suitable candidates for these posts kept in the PMO. After 25 years of service in the IAS, both in the state and at the Centre, I have learnt that the Governors do not have much work or power except during President's Rule. In the states, they give oath to ministers, judges, and to people holding constitutional positions; approve appointments of state public service members, vice chancellors etc. Other than that, they do not have many functions and perform only ceremonial duties such as taking salute on Republic Day.

I have not found any document that mentions the necessary qualifications for appointment as Governor. The Governor holds office at the pleasure of the President of India, which implies the Government of India. As such, it is difficult to argue whether a person is less qualified than another person. How a Governor handles a constitutional crisis in a state brings out his competence. Only past constitutional crisis cases and judgments of the Hon'ble Supreme Court or High Courts can provide guidelines regarding this. I used to be amused listening to people who would explain to me their competence to hold these posts.

One day I got a call to come to the office chamber of the Principal Secretary. When I entered, I found the Governor of Arunachal Pradesh sitting with a few papers in his hand. The Principal Secretary informed me that the Governor had a proposal for a water supply scheme to be sanctioned by the Government of India. He had requested the PMO for help and support. I looked at the water supply scheme in surprise, as it was for a village and at a cost of about Rs 6 lakh. I informed the Principal

Secretary that rural water supply schemes are covered under the state plans, and the Planning Commission gives adequate funds for them. Many such schemes are annually taken up by the state's Water Supply Department and are funded by the state government. The Centre did not have any fund to sanction such schemes for states. After listening to me, the Principal Secretary asked the Governor to ask the Chief Minister or Chief Secretary to provide funds to implement the scheme. Once the Governor left, I told the Principal Secretary that it appeared that the Governor was inventing excuses to extend his stay in Delhi.

PENSION FOR GOVERNORS

There was a frequent demand from Governors of states for sanctioning pension and other post-retirement benefits. I had processed this matter in the PMO for many years. As and when there used to be a Governors' conference this issue used to come up. The internal finance wing of MHA had rejected the proposal on two grounds. First, the Governors are not selected by a selection process but appointed, unlike the members of civil services who receive pensions. Secondly, they were not elected like the MLAs and MPs who also get pensions. Therefore, the appointing process did not fulfil the two basic guiding principles, decided through convention, for grant of pension. I was happy to read the unambiguous comments by the internal finance wing of MHA. During my tenure, I must have processed this proposal several times, and every time the sitting PM agreed with the arguments and rejected the demand. I always felt that the Governors did not deserve the pension and retirement benefits and was surprised at the way these benefits were pursued relentlessly. I was informed that later on during the UPA regime, the retirement benefits were finally given.

THE GOVERNOR'S REPORT

The Governor sends a monthly report to the President of India, the Prime Minister, and the Home Minister about various matters relating to the state. These reports cover security, law and order matters, general and specific economic development issues, functioning of the state government, and any other issues which are important enough to be brought to the notice of the Central government. There is a broad format prescribed to prepare the report, including the topics which should be covered. Generally, these reports are routine in nature and mention matters of the preceding month. Even then these reports are marked as secret or confidential, purely on the ground that these are communications from a Governor to the President and Prime Minister of India. More often than not, there is nothing substantial in these reports and I wondered if anyone read these lengthy reports fully. The reports have become so routine that they have lost their significance. In some specific cases of urgent importance, the Government of India could call for special reports from the Governors such as in cases of failure of constitutional machinery in the state, or a major law and order problem.

On one occasion, during a cursory glance at the Manipur Governor's report, I saw a worrisome paragraph. According to this, about nine subdivisions of Manipur were being called a 'Liberated Area', as the writ of the state government did not run here, and the influence of different militant groups was strong. This was a strong statement from the Governor and surprisingly, he did not mention any action taken by him, or by the state government, to 'liberate' the so called 'liberated areas' from the stranglehold of the militants. This seemed strange and I thought it a matter worth pursuing through MHA.

I requested MHA to ask the Governor regarding the action taken to clear the 'Liberated Area' and inform the PMO about it. The PMO neither received any intimation from MHA, nor from the Governor's office about this. I reminded the Special Secretary MHA about this. This was the only case I remember in my eight years in PMO where a constitutional functionary such as the Governor of a state did not act after informing the President and PM about a serious situation in his state where the writ of the state did not run.

I may mention here that when Manipur was facing a law and order crisis in August 2004 following the 'alleged' murder of Th. Manorama

Devi, the state Governor was not present in the state for many crucial days. When the then PM convened a meeting with the Home Minister, Defence Minister and other senior officials, it was decided to change the Governor and appoint Dr S. S. Sidhu as Governor of Manipur.

LOTTERIES AND LOSS OF REVENUE

To raise revenue, during the latter part of the 1990s, many states started organising lotteries, some more than a dozen lottery draws daily. To organise the printing of tickets, their sale and lottery draws, etc., the states appointed lottery agents through open tenders who remitted the revenue receipts to the state. Over the years, the same lottery agents were appointed again and again which gave rise to serious reservations about its credibility in the government. The MHA decided to ban the lottery by the states.

The Comptroller and Auditor General of India (CAG), while auditing these lotteries, found serious irregularities in the system of lottery management of the states. The CAG reports routinely mentioned revenue losses to the states running into thousands of crores. In its report on Nagaland, the CAG mentioned the revenue loss of about Rs 28,500 crore to the state exchequer from lotteries in the previous seven years. This revenue loss was based on calculation and certain assumptions about sale of tickets, distribution of prizes, etc. This notional revenue loss calculation was an astronomical figure and too high to be believed. As per the procedure, the CAG report is discussed in the Public Accounts Committee (PAC) which is assisted by the Accountant General (AG) and his staff. In the PAC meetings, the concerned departments are given a chance to explain their views. In this case also, the report of the CAG required discussion in the PAC of Nagaland Legislative Assembly as per the procedure laid down for handling such matters. The PAC reports are then presented to the Legislative Assembly where their recommendations are discussed and then either accepted, rejected, or modified.

The Governor of Nagaland sent a letter to the PM containing the CAG Report relating to the revenue loss due to lotteries. It seemed he possibly wanted to score a point against the CM. At that time, the Congress was the ruling party in Nagaland, and the government at the Centre was led by BJP. The Governor, a retired IPS officer of Punjab cadre, was perhaps not familiar with the procedure followed to deal with CAG reports. Perhaps he forgot that the PM was not his counterpart and that he had to communicate through the standardised format of monthly reports.

I was asked by the PM about the action which PMO could take on the letter from the Governor. I informed him that after acknowledging the letter as routine, the PMO would send the letter to MHA. As far as any action on the CAG report relating to financial loss, the action lay with the PAC of the Nagaland Legislative Assembly, and Government of India could not do anything. I informed the Governor to not write letters in routine to the PM, as the latter was not his counterpart. I also informed him that any query by the PMO to Governor would be through the MHA only.

For a state with a budget of about Rs 3,000 crore per annum, to say a loss of Rs 28,500 crore in seven years was an exaggeration by the CAG. Admittedly, there were allegations of corruption in the lottery management by the state, but the revenue loss could not be Rs 4,000 crore per annum for Nagaland only. The extent of loss calculated by the CAG appeared too exaggerated and seemed like a bad joke. This remained a matter of casual discussions in PMO for many days. One of the officers opined one day that if the corruption was of such high order then the CM or other persons allegedly involved could have purchased an island. So much for loss calculation by CAG!

This, and other incidents relating to other Governors, made me wonder why politicians and retired bureaucrats wanted the position in the first place. The Governors were neither elected nor selected through a rigorous system but appointed by the executive and some through lobbying. In majority of the cases, it was as if the governorships were given to those whom the Union government wanted to rehabilitate. It was a nominated post with perks and privileges inconsistent with the duties and responsibilities it entailed.

24

JAMMU AND KASHMIR: DEVELOPMENT AND SECURITY ISSUES

After Vajpayee took over as PM, first in 1998 and later in 1999, he paid special attention to resolve the issues relating to the state of Jammu and Kashmir. A separate department for Jammu and Kashmir affairs was constituted to handle all relevant matters regarding the state. A.S. Dulat, former Special Director Intelligence Bureau and former RAW Chief, who had in depth knowledge of the state, was appointed as Adviser in PMO for Jammu and Kashmir. PM Vajpayee's liberal views on various issues and Brajesh Mishra's diplomatic skills were the best assets available in the PMO for any meaningful initiative about the state.

A number of meetings were held at the official and political levels to discuss ways and means to develop a strategy, and also to reduce the tensions in the state. An action plan was prepared to address all aspects in a time bound manner. The Vajpayee government was also keen to bring normalcy in relations with Pakistan, thinking this would in turn help in improving the security environment in Jammu and Kashmir.

Both the PM's visit to Lahore in February 1999 and the Lahore Declaration signed by India and Pakistan created a lot of optimism for bilateral relations. The Lahore visit which was on the invitation of the then Pakistan Prime Minister Nawaz Sharif, reflected on the sincerity of Vajpayee to improve relations with Pakistan. But the goodwill created by the Lahore visit was short lived, and the misadventure by Pakistan in Kargil showed its real intentions and vitiated the atmosphere. Despite this, PM Vajpayee pushed forward efforts to improve relations with Pakistan. I often heard him reiterate that neighbours cannot be selected by one's own choice. They are there and they will remain there as neighbours in the future too. Hence, he stressed on the need for living in peace with Pakistan. His continued efforts culminated in the Agra Summit in July 2001 with Pervez Musharraf, the then President of Pakistan. This summit was not successful because of a variety of reasons. Despite the failure of the talks, Pervez Musharraf agreed with the peace call given by PM Vajpayee and invited the Indian Prime Minister to visit Pakistan. Before his departure for Pakistan, President Pervez Musharraf said that the issues between Pakistan and India were complicated and hence could not be resolved in a short time.

PM Vajpayee was optimistic and had been striving to improve the situation in the state. A three-pronged strategy was prepared for Jammu and Kashmir, which included political level talks at formal and informal levels with all stakeholders, implementing major economic as well as infrastructure development projects, creating employment opportunities, and tackling law and order situation to reduce violence level in the state.

After some good preparatory work, the Prime Minister's visit to the state was planned for May 2002. The focus was to give development a big push. At least six months preceding the summer of 2002, all of us at the PMO had begun to review important projects, programmes and schemes pertaining to Jammu and Kashmir. Numerous discussions were held with concerned ministries to expedite infrastructure development projects, increase employment opportunities, and to improve the security environment in the state.

As I was in charge of Jammu and Kashmir, I delved deep into the different aspects of the issues which would be discussed by the PM at his level. A schedule for each meeting and the agenda was detailed and prepared for the visit. During the three-day visit, the PM was to meet with the Chief Minister and his council of ministers, representatives of political parties and important NGOs, and visit the army posts near the Line of Control (LoC) and address a public meeting. The visit was planned as a comprehensive one to cover all aspects of the strategy and to meet a cross section of the people of Jammu and Kashmir.

PRIME MINISTER VAJPAYEE MEETS KASHMIRI PANDITS

It was in the evening of the first day of the visit and a number of delegations and individuals wanted to meet the PM. These meetings were arranged in the Srinagar Raj Bhavan. The Private Secretary to PM informed me that he wanted to look at the golf course in Srinagar and try his hand there. As such, I would be covering all the PM's meetings alone and provide all assistance needed. Even if the PS to PM was there in these meetings, I had to be present in PMs meetings as the officer-in-charge of Jammu and Kashmir in the PMO. I would have to brief the PM on the status of various issues raised in the meetings by various delegations, and the possible actions which could be taken. I was to also note down any direction by the PM in respect to any point raised by any delegation, and then take follow up action. The last meeting of the day started after 7:30 pm with a delegation of Kashmiri Pandits.

The delegation consisted of about 10 people who came wearing saffron-coloured turbans and looked majestic. The PM warmly greeted them and invited them to sit. The members of the delegation included eminent Kashmiri Pandits and different organisations representing the community. Raman Mattoo, who was an MLA and had been a Minister of State (Tourism) in the state government, was also a part of the delegation. After they settled in, they began to recount their problems. The members of the delegation highlighted various incidents for about half an hour and the PM listened attentively. They informed him about 878 incidents of desecration or demolition of temples in Kashmir. They spoke of being very scared of sleeping in their houses at night even in Srinagar because of frequent incidents. They recounted how they sent their young girls to sleep in neighbours' houses in the night. They narrated incidents of violence against Kashmiri Pandits and their family members, while Prime Minister attentively listened to their woes.

The Kashmiri Pandits live all across Kashmir and are not limited to any specific region. The Hindus and the Muslims have traditionally lived in harmony in the remote villages of the state. Since they were not staying in clusters, it was not possible to provide security to each Kashmiri Pandit family. They became tempting targets for militants, who begun to single them out in these remote villages and create panic. The community had no choice but to flee to Jammu or big cities like Delhi.

After listening to them for more than half an hour, the PM asked for their views on possible solutions to their problems. They, however, did not have any solution in mind. It was difficult to imagine that this was what citizens in India had to face and the government was not able to do anything. After about 45 minutes the delegation left while promising to submit a proposal of possible solutions. It was around 8:30 p.m. by the time the delegation left. I found the PM in a pensive mood. After a while he rose up saying, *Harey Ram, Harey Ram! Is desh ka kya hoga?* (Good heavens! What will happen to this country?). His eyes were moist, and I sensed a heaviness in his voice. He too seemed helpless to provide any solution to ease the pain of the Kashmiri Pandits. This was the last delegation to meet the PM that day. I stepped out and asked his personal peon to come in and escort him to the room.

Through the thick fog outside, all I could see was the blurred lights of the lamps. It was a very eventful meeting, but it also filled me with sadness. I kept thinking about possible solutions to protect such a spread-out population. The only possible solution that came to me was their protection by the majority Muslim community.

I had requested the delegation to suggest some possible solution which the government could consider and asked Raman Mattoo to expedite the submission of suggestions as a follow up to the meeting. Despite following up with the Minister and the delegation, the PMO did not get any concrete suggestion which could be taken forward. It seemed that the Kashmiri Pandits also did not have any suggestion for the Government of India. The situation was complicated. The conditions in which Kashmiri Pandits were living in Kashmir was very scary and painful. Instead, after some time, the PMO got requests to provide temporary relief to the Kashmiri migrants or internally displaced Kashmiris staying in Delhi and other places. These requests revolved around giving second cylinder of LPG gas to each family, reserving seats in medical and engineering colleges in other states for the children of Kashmiri internally displaced persons, etc. These suggestions, I felt, would encourage more Kashmiri Pandits to leave the valley and go to Delhi or to Jammu. However, given the dispersed settlements of the community across Kashmir, it was neither desirable nor possible to ask Kashmiri Pandits to stay in segregated villages.

BREAKFAST CONVERSATIONS

Much care was given to provide a healthy breakfast to the Prime Minister at the Raj Bhavan. The PM was seated at the head of the table and I at the opposite end. The staff at the Raj Bhawan served us sprouted grams for breakfast. I had my apprehensions when suddenly, I heard the PM saying, *Nastey mein hum to chapatis ya paranthey ya puri khayengey* (We will have chapatis or paranthas or puris for breakfast). This was like music to my ears. With a whole day's work ahead, it was necessary to have a good breakfast. After some time, puris, bread and paranthas were served with vegetables.

Lt Gen S.K. Sinha (Retd.), Governor of Jammu and Kashmir, was an experienced army veteran and had a lot of stories to narrate about his army days. He was earlier the Governor of Assam, where I had met him a few times at Assam Raj Bhawan during the Prime Minister's visits. At the breakfast table, the Governor referred to his book and started to recount some stories from it. The Prime Minister quipped in good humour, *Army ke General books kyon likhte hai?* (Why do Army Generals have to write books when they are in such high positions?). The PM was indirectly asking whether the army officers had adequate work on their hands in these positions. I verbalised what was intended and said, 'Sir, one possible reason could be that they do not have adequate work at that level. May be they have a lot of free time.' Immediately Governor Sinha rebutted, saying he did not agree with the view, and said they actually wanted to share the knowledge with their colleagues and the public.

BAGLIHAR PROJECT COMPLETION

Next day, Farooq Abdullah, the Chief Minister of Jammu and Kashmir, briefed the PM about various development projects taken up by the state government. While doing so, he informed the PM about the progress of the Baglihar Hydroelectric Project and requested for Rs 623 crore as financial assistance to complete it. The state government had already spent about Rs 1,500 crore from its resources on the project.

The Baglihar Hydroelectric Power Project is a run-of-the-river power project on the Chenab River in Doda district of Jammu and Kashmir. This project was conceived in 1992, approved in 1996, and construction began in 1999. A state-sector project, it was being constructed by the state government through its own resources. Unfortunately, due to inadequate resources it was not able to maintain the tempo of progress, and the work on the project slowed down. It was in this context that the Chief Minister had asked the PM for additional grants from the Centre, stating that this would enable project to be completed within two years. Looking at any further delay in completion of the project as a loss to the nation in terms of loss in electricity generation, PM Vajpayee agreed to the request. On reaching New Delhi, I sent a note to the Ministry of Finance informing them of PM's approval to release of Rs 623 crore to Jammu and Kashmir for Baglihar Project as a special case.

DUBIOUS ROLE OF SOME OFFICIALS

With the PM's announcement of the special grant for the Baglihar Project, the Finance Ministry started processing the release of money to the Jammu and Kashmir government. While this was happening, I was informed that the Department of Economic Affairs (DEA) wanted a particular private consultant to reappraise the Baglihar Hydroelectric Project before the grant could be released. On further enquiry, I learnt that the particular consultant would charge 2 per cent of the total cost of the project as an appraisal fee, which in this case would be about Rs 45 crore.

To me, this was not only a strange arrangement but also a very high fee. The Baglihar Project was nearing completion and charging a fee on the already incurred cost of the project was ridiculous. Moreover, if the consultant was to be given Rs 45 crore as appraisal fee, the Centre would have to pay Rs 45 crore in addition to the Rs 623 crore which was to be provided. The DEA could get this evaluation done, if it wanted, at a nominal fee from the Power Finance Corporation Ltd (PFC). In the case of a project nearing completion, such as this, it would be a few lakh rupees. I informed the Secretary Power and Additional Chief Secretary Finance of Jammu and Kashmir not to give any money to the consultant and if needed, take the help of the PFC. The PM had agreed to provide the fund in national interest since the water from Chenab was flowing into Pakistan without generating any power.

Somehow, the information about my talks with the Secretary Power and Additional Chief Secretary Finance of Jammu and Kashmir reached the Additional Secretary in the DEA. He complained to Ashok Saikia, Additional Secretary in the PMO, that I was interfering in the process of the release of funds for the Baglihar Project. I apprised Saikia of the whole case and he advised me to go ahead as per my plan. After my firm stand and brief to the Jammu and Kashmir government to not shell out any amount to the private consultant, the DEA officer and the private consultant developed cold feet. The Baglihar Project authorities submitted the initial appraisal reports and the completion cost proforma cash inflow and outflow profiles, and the financial aid of Rs 623 crore was released. This case made me aware about the influence of some private consultants in some government departments and how touchy some senior officers could be if someone crosses their path even in good faith. I was lucky that I faced no rebuke as I was sitting in the PMO.

JAMMU-BARAMULLA RAILWAY LINE – A 345-KM NATIONAL PROJECT

One of the projects explained to the PM during his visit was the long delay in taking up work on the Jammu-Baramulla railway line. In 1994, the Ministry of Railways had started work on this line with a meagre allocation of about Rs 20 crore per annum, whereas the project cost was around Rs 4,500 crore. It was surprising as to how a project costing Rs 4,500 crore was expected to be completed with about Rs 20 crore budgetary provisions per annum.

Such a small fund for a project of this size seemed like a joke. After discussions, the PM agreed that the Jammu-Baramulla Project could be funded from the national Budget outside the Railway Budget and be taken up as a national project. Only then could adequate funds be provided to complete it, since the Railway Ministry did not have adequate funds. It was also decided to provide about Rs 1,000 crore every year so that the project could be completed in five years or so. Before leaving Srinagar, the PM announced the full funding for the railway project from the national Budget and set the deadline as 15 August 2007 for the first train to enter Kashmir valley at Qazigund.

After the PM's announcement, adequate funds were provided for the project. Since the railway line passed through tough hilly terrain, there were delays and difficulties in taking up different stretches of the project. As against the original proposed target of 15 August 2007, the project is now expected to be completed by 2020. The August 2007 target was too ambitious and was fixed arbitrarily to start work at full speed. Everyone knew that the project would take 15 years or so even though some stretches such as Jammu-Udhampur, Katra, etc., could be completed earlier. This was a bold decision by PM Vajpayee and gave life to a dead project. After his announcement, the PMO started monitoring this project to see if it could be completed as per the PM's announcement.

A VISIT TO THE BORDER

On the second day of his Kashmir stay the PM visited areas near the Line of Control (LoC). Brajesh Mishra also accompanied the PM on that day. During his visit to these areas, he was to address a gathering of army jawans. I too was a part of the visit, as was Sudheendra Kulkarni, who had prepared the PM's speech in Hindi. As soon as the helicopters landed at the site the senior army officers, including the Corp Commander, received the PM. I was told that we were a couple of kilometres away from the LoC. In fact while landing or taking off, the helicopters from Indian side could see the Pakistan Occupied Kashmir (PoK) and Pakistani positions. The terrain did not appear inhospitable and all around was thick forest and hills with gentle slopes. The army had constructed temporary barracks for accommodation and storing equipments. An area had been cleared to land helicopters belonging to the PM's entourage. Even while flying to these areas, I did not find many villages en route. It seemed that the area was sparsely populated.

Immediately after landing, the PM had refreshments and a brief meeting with the army officers. The army commander then took the PM and his entourage to a big room to show the equipment and weapons which the army had seized from the intruders who came from across the LoC. These included night vision equipments, sleeping bags, weapons etc. Many of these had Pakistani markings. The officers had listed the dates on which they had seized each equipment and weapon. The equipment and weapons were shown to the PM to convey the point that Pakistan was actively encouraging intruders to enter India and providing them with weapons. The officers also informed the PM about the number of training camps in PoK and Pakistan.

After this briefing meeting, the PM addressed a gathering of officers and jawans. Sudheendra Kulkarni had prepared the PM's speech in Hindi. While the speech was routine, a few lines the PM spoke made the situation war like. I am sure these were discussed with Brajesh Mishra beforehand. The PM spoke of an *aar paar ki ladai* (fight to the finish) with Pakistan', which meant a decisive battle with Pakistan once and for all. When I heard him speak, I immediately sensed that the PM had spoken strong words. I saw a few people in the Prime Minister's entourage clapping and thumping thighs with pride. It appeared that Pakistan sponsored militants had become very active in 2001. In May 2002, the militants had massacred 31 people including civilians, soldiers and their family members in Kaluchak in Jammu, making the situation in Kashmir unbearable, thus escalating the crisis. After visiting the injured jawans in the hospital, the PM had then described the Kaluchak attack as terribly inhumane and brutal.

On our return to the Raj Bhavan, I saw the PM and the Principal Secretary in intense discussion. After sometime, Brajesh Mishra came out and asked to be connected to Condoleezza Rice, the National Security Adviser to USA President George Bush. Among others, I saw our tour officer Shankar trying to connect the phone. Connecting to Condoleezza Rice was not easy as she was in Europe and to get to her one had to go through the White House. Our officer managed to do so after the mandatory security vetting.

Brajesh Mishra went inside the room to take a call and came out after some time. I realised that the situation was serious, and there could be some unavoidable issues of which he wanted to brief Condoleezza Rice urgently. After the PM came to Delhi, the issue of *aar paar ki ladai* kept getting raised for some time. India and Pakistan moved their army units near the border, and it appeared that the countries could go to war. But eventually, the situation cooled down and both the countries withdrew their armies from the border without a shot being fired.

JAMMU AND KASHMIR DEVELOPMENT PACKAGE

At the end of his three-day visit to the state, PM Vajpayee announced a Rs 6,165-crore-package for Jammu and Kashmir. This included the Jammu-Baramulla railway line, double laning of Jammu Tawi-Jallandhar railway line, construction of an all-weather 474-km road to Leh via Manali at a cost of Rs 1335 crore, including construction of the Rohtang Tunnel, Batote to Kishtwar-Sinthan Pass–Khanabal roads, technology mission for horticulture, export promotion for walnuts and apples, promotion of Kani shawl and cottage industries of wool Pashmina, sericulture, handicraft and carpet weaving; strengthening Border Area Development Programme, raising of two India Reserve Battalions, strengthening of Village Development Committees (VDCs) and enhancement of assistance for Kashmiri migrants.

The projects and schemes mentioned in the PM's package were monitored by the PMO regularly. The concerned ministries and departments were asked to monitor the implementation of the projects and schemes and send their officers to the state regularly. In cases such as the Rohtang Tunnel, meetings were conducted by the Principal Secretary so that project could be started early. Work on Baglihar Hydroelectric project started as the assistance of Rs 623 crore was released by the Ministry of Finance. The work on Baramulla railway line started at full speed and the Railway Board assigned additional manpower to the project. Even though the PM had mentioned that the first train should enter the Kashmir valley on 15 August 2007 through Qazigund, it appeared a difficult task to meet this deadline as the terrain through which the railway line was passing is very difficult. Initially, it took time to decide the route from Jammu to Qazigund as various alignments were suggested, with some having short routes but more tunnelling work, while others had less tunnelling work but longer railway lines. The second proposition comprising of longer railway line and fewer tunnels also served more population in the state and would go near the border with Pakistan.

The technology mission on horticulture which had been successfully implemented in the north-eastern states was started immediately in Jammu and Kashmir too. Work on Batote to Kishtwar-Sinthan Pass–Khanabal road was started immediately. As the PM had specially directed that there would be no shortage of funds for projects in Jammu and Kashmir, these progressed fast. For a change, many officers from the ministries and departments of the Government of India started visiting projects sites in the state.

25

MORE EMPHASIS ON JAMMU AND KASHMIR

THE 2003 INITIATIVE

The Centre had taken many initiatives to provide a secure environment in the state, as well as initiated a number of infrastructure and economic development and employment generating projects during 2002. It was expected that the concerted efforts of the government would help in improving the situation in the state. Over the years, it was noticed by the security forces that during the summer months, with the melting of snow, the influx of terrorists from PoK and Pakistan increased. After infiltration, these militants with the support of local sympathizers, used to indulge in incidents of violence. There were also reports of a large number of training camps for terrorists in PoK and Pakistan. The Department of Jammu and Kashmir Affairs, which was facilitating all issues related to Jammu and Kashmir, had prepared an action plan that envisaged a multi-dimensional approach to tackle militancy and terrorist activities in the state. I monitored it regularly. In addition, there were parallel efforts made through Track II diplomacy handled by Principal Secretary Brajesh Mishra with the help of his trusted persons in the PMO and Ministry of External Affairs about which I was not aware, as I was not handling external affairs matters in the PMO.

During my eight years in the PMO, I saw four governments making efforts to tackle violence through a variety of ways, but nothing succeeded. Sometimes, the violence decreased and then suddenly, it would spiral out of control. This continued despite all efforts to stop it. With each incident of violence the intensity increased as compared to the last one, and more and more Kashmiri Pandits kept leaving the valley. Even though some attempts were made to convince them to go back, it was without any success. That seemed to be the bitter truth of Jammu and Kashmir.

In the beginning of 2003, there were reports that a large number of Muslims were coming and settling near the railway lines in the Jammu area. There was no mechanism to evict these people except in those cases where the squatters were on railway land. While all people from Jammu and Kashmir had a right to settle wherever they wanted to in their state, some people were getting worried that the migration of Muslims from Kashmir to Jammu might change the demographic composition of Jammu. This issue was raising tension in the Jammu region of the state. The Hindu leaders were apprehensive of becoming a minority even in the Jammu region.

I felt that the initiative by PM Vajpayee, when General Musharraf was the President of Pakistan, was one of the best opportunities to settle this matter once and for all. Perhaps, no other leader in India could charter a new territory and settle the Jammu and Kashmir matter permanently. The resolution of Jammu and Kashmir related issues required new initiatives and for that, I felt the combination of PM Vajpayee and Brajesh Mishra was a formidable one which could have resolved it.

A SECOND VISIT TO THE VALLEY

In April 2003, the PM decided to visit Kashmir again. This time he was to address a public rally, as well as the Kashmir University convocation in Srinagar. Six months prior to the visit, elections were held in Jammu and Kashmir and Mufti Mohammad Sayeed, of the People's Democratic Party (PDP), took over as the Chief Minister of the state. There was some criticism of the PDP government about its 'healing touch' policy, which many thought as going soft on militants and separatists. The new state government wanted the PM to take new initiative to involve separatists also in the peace process and talks. That was why a public meeting was held where the PM was to address the public.

The Prime Minister addressed a public meeting at Sher-e-Kashmir cricket stadium which was attended by more than 25,000 persons. This was perhaps the first time in 15 years that a Prime Minister had addressed a public rally in Srinagar. In a forceful speech, PM Vajpayee said that the government had made all efforts to build a harmonious relationship with Pakistan. He said:

> 'As Prime Minister of the country I wanted to have friendly relations with our neighbours and I went to Lahore, but it was returned with Kargil. We still continued and invited General Pervez Musharraf to Agra but again failed... We are again extending a hand of friendship, but hands should be extended from both the sides. Both sides should decide to live together. We have everything which makes us to have good relations.'

Referring to the militants and the separatists, the PM said that the gun was no solution to any problem. He also reiterated the Centre's resolve to hold talks with the people of Jammu and Kashmir and assured complete support to the state government. Without naming any separatist or militant group, he reiterated New Delhi's promise to hold a dialogue on both internal and external problems. 'Not only are our doors, but also our hearts are always open for you. You can come to us with your grievances,' he said while reiterating that 'no guns but only brotherhood can resolve the issues confronting us.'

The PM complimented Chief Minister Mufti Mohammad Sayeed's government and announced that the Centre would work in tandem with them as it was the duty of the Central government to make the state government a success. He also complimented the people of Jammu and Kashmir for exercising their franchise at grave risk to their lives and even daring death. Taking full credit for holding free and fair elections, he referred to his Red Fort speech in which he had exhorted people to participate with zeal in the elections. He also assured the people that special attention would be paid to the state in addressing the problem of unemployment.

CONVOCATION OF KASHMIR UNIVERSITY

The PM attended the 16th Convocation of the University of Kashmir. N.R. Narayan Murthy, the founder of INFOSYS, was conferred the degree of D.Litt by the University. The PM, in his address to the gathering, stressed on continuous learning in life, communal harmony and preserving the beauty of Kashmir. In his address he said that 'the Convocation might connote the end of formal education, but not of education as such. Learning is a lifelong activity. Prophet Mohammed exhorted everyone, woman and man alike, to pursue learning from cradle to grave, and to cross every frontier to seek *ilm* (knowledge). It is a happy coincidence that your university is located near Hazaratbal, which is famous because of its association with the Prophet of Islam'.

Exhorting people not to disturb the academic atmosphere of the University, he said that the very fact that the Convocation was taking place after a gap of six long years was an indication of the troubled times in which students had to study, the teachers had to teach, and the administrators of the university had to function. It was the responsibility of academicians, scholars, artists, cultural personalities, mass media and political workers to highlight the age-old traditions of communal harmony and national unity in Kashmir and the rest of India. He also advised that death and destruction cannot always claim supremacy over life and creation, and that darkness cannot keep light away forever.

Referring to the beauty of Kashmir, the PM said that anyone who had experienced the beauty and serenity of Jammu and Kashmir was bound to conclude that God had been partial to this place, making it the paradise on earth. However, the same person, looking at the strife and violence that has marred the state's tranquillity might also wonder why had peace eluded this paradise for so long? Referring to the spiritual past of Kashmir, he said that it was only in Kashmir that the Rishi order recognises Hindu and Muslim spiritual masters alike. Nooruddin Shaikh, the greatest saint of Kashmir, was also known as Nand Rishi. His appeal to the people 'to break the sword and forge it into a sickle', reads as if it was coined not only for Kashmir of today, but also for the world of today.

PM Vajpayee made repeated efforts to usher in peace in Jammu and Kashmir. He was politically powerful, liberal and understood the reality of the situation in India, as well as South Asia, very well. He had earlier been the Minister of External Affairs and knew very well that India would have to live in peace with its neighbours, including Pakistan, and that this was in the interest of all the countries of South Asia. He extended his hand of friendship repeatedly to Pakistan. He did not lose hope and continued to take various initiatives to achieve this. He understood the position of hardliners in both India and Pakistan on the Jammu and Kashmir issue.

PM Vajpayee was widely respected by leaders of all political parties. The presence of Brajesh Mishra as Principal Secretary, who knew the intricacies of international relations and Track II diplomacy well, was of tremendous advantage to the government. If PM Vajpayee was able to settle the issue of Jammu and Kashmir with Pakistan, it would have been easy to also take on board other Opposition parties about the settlement. Alas! It did not happen in spite of the best efforts of the PM. The resolution of Kashmir issues would require someone with political views and the maturity of PM Vajpayee, without that it would be difficult.

26

IT'S ALL ABOUT RULES

Like my colleagues serving the Government of India, I too thought that everyone who works in the government is well conversant with the rules and regulations regarding its working. However, after serving a few years in the PMO, I realised that many officers worked based on precedents and did not update their knowledge of rules, regulations and procedures of working in the government system. In a few instances, I was shocked at the ignorance of officials regarding the procedures laid out in various government documents such as the *Government of India (Allocation of Business) Rules* and *the Government of India (Transaction of Business) Rules* (*ToB Rules*). Many of them were senior officials who were neither keen to find out for themselves nor insisted their juniors check the rules before processing the proposals. To me this seemed quite serious.

The instances that I mention highlight the ignorance about rules. These are not mentioned to show anybody in poor light but to reflect the general malaise of the prevalent system where a *chalta hai* (it's ok) attitude is adopted quite often. Seniors as well as juniors want to process proposals without looking at the rules and finish work. Many officials were not concerned about innovating and documenting procedures that should be followed in all cases in the future.

VLADIMIR PUTIN VISITS INDIA

In October 2000, Russian President Vladimir Putin visited India. I came to hear that the MEA was considering a proposal to remit the life sentence of one of the people convicted and sentenced to life imprisonment in the Purulia Arms drop case. India was still under US sanctions because of the nuclear tests of May 1998. Perhaps, the Government of India wanted better relations with Russia and hence the proposal to remit the sentence of the Russian was being considered by the MEA. This type of counter balancing of relations is generally done in external affairs and international relations.

The MEA initiated the proposal before the arrival of Putin. As per the *Government of India (Allocation of Business) Rules* and *the Government of India (Transaction of Business) Rules*, the President of India can remit a jail sentence. However, according to the *ToB Rules*, the remission of jail term is done by the Home Minister and the order is issued in the name of the President of India. The MEA officials were under the impression that the file would have to be sent to President of India. The file reached the Principal Secretary after the MEA's approval and I was asked to process the proposal for taking the President's approval. I showed the Principal Secretary a copy of the *ToB Rules* and informed him that this proposal would require approval of the Home Minister, hence, the proposal has to be sent to MHA by MEA. Based on the proposal from MEA, the MHA would take approval of the Home Minister and issue necessary orders, if any.

It was only after my intervention that the proposal for remission of sentence was sent back to MEA. In my presence, the Principal Secretary rang up the MEA official and advised him to read the *ToB Rules* and follow it. I wondered if anybody in the MEA had read it. The incorrect processing of the proposal happened because they were not aware of the procedure given in the relevant rule book.

Sometime after this, some officials from the MEA approached me to get a copy of the *ToB Rules*. I had one copy, which was overwritten and stapled with amendments all over. I told them that I could not give my copy as these were marked confidential and it was a numbered copy that had been issued to me. I advised them to get one from the Cabinet Secretariat or from the Administration wing in MEA. It seemed that the book was printed long back and perhaps nobody had bothered to reprint these annually.

CONSTITUTION OF A CONVENIENT COMMITTEE

There are committees constituted by the Government of India for specific purposes. Whenever these are set up, the 'terms of reference' of these committees are invariably specified in the orders constituting the committees. In addition to these specific committees constituted by the different ministries from time to time, there are committees such as Committee of Secretaries, popularly known as COS, chaired by the Cabinet Secretary which holds meetings to discuss inter departmental matters or other important matters.

Based on the discussions and decisions in such committee meetings, the concerned ministries, or departments act by following procedures as has been laid down. There is a set procedure followed in the Government of India, and the members of Central Secretariat Service (CSS) and lower services are aware of the procedure. In one instance, a Minister holding an independent charge constituted a committee to discuss issues, many of which required approval or concurrences of other ministries and departments. After the meeting, surprisingly, the minutes were sent to the PMO for approval before the Minister concerned acted on it. It seemed the Minister and the Ministry thought that an approval of the minutes implied that the proposals in the minutes too were approved by the PMO and the PM. But that could not be the case.

A few days later, I was informed that a reminder had been received in PMO from the office of the Minister to get approval of PMO for the minutes. The Minister approached the Principal Secretary, who advised me to look into the proposal. I checked and found that the minutes contained several inter-ministerial issues, which could not be resolved by the said Ministry on its own. Some of these issues related to finance and other departments. Surprisingly, the officers from these concerned ministries were not part of the meeting when the issues were discussed. It appeared that the Minister had invited whosoever he felt convenient to decide on the issues confronting his Ministry and suggested decisions in that meeting.

This is not the way the inter-ministerial, inter-departmental committees are constituted, and issues resolved. Moreover, PMO does not approve the minutes of these meetings held in different ministries and chaired by different ministers. It is up to the concerned ministries to approve those minutes and take follow up actions. Any issue or matter, which as per the *Government of India (Allocation of Business) Rules,* was outside the domain of that department or Ministry, the matter would be handled by concerned Ministry or department authorised to handle it. In case of any dispute or overlapping jurisdictions of subjects or new topics or items, the matter would be referred to the Cabinet Secretary, who would decide the relevant department or Ministry to handle the matter. In this case, the Minister was incorrectly trying to seek approval of PMO for minutes of meeting which was chaired by him in his Ministry. This was strange but it happened. The PMO did not take any action and returned the file despite pressures exerted from different sources.

ALLOCATION DELAY FOR KARGIL MARTYRS' FAMILIES

I was handling matters relating to Petroleum and Natural Gas throughout my tenure in the PMO. After the Kargil War, the Prime Minister, in a very humane gesture, announced that families of all 527 war martyrs would be provided a petrol pump or gas agency to enable their families to earn a reasonable livelihood. The Ministry of Petroleum and Natural Gas was advised from the PMO to start the process of allocating these in consultation with army authorities. I was asked to monitor the progress and brief the Principal Secretary from time to time.

The procedure for allotment of petroleum product outlets was two-fold. First, it involved contacting Director General of Rehabilitation, Army Area Commanders and other army authorities, who would meet the family members of the martyrs and identify the person in whose name the petrol pump or gas agency was to be allotted. If these are to be in joint ownership, the same had to be discussed and proposed accordingly. Secondly, the oil marketing companies had been advised to suggest suitable locations to be serviced by such petrol pumps or gas agencies. It was supposed to be a quick operation but as is the system in our country, it took a really long time.

Whenever I reviewed the progress, I was surprised to find that the system of identifying the beneficiaries and the locations had become very complicated. There were disputes among family members about the actual beneficiaries. Should it be the wife alone, or should the father and mother also be included? In poor families, it was quite difficult to find a solution. Then there was the issue of the location of petrol pumps and the availability of land. In the case of gas agencies, it was easy to find a suitable place and a store for the gas cylinders. However, when it came to selecting a suitable location along the road for a petrol pump it took time. Often suitable plots of land for a petrol pump along a road could belong to private person who would not part with it. Sometimes the suitable land would be far away from where the martyr's family lived or wanted a petrol pump. The issues of commercial viability of petrol pumps and the availability of land by the roadside, delayed the selection of sites and allotment of petrol pumps.

Even after a few years, many of the petrol pumps and gas agencies had not been established. I reminded the Principal Secretary a few times to remind Chief of the Army Staff to expedite the process. I am sure that he must have reminded the appropriate authorities, but it lingered on. I did not expect it to be done in a short time, but I had not imagined this long a delay either.

CARELESSNESS IN PREPARING CCEA NOTE

Many a time at the PMO we would receive notes for Cabinet or Cabinet Committees very late. We had to then go through the notes hurriedly for the Cabinet and prepare our comments, then send these to the PM and the Principal Secretary before the Cabinet meetings. Often I used to feel hard pressed for time, but as and when I would get the notes I checked the data and the figures quite carefully for any mistakes in calculation. Since these notes were scrutinised by various ministries, Planning Commission, and the Ministry of Finance before reaching me, the calculations and the figures used to be correct. Even then I checked the crucial calculations before sending my comments to the PM and the Principal Secretary. The advice of B.N. Yugandhar that the PMO is a zero-error office was deeply embedded in me, and I would check and verify everything for facts and accuracy before it was put up to the PM.

The Ministry of Railways sent a note to be placed before Cabinet Committee for Economic Affairs (CCEA) for fabrication of cement concrete spacers and sleepers for railway lines in place of iron and wooden spacers and sleepers. I got copies of the CCEA note on a Saturday morning and the CCEA meeting was slated to be held in the evening. It was a small note containing a few pages, and both the Ministry of Finance and the Planning Commission had agreed to the proposal contained in the note.

I looked at the proposal and found that each sleeper cost about Rs 187, whereas it was mentioned that each piece would consume about five bags of cement, sizeable stone chips, sand and also some reinforcements of iron rods. Each bag of cement costed over Rs 125 and even cement cost for each piece of sleeper was more than Rs 750. I was surprised at such a low cost of each spacer. I did my own calculation and found that the decimal in the calculations was incorrectly placed and instead of arriving at Rs 1,870 per piece, the cost per piece was calculated as Rs 187 per sleeper. I wondered how this note for the CCEA with such a glaring mistake could pass through so many hands and the Cabinet Secretariat, which was supposed to scrutinise the note for its veracity.

Moreover, there is a Chief Financial Adviser in the Railway Board who was also supposed to check this. Why did no one wonder how a sleeper that consumed five bags of cement would cost less than cost of two bags? Perhaps, everybody from the Ministry of Railways to others, took it for granted that the juniors must have checked the calculations, approved the note, and sent it forward to CCEA for seeking expenditure sanction to the proposal.

As soon as I spotted the mistake, I rang up the Cabinet Secretariat officials and the office of Chairman Railway Board and the Chief Financial Adviser. They too were shocked. I found the primary responsibility for this mistake was of the Chief Financial Adviser in the Ministry of Railways. The Chairman Railway Board was furious and did not want to be faulted for such a silly mistake. Moreover, if this leaked out to the media, it could attract adverse criticism about the casual functioning of the Railway Board and the Cabinet Secretariat. Within a few hours the CCEA note was withdrawn and a rectified one sent. The proposal was approved by the CCEA the same evening.

Many a time, senior officers do not check the details and assume their juniors have checked these properly. This may not be the case always and mistakes can reach the top due to this casual approach. The *chalta hai* attitude can lead to serious problems.

27

PEOPLE AND PERSONALITIES

TEHELKA EXPOSE AND THE PM'S CONFERENCE

The Ministry of Environment and Forest under T.R. Balu, had convened a conference of Environment and Forest Ministers of states and Union Territories to discuss matters relating to timely forest and environment clearances of development projects, and for formulating new guidelines for environment and forest clearances at the state and national level. The meeting was held in the Main Hall of the Parliament House Annexe. Mr Balu was pushing through the agenda very fast even though a few states had reservations on some of the issues given in it.

Midway through the meeting, I received a message for the PM from a junior officer in the PMO. A TV clip was being repeatedly shown in the news wherein BJP party president Bangaru Laxman was accepting money in lieu of some defence contract. I conveyed the news to the PM. He heard me but neither showed any emotions nor ended the conference abruptly. He continued with the conference but asked the Union Minister to finish as early as possible. The news was a big setback for the BJP whose president was caught on tape accepting bribe. He was convicted by a Special CBI Court later in 2012 under Prevention of Corruption Act and sentenced to four years in jail.

DGP JUMPS SECURITY PROTOCOL

The PM was visiting a school during his tour of Karnataka in 2001-02. I was with him during the tour. There is a standard security drill laid out for the PM's travel, whether by car or by aeroplane, known to all police officers. This drill includes the names of people who would come near him, how the PM has to come out of the car, which Special Protection Group (SPG) person would open the door of the car and when. The SPG is a well-trained and an efficient protection unit whose responsibility is to protect the PM. When the PM's visits are planned, a detailed rehearsal is done in advance and loose ends are tied by the SPG along with the state police. So much so that though I was Joint Secretary to the PM and used to be present in his meetings, brief him on subjects of my areas of responsibility, sometimes even alone, even then the SPG would not trust me if I came in their way during the movement of the PM. They did not tolerate any breach in their security protocol. Ordinarily, only the SPG personnel are allowed to go near the PM with weapons. The decision or advice of the SPG officer in charge with the PM is taken as final, and the states and other agencies hosting the PM do not challenge it. The state government agencies including security organisations go by the procedure approved by the SPG.

When the PM's convoy reached the school a strange thing happened. Quite unexpectedly, the DGP of Karnataka, who was waiting near the alighting point, rushed forward to open the door of the PM's car. In his eagerness, he forgot that there was a well-laid-out standard operating procedure (SOP) even for opening the door of the PM's car. The DGP Karnataka violated the security protocol, rather strange for him as head of the Karnataka Police Force he should have been aware of the SOP. As soon as he tried to approach the PM's car door, the SPG personnel pushed him away from the car. The DGP got the shock of his life because he had not expected this. Instead of being apologetic, he felt insulted and left the PM's entourage as well as the venue of the meeting. During the remaining leg of the tour, another senior officer from Karnataka police accompanied the PM's convoy.

While the meeting in the school was going on, I. J. Nagia, IPS, Joint Director SPG and my batchmate told me that the DGP was upset for being insulted. Nagia appreciated the SPG personnel who followed the SOP during the visit. The SPG personnel did his duty and needed to be commended. It seemed the DGP Karnataka did not appreciate it nor had any remorse for the serious breach of SOP he had committed.

RECOMMENDATIONS FOR PADMA AWARDS

Every year, Padma Awards (Padma Shree, Padma Bhushan, and Padma Vibhushan) are announced on the Republic Day. In 1996-99, procedures were laid down for inviting names and constitution of the awards committee for Padma awards. As per these guidelines, the MHA invites names from states, individuals and other functionaries in the Government of India for consideration for Padma awards. For the announcement on Republic Day in 2000, the MHA invited names in July 1999 and in the PMO too we got a letter to suggest names to be placed before the awards committee.

I sent a note to the PM's Private Secretary to recommend names for Padma Awards. I assumed the PM would have a number of names to recommend. I did not receive any word from him despite several reminders. I spoke to the Principal Secretary about this. He advised me to prepare a list of names of those who had contributed in public administration and other areas, and send it to PM. I immediately contacted G. K. Pillai and requested him to suggest some names from the North-East. He sent about half a dozen names which included Patricia Mukhim from Meghalaya, Neidonuo Angami, President of Naga Mothers Association, and Brigadier T. Sailo from Mizoram along with a brief bio data of each of them. I forwarded the file to PM and suggested that PMO could recommend these names for placing before the awards committee.

When I got back the file with the approved list, only one name was added. The PM did not have any name to favour. My respect for PM Vajpayee went sky high. Here was a man with a large heart, a liberal person who did not allow even his closest confidantes to influence any awards or ask for favours.

ANTI-GOVERNMENT IS NOT ANTI-NATIONAL

The PMO sent the list of names to MHA to be placed before the awards committee. Once recommended, the names are sent for verification to the state police, Intelligence Bureau, Income Tax Department, etc. before finally announcing their selection for Padma awards. It was at this stage that I heard a strange view from a senior officer in the Meghalaya government. He said that the Meghalaya government was not happy with Patricia Mukhim as she criticises the state government's actions and decisions through her writings in newspapers. In fact, he said that Patricia Mukhim was an anti-national, as she was anti-state government. I do not know whether the Meghalaya government had also formally mentioned this in the police verification. I also heard that the Chief Secretary of the state had commented that some of her writings were anti-national and hence, she could not be considered for the Padma award. This was completely untrue. She had written sometimes against some actions of the state government and there is nothing wrong in that. Writing against the state government did not mean that the writer is anti-national. If the government actions are wrong, every right-thinking person has a right to write or speak against the wrong actions. I heard Ashok Saikia speak out aloud that the state government should take such writings in the correct perspective and must not brand people who opposed its policies as anti-national.

Though I have never met Patricia Mukhim, I heard a lot of good things about her later. There is a difference between being anti-national and being anti-government. Officials at higher level in the state government have to be broad minded and give adequate space to all shades of opinions or views against or in favour of government actions.

In this case, the utterances of some of the senior officers in Meghalaya showed them in poor light.

PRESIDENT'S POLICE MEDAL FOR R.K. RAGHAVAN IPS

On each Independence Day and Republic Day, selected police officers are honoured with gallantry medals and service medals. The two police service medals are Police Medal for Meritorious Service and President's Police Medal for Distinguished Service. Based on the service records and Annual Confidential Reports of the officers, the Police Medal for Meritorious Service is awarded for a meritorious record of at least fifteen years in the state police, Central police or security organisation. The President's Police Medal for Distinguished Service is awarded for long and distinguished service to an individual who has served for at least 21 years in any of these services or organisations. The person must be a prior recipient of the Police Medal for Meritorious Service and must have held that medal for at least six years.

Once proposals are received from the state governments and police organisations in the MHA, it is placed before a high-level committee chaired by the Home Secretary and heads of Central police organisations such as Intelligence Bureau, Central Reserve Paramilitary Force, Border Security Force, and some other senior officers of MHA.

In 1999, proposals received from different organisations were processed as usual in the MHA for the Republic Day announcement. I received the proposal file from MHA and processed as routine case without any material contributions. I was then informed by the Principal Secretary that the name of the recently appointed CBI Director R. K. Raghavan, who had distinguished service record, was surprisingly not recommended for the President's Police Medal for Distinguished Service.

There was a lot of concern and discussion about fair and objective selection and appointment of the CBI Director in 1998-99. It would look very strange that a person who had not even received President's Police Medal for Distinguished Service had been appointed as the CBI Director. People would impute motives to the appointment, raise doubt about the outstanding record of the newly appointed CBI Director, and may even question the Centre's decision.

The Principal Secretary advised me to inform the Home Secretary to review the recommendations of the committee and include Raghavan's name as one of the recommended people. I rang up the Home Secretary and told him the reason. He was slightly irritated and did not seem keen to hold the review meeting of the committee as some members were not in North Block and, it was possible, that the heads of Central police organisations might not be available for the review meeting. Nevertheless, I sent back the file to him not very sure about the actions that would be taken by MHA on the file. Surprisingly, I got the revised proposal with the name of Raghavan recommended for President's Police Medal for Distinguished Service. I then processed the file for approvals and the revised proposal was approved.

This case was the only one during my tenure where the PMO advised the Home Secretary to review recommendations of the committee under his chairmanship. Raghavan might have been excluded inadvertently or on its own merit. I am not aware about that. I also want to make it clear here that I am not making any comment on the record or suitability of Raghavan for the President's Police Medal for Distinguished Service.

'WHOSE MAN IS HE?' ASKS THE PM

I was in my office in the South Block in 2003, when I got a call one day from the PM's office in 7 RCR. It was his PS who informed me that Lt Gen Ajay Singh, the Governor of Assam, had come to call on the PM and was waiting in the lounge. He said that the PM wanted to know the person on whose recommendation the Lieutenant General was appointed as Governor. To quote the PS he said, 'The PM wants to know as to whose man is this Governor?' It seemed the PM wanted to ask the Governor something at the time of his courtesy call. I knew that when the proposal for the Lieutenant General's appointment was processed, the PM was on tour in Europe and I had faxed the relevant papers to him. We had to guess and do a few eliminations to arrive at the answer.

After a few minutes we were able to know that it was Jaswant Singh who had recommended the Governor. I informed the PS, and then the Governor called on PM. This incident amused me as I could not ask the same question from the Governor for briefing the PM. All Governors and Lieutenant Governors invariably are appointed by the government on the recommendations of influential political personalities, or to favour certain groups within the political party in power, or to favour a coalition partner of the ruling party in power. There is no selection criteria for Governors, it is the prerogative of the PM.

TELECOM CZARS MEET PRINCIPAL SECRETARY

In January 2003, the Prime Minister was on tour of Andaman and Nicobar Islands. During this tour, a serious telecommunications crisis developed in northern India. MTNL and BSNL refused to allow the inter-connections of telephones from other private companies such as Airtel, Aircel, etc. through the switches located in the premises of MTNL in Delhi. As a result, private mobile phone users could not contact the telephones of any other service providers. This created a serious communication problem and a hue and cry among public.

The chairmen of major private telecommunications firms, including Sunil Bharati Mittal and Anil Ambani, called on the Principal Secretary and briefed him about the situation. I also attended the meeting and recorded the issues. It appeared that both MTNL and BSNL had arbitrarily imposed some restrictions, which could not be explained by the Secretary, Telecommunications in the meeting. The unexplained reasons behind the crisis seemed to be self-created by the Ministry of Telecommunications. The Principal Secretary spoke to the PM about this and the inconvenience to public this had created.

I could sense the seriousness as the private telecommunications operators had made large investments in infrastructure. It appeared that they were being blackmailed by the Ministry or somebody in the Ministry. However, due to the huge public outcry, the issues relating to restrictions on interconnections were resolved after the intervention by the Principal Secretary. This incident dented the image of the Telecommunications Ministry. There were some whispers about who was behind this crisis. At PMO, people were quite upset at the crisis created out of nothing. Later, I heard that this incident along with pressure from private telecommunications operators led to removal of the then Telecommunications Minister from the Ministry in 2003.

A DHARNA OUTSIDE PM'S OFFICE

It is necessary to fix minimum prices so that farmers are not victims of distress sale. Distress sale could also discourage the farmers from growing paddy and wheat, which are essential for food security of the country. In Punjab, the farmers go in a big way to grow paddy and wheat. The Central agencies like Food Corporation of India (FCI) and state procurement agencies procure paddy and wheat at a price fixed by the government. During the tenure of PM Vajpayee, at one point there was discontentment among the farmers because of the low Minimum Support Price (MSP) for paddy and wheat, especially among farmers from Punjab. Since farmers play a major role in the formation of government and could make or break governments in Punjab, these matters were never allowed to fester.

The Punjab Chief Minister Capt. Amarinder Singh was not satisfied with the stand of the Union government on the low MSP in 2002. Since he neither got a proper response from the government nor an assurance to review the MSP upwards, he decided to sit on a dharna at the junction of the then Race Course Road. I was in 7 RCR at that time. I saw that the Prime Minister was a little disturbed and did not feel comfortable at the thought of the Chief Minister of a state sitting in protest in front of the PM's office to draw attention to the farmers' concerns. He asked his officers to request the CM to come in and discuss the issue. PM was even eager to go outside and meet the Punjab CM and request him to come in PM office and discuss the matter. PM Vajpayee was a large-hearted individual who dealt with politicians from other political parties as a true statesman would.

28

DEALING WITH COMPLEXITIES

VETTING THE PM'S STATEMENTS

The PM used to visit Manali and stay at his daughter's residence. These were visits for relaxation and stepping away from the hectic and tight routines of the PMO. For a while, I was also handling matters and issues relating to Himachal Pradesh in the PMO. Often the Himachal Pradesh CM and other state dignitaries would visit him as per protocol and for courtesy calls. It was but natural for the CM to raise issues of development of the state. During one such visit, the CM discussed certain issues with the PM and a statement was issued at the end of his stay at Manali.

The last point in PM's statement was that he had given his approval to the Himachal Pradesh government to allot hydroelectric projects up to 300 MW without call of tenders. It seemed this point was included in the PM's statement without either understanding its financial implications or the feasibility of such an announcement. The PM's statement was prepared and finalised without consulting either me or the senior officers in the PMO. I saw the statement and realised that this was not actionable as the PM did not have the power to authorise this.

The next day, I got a copy of the PM's statement and at the same time I began to get reminders from the Himachal Pradesh government to issue orders from the PMO regarding the PM's approval of this. I knew that the cost of construction one MW of Hydroelectric project was about Rs 5-6 crore. Going by this thumb rule, the cost of 300 MW hydroelectric project would be between Rs 1,500 crore and Rs 1,800 crore. There was no law or financial rule which empowered the PM to authorise any state or person to award work without call of tender, leave aside a project of such big magnitude.

I processed file through the Secretary to PM and proposed that nothing should be issued from the PMO citing that the PM did not have this power. After a few days, the PS to the PM sent the file back to me and informed me that the PMO should issue a letter as per the PM's announcement at Manali. The CM who was camping in Delhi was sending reminders for the letter to be issued quickly. I made a proposal once again suggesting that since the PM did not have such power the PMO should not issue such a letter. This time I sent the file through the Principal Secretary. A few days later, when I got the file back it was stated that the PM desired the letter be issued in line with his announcement. I realised the serious implications of preparing PM's speeches without considering financial rules. His statement was prepared by those who prepare his speeches and was not vetted by the concerned Joint Secretary.

When I realised that neither the Principal Secretary nor the Secretary would be able to help me convince the PM about the non-workability of his announcement, I informed Ashok Saikia about this issue. I showed him the file and told him that both the CM and CS of Himachal Pradesh were camping in Delhi to get the letter from the PMO. I informed him of the reminders I got from the office of the Resident Commissioner Himachal Pradesh, and a few times from the PS to the PM regarding this. I shared with him my apprehension that the CM might be reminding the PM on this issue repeatedly and hence the PM's Office was sending repeated reminders.

Ashok Saikia rang up the CM of Himachal Pradesh. He was very blunt and told the gentleman the impossibility of issuing orders from the PMO for such financial matters. He said, 'Do you want this old man (referring to the PM) to go to jail? Who has the power to authorise you the award of work without calling tenders up to Rs 1,800 crore? Your file is with me and you can tell the PM that I am not putting up the file and the PMO will not issue any such letter come what may.' Saying this he disconnected the call. I was told later that when the CM met Ashok Saikia, the latter repeated the same words. I neither saw the file nor was there any reminder from the Himachal Pradesh government again. I realised that Ashok Saikia had a much better personal relationship with PM Vajpayee than Brajesh Mishra.

CHANDRABABU NAIDU PLAYS HIS CARDS WELL

The TDP, headed by N. Chandrababu Naidu, was part of the NDA but did not join the Vajpayee government despite having 29 MPs in the Lok Sabha. The TDP preferred the post of the Lok Sabha Speaker. C. M. Balayogi of the TDP was Lok Sabha Speaker in 1998 and 1999. As ill luck would have it, Balayogi died in a helicopter crash in Krishna District in 2002.

I found Chandrababu Naidu a hardworking and clear-headed politician. He did not want any ministerial berths for his party. He wanted to derive maximum benefit from NDA government by way of assistance for new projects in Andhra Pradesh. He had realised that he could get more benefits from the Union government if he did not have any minister in the Cabinet. This would give him a greater leverage with the PM. I found that this strategy worked well for him and for Andhra Pradesh.

A few weeks after the Vajpayee government was sworn in, Chandrababu Naidu met the PM along with the TDP MPs and some officials of Andhra Pradesh government and K. Yerran Naidu, the leader of the TDP Parliamentary Board and a trusted lieutenant of Chandrababu Naidu. I remember we had to make a makeshift arrangement for the meeting in 7 RCR, since Panchvati had not been constructed. I have not seen so many persons ever attend a PM's meeting.

Only Chandrababu spoke in the meeting, and a few times Yerran Naidu intervened and spoke about some requests for projects. Chandrababu Naidu gave a list of more than 40 issues, projects and programmes. He requested the PM to address them and identify one nodal officer in the PMO, who would specially be in charge of pursuing these. The Principal Secretary informed them that Jarnail Singh would be the focal point for all issues relating to Andhra Pradesh. I was asked to take advice and help of OSD to PM as and when required. Since Chandrababu Naidu visited Delhi often, I regularly updated the progress of action taken in consultation with all concerned agencies, ministries and departments.

I held frequent meetings in the PMO in this regard and made sure that the minutes of the meetings and decisions taken were conveyed on the same day to all concerned. Yerran Naidu often came to my office to know the latest position. After a few monthly meetings, Chandrababu Naidu noted with satisfaction in a meeting that there was good progress on most of the issues and projects requested by him.

Rajarshi Bhattacharya, the Resident Commissioner of Andhra Pradesh in Delhi, was updated from the PMO and he in turn updated the state government. Chandrababu Naidu reviewed the projects in Hyderabad and had advised Yerran Naidu to pursue hard with the PMO regularly. After a few years, all of the forty projects except one, were brought to logical conclusions. I was very happy. It had been a very difficult task every fortnight to face Chandrababu Naidu in meetings with the PM.

PM'S NO TO TOBACCO CULTIVATION

One of the proposals given in the Andhra CM's list was the encouragement to grow more tobacco by giving subsidy and fixing minimum support price as was being done for wheat and paddy. I kept on pursuing this proposal with the Ministry of Commerce, but I did not get any positive response. Although the issues raised by the CM were discussed and the

PM informed, but surprisingly, the PM never asked us to encourage the production of tobacco. The Ministry of Commerce and other concerned ministries were also reluctant to agree to any of the suggestions given by the Andhra Pradesh in this regard. During one of the PM's planned visits and address to farmers of the Andhra Pradesh, he mentioned that his father had died of throat cancer presumably as he used to chew tobacco leaves. The PM said this was the reason he did not encourage the production of tobacco by farmers in south India. He wanted them to start growing alternate crops which could be equal or more remunerative, but also good for human health.

There was drought in some parts of Andhra Pradesh during 2000-01, and clear cut guidelines to declare drought were given by the Government of India. Surprisingly, the state government was quite quick in declaring drought in the different districts and areas. As and when the drought was declared, a substantial quantity of rice became available to the state for the drought affected people. Strangely enough, I heard a murmur in the corridors of the PMO. Some officers handling Food Corporation of India (FCI) wondered why in a drought-hit state food procurement had not reduced as sharply as it should have been in such areas. There was a possibility that the rice taken from the Central government for drought relief was coming back to the procurement agencies through some unscrupulous elements in the state administration with and without collusion with the FCI personnel.

THE INFORMATION TECHNOLOGY HUB

Andhra Pradesh government was developing Hyderabad as an alternate Information Technology hub, similar to Bangalore. Chandrababu Naidu was making all efforts, providing incentives, and offering better locations to Indian and Foreign IT companies. The proposal to set up a National Institute of Smart Government (NISG) was pursued vigorously by the CM. It was decided that NISG should be set up as a Public Private Partnership Project (PPP Project) jointly between governments of India and Andhra Pradesh, and the National Association of Software and

Service Companies (NASSCOM) to promote e-governance in both the national and state government departments. Since it was Chandrababu Naidu who was trying to build Hyderabad as a magnet counter to Bangalore for IT sector, it was decided to set up NISG at Hyderabad.

A NEW AIRPORT AT HYDERABAD

If Hyderabad was to have a status similar to Mumbai or Bangalore, the city should have international flights and an international airport of a reasonable standard. I had seen the CM raising the issue of international flights to Hyderabad, but the Ministry of Civil Aviation had developed a complicated system of seat sharing and approval of flights and most of the time the CM's request was not agreed to. In one instance, the CM informed the PM that Malaysia Airlines was interested in operating direct flights between Kuala Lumpur and Hyderabad. The Ministry of Civil Aviation resisted this with the same logic of seat sharing and bilateral arrangements implying that if Air India could not operate flights between Hyderabad and Kuala Lumpur, the Malaysia Airlines could also not do so. This logic and insistence on reciprocity was one of the reasons for delay in approval of flights and possibly the reason for slow growth of air traffic in some places in India.

Hyderabad needed the new international airport as the old airport did not have adequate space for expansion required for landing the latest aeroplanes. Further, funding issues cropped up before the work started on the new airport. It was decided that the new international airport would be designed, built and operated by a joint venture company with the private sector having major equity. It was proposed to impose Additional Development Charges (ADCs) on passengers using the existing airport. When the proposal was discussed in the PMO, it appeared strange that existing passengers were to pay ADCs for the development of a new airport at a different location. After initial hesitation, the ADC route was used to part fund the new airport. I was quite sure that if some passenger approached the Consumer Court this ADC might be held illegal and without locus standi and therefore, possibly scrapped. But it continued and a new airport was built in Hyderabad.

POSTINGS IN PMO: REAPING THE BENEFITS

During my tenure, I found many officers joined the PMO and were rewarded with postings abroad, which many outside the PMO would find it hard to come by. The posts preferred by bureaucrats were Minister (Economic) in our Embassies in Europe and the USA, positions in World Bank, Asian Development Bank, IMF, United Nations bodies, etc. These jobs entitle the appointees to a salary in dollars, and for some even pensions after completing service. Many of my colleagues from PMO joined some of these foreign posts and left the PMO.

I was asked by the Principal Secretary one day, if I was interested in any foreign posting. I said no. For me and some of my other colleagues, the PMO posting was more difficult to get as compared to foreign postings.

CHIEF MINISTER'S PURPOSELESS MEETING

W. Nipamacha Singh became the Chief Minister of Manipur in 1997 replacing Rishang Keishing through a combination of use of power of the Speaker for disqualification of MLAs and the fragile political system in Manipur where MLAs could switch sides very quickly. He was a sincere and simple person and many a times, did not hesitate to speak the truth in front of his adversaries. When he became the Chief Minister, he was also heading Manipur State Congress Party (MSCP). Surprisingly, during his term the Manipur State Congress Party was allotted a piece of land in Nityaipat Chuthek near Imphal Raj Bhawan, where 19 electricity department quarters were demolished during 1994 President's Rule by me, for the construction of a public library and a reading and recreation park for elderly people. Later, another politician with an uncanny knack for manipulations occupied the office of MSCP and converted it as the office of the BJP. I have always felt this as the biggest disservice to the people of Manipur by some of these politicians.

In 1999, W. Nipamacha Singh called on PM Vajpayee along with his colleagues from the MSCP. The meeting was held in the PM's office room in the Parliament. After exchanging pleasantries, the CM Manipur explained the position of his party vis-à-vis NDA government at the Centre. Then he rolled out a handmade map of Manipur and spread it on the table and started explaining the boundaries of different districts and the tribes in each district of Manipur. The PM did not understand the context of the map of Manipur and the issues which the CM was explaining. Then CM pointed out the location of Sadar Hill where a demand and proposal to create a district, primarily to meet the aspirations of Kuki community was underway. He informed the PM about the determination of his government to create Sadar Hills District but expressed fears of backlash from the Nagas. At this point the PM asked him, 'Why are you creating a new district if you fear trouble and agitations? If the state government cannot control the situation and maintain peace then do not do any such thing?'

Unfortunately, the CM was unable to convey clearly what he required. There had been agitations, bandhs and national highway blockades organised to demand the district. However, the Nagas of Senapati district and other districts had been opposing this on the ground that the land where the Sadar Hills district was to be created belonged to the Nagas. The Nagas had also threatened to impose indefinite blockades on all highways of Manipur if the state government went ahead with the creation of Sadar Hills. They held the view that the creation of Sadar Hills Autonomous District in 1971 was a mistake done by a Committee in 1971 headed by an IAS officer.

The CM was raising an issue, the full authority of which lay with the state government. He should have, instead, asked for adequate police protection to open the highways in case of a blockade. The PM looked at me and asked for any other point which the delegation wanted to discuss. I told him that the creation or non-creation of a revenue district or any new sub-division was within the power of the Manipur state government and that the Central government did not have anything to do with that. One of the ministers accompanying CM rolled back the map and the delegation left the office. I have never seen a meeting as purposeless as this. Perhaps someone should have advised the CM and his ministerial colleagues to do their homework and come ready with talking points so that the meeting did not end on such a dry note.

NAGALAND AND RESOLVING MIALAND ISSUE

S. C. Jamir had been Chief Minister of Nagaland for many years. A very polished gentleman, he was always to the point and came well prepared to meet the PM. I found that he had excellent relations with prime ministers from different parties. In November 1999, he met the PM and raised an issue regarding many Muslims in Nagaland allegedly from Bangladesh. He said there were about 1,50,000 Muslims in a place called Mialand in Nagaland and wanted the PM's help to remove them from Nagaland. According to him many of them are running small shops like pan shops, working as labour and their ever-increasing number was worrying for the government of Nagaland. He also referred to the encroachments on the reserve forest land by them.

We knew that there were Muslims in Nagaland but did not know that they were so many and that most of them were concentrated in one place called Mialand. To the queries of the PM, CM Jamir informed him that over the years Naga farmers had been bringing in farm labourers mostly from the Muslim community from Assam, who were originally from Bangladesh and allowing them to stay in their fields. With time the Naga farmers increased their demand for these labourers and the process has continued for years. Since these immigrant labourers were hard working, the Naga girls preferred to marry them and had children from such marriages. Over the years, their numbers and their children had increased to about 1,50,000. Many of the people, which the Nagaland CM was referring to were born and brought up in Nagaland and as such could not be called foreigners or evicted from Nagaland or from India. This appeared a tricky issue to handle.

Some MLAs, including Thomas Ngullie, from Nagaland had also met me and discussed this issue and its effect on the culture and history of Nagas. I advised them to go into the reasons for this phenomenon and take steps to stop Mialand from happening elsewhere in Nagaland. They too knew the reasons and perhaps did not want to openly admit it. My suggestion was to undertake a study by research students of Nagaland University about the area called Mialand. The real reason was that the local Naga farmers were not keen to work in the fields and brought in labourers to cultivate their fields, increasing their dependence on migrant labour over the years. Though those in Mialand could not be removed, a research study could bring out the main reasons behind this phenomenon and adequate steps could be taken to prevent further occurrence. However, nothing happened, and the issue was never raised again by CM or MLAs with PMO.

Such situations happen when the politicians do not want to face reality. The Chief Minister and his MLAs were worried about the increasing Muslim population changing the demographic pattern of some areas in Nagaland. This was true but action to prevent such things lay solely with them.

29

RESOLVING CHALLENGES: A NEW APPROACH

CHANDRAYAAN I

We were flying to Bangalore where the PM had a few engagements. During the journey from New Delhi to Bangalore, Sudheendra Kulkarni, OSD in PMO, was giving finishing touches to some of the PM's speeches. While he was modifying the speech, I told him to include some ideas which should be exciting and push the frontiers of development. In the normal course, bureaucrats find it difficult to include somewhat impossible tasks in their targets. I suggested that he include in the speech that India would send a rocket to the moon. He looked at me and wrote the word *Chandrayaan* in Hindi. After writing it he went into the PM's cabin. The PM too agreed to include Chandrayaan in the speech. Later, during his speech, the PM announced India would send a spacecraft to the moon.

I am sure if Sudheendra had not mentioned this in the speech it would have been delayed and not taken front seat. As soon as the PM made the announcement the whole government machinery went ahead with the project in full force.

PESTICIDES IN SOFT DRINKS

The Centre for Science and Environment (CSE), a private institute, detailed some astonishing facts about the extent of pesticide contamination in soft drinks sold in India. The CSE study found high levels of toxic pesticides and insecticides, high enough to cause cancer, damage the nervous and reproductive systems, create birth defects and severe disruption of the immune system. Market leaders Coca-Cola and Pepsi had almost similar concentrations of pesticide residues. At the same time CSE also tested two soft drink brands sold in the US, to see if they contained pesticides and found they did not. The CSE blamed US-based MNCs of adopting dual standards when it came to developing countries and the consumption standards in their home country.

There was an uproar in the Parliament when this report appeared, and the media picked it up in a big way. Cutting across party lines, the Members of Parliament expressed concern about the startling revelations of the CSE study, given the popularity of these brands among the younger generation. Some MPs even demanded a ban on soft drinks while others questioned why these companies were allowed to maintain a quality standard in India that was lower than what was acceptable in the developed world. The Parliament was quick to banish from its premises all soft drinks. Orders were also issued for the removal of the refrigerators of the two companies and any other promotional material they may have put up in its canteens.

The issue of insecticides in soft drinks came up soon after the close of the question hour and at least 20 Members had given notices to speak on the subject. Conceding the importance of the issue, Speaker Manohar Joshi allowed a discussion. Some MPs demanded a legislation regulating soft drinks in the country and made out a case for providing security to the Director of CSE for coming out with such a report. While there was near unanimity in the House on the issue, a discordant note was struck by some BJP MPs who accused the Opposition of politicising the issue. Soon after a Joint Parliamentary Committee (JPC) was set up to discuss the issue and give its report. When the news about this matter was reported to the PM, he spoke in a somewhat sarcastic tone, 'Pressure groups would now make money from the MNCs. JPC is a not correct route'. It appeared to everyone that the JPC route would take a long time to resolve the issue.

IMDT ACT

The Illegal Migrants (Determination by Tribunal) (IMDT) Act 1983 contained procedures for detection and expulsion of illegal immigrants from Assam. This Act provided special protection against harassment to 'minorities' affected by the Assam agitation. It was only applicable to the state of Assam, whereas in other states, detection of foreigners is done under the Foreigners Act, 1946. While under the Foreigners Act 1946, the onus of proving whether a person is a foreigner or not lies upon the person, under IMDT Act the burden of proving the citizenship or otherwise rested on the accuser and the police and not the accused. This was a major departure and proved to be the most difficult to detect foreigners. Further, there were other provisions under the Act which made the work of the police as well as the accuser difficult. According to these the accuser must reside within a 3-km radius of the accused, fill out a complaint form (for a maximum of 10 persons one accuser was allowed), and pay a fee of Rs 10. If a suspected illegal migrant is thus accused, he is required by the Act to simply produce a ration card to prove his Indian citizenship. If a case is made out then a system of tribunals made up of retired judges would finally decide on deportation based on the facts. The IMDT Act also provided that 'if the application is found frivolous or vexatious' the Central government may not accept it. The IMDT Act excluded migrants who entered India before 25 March 1971 from its purview. Even for the post-1971 migrants, the procedure for deporting was tough and seemed rather impossible.

Even though enquiries were initiated in 3,10,759 cases under the Act, only 10,015 persons were declared illegal migrants and only 1,481 illegal migrants were physically expelled from 1983 to April 2000. Compared to Assam, West Bengal, where Foreigners Act was applicable, around 4,90,000 persons were deported in the same period. It was becoming apparent that the IMDT Act was advantageous for illegal migrants as any proceedings initiated against them not only ended in their favour but enabled them to have a document with official sanctity for their claim to citizenship. The Government of India through MHA was providing funds for stopping illegal entry of Bangladeshis. For that purpose, a force was raised, and this was supposed to help in stopping the entry of Bangladeshis and in detection of illegal migrants. However, it proved to be worthless.

During a discussion in a meeting with MHA officials, we were informed that most people employed under the MHA-funded scheme for stopping illegal migrants into India from Bangladesh, identifying them and proceeding against them, were being used by senior officers in Assam for helping them in their family chores or as personal attendants. So while on the one hand the state government vehemently asked for help and assistance of the Cenre to stop infiltration from Bangladesh and for the deportation of the illegal migrants, the Assam state officials and the Assam government did not play an active role in this regard.

STANDING BY THE HONEST AND THE UPRIGHT

J. Jayalalithaa, the Chief Minister of Tamil Nadu, had a special aura surrounding her. She arrived for her meetings with the PM in her own inimitable style. A person would carry a bouquet, and a few others would carry her files. She walked slowly and in a majestic way. There were no indication whether she was happy or unhappy with any decision or argument. The impression I got about her was that she expected all her requests to be agreed to by the PM. I could also sense this from the way officers accompanying her used to run around her and be mindful of her every small gesture. Her meeting with the PM was arranged in the central portion of Panchvati, a newly constructed hall, which could be divided into three separate rooms with wooden partitions. Since I oversaw southern states in the PMO, I was there to assist the PM along with his Secretary. In the meeting she raised issues relating to the state and the meeting went off well.

P. Shankar IAS was working as Secretary, Ministry of Petroleum and Natural Gas in the Central Government when Ms Jayalalithaa took over as Chief Minister. On the request of Tamil Nadu government, he had reverted back to his cadre state Tamil Nadu and the state government appointed him as Chief Secretary in June 2001. P. Shankar was a straightforward and upright officer. I had interacted with him while dealing with the Ministry of Petroleum and Natural Gas in the PMO. However, it seemed working with the CM Jayalalithaa was not easy. After some months of working as Chief Secretary, there was a news report that P. Shankar had sought voluntary retirement from service.

This seemed strange, as less than a year back he was very confidently working and did not exhibit any signs of possible voluntary retirement. The news report also mentioned his uneasy working relation with the Chief Minister though it was the CM who had requested for his reversion to Tamil Nadu and appointed him as Chief Secretary. It was apparent that he was pressurised to seek voluntary retirement. PM Vajpayee apparently knew about it and knew P. Shankar too very well and had an excellent opinion about him. When the meeting with the CM was over, PM asked her about the reported resignation of P. Shankar. To this she replied that Shankar had resigned voluntarily. The PM did not press any further and the talk ended there, and Ms Jayalalitha left the meeting room.

PM Vajpayee did not believe the CM. He did not leave the meeting room and kept standing there. This was very unusual for him. He walked up to his secretary who was standing next to me. He spoke in Hindi and said that the Tamil Nadu Chief Minister was not speaking the truth about P. Shankar's resignation. He also said that his information was that Shankar had been forced to resign from service.

Immediately, standing there in the room, he advised a senior officer to contact Shankar and ask him to withdraw his resignation if he had submitted it. He also said that Shankar could work in Rashtrapati Bhavan with the newly elected President A. P. J. Kalam as his Secretary. Shankar was informed about this the same day.

President Kalam preferred to bring in P.M. Nair IAS, as Secretary to President, so P. Shankar was appointed as Secretary, Planning Commission. Even though President Kalam was elected with the support of PM Vajpayee as President of India, the PM did not impose his views on the President regarding posting of Secretary to President.

SABOTAGING APPOINTMENTS

A strange phenomenon that I noticed quite often in the PMO was the sudden increase in complaints against officers who used to be under consideration for senior positions in important Public Sector Undertakings. After a few months in the PMO, I realised that some of those who did not make the grade could be behind the complaints with a view to delay or sabotage the appointment process. There was well-laid-out procedure and process to handle such complaints.

Even though I did not handle ACC cases, yet as I was handling ministries of Petroleum and Natural Gas and Power, the complaint against the appointment of Subir Raha as CMD of Oil and Natural Gas Commission Limited (ONGC) was incorrectly marked to me at the dak stage. I immediately guessed that his appointment might be under process somewhere and in an advanced stage. On checking with ACC cases processing officer, I found the proposal for his appointment had reached the PMO and this complaint was to sabotage the appointment process. A similar thing happened in the case of M.A. Pathan. The complaints against him reached the PMO just when the process for his appointment as Chairman of IOC was under consideration of ACC. In all likelihood, no authority in ACC would take cognizance of such complaints at such a late stage.

Rajindra Singh was CMD of National Thermal Power Corporation Limited (NTPC). He was rated as an outstanding engineer dedicated to the growth of the power sector, especially NTPC. He used to come to the PMO and meet me sometimes as I was dealing with issues of the power sector. He was a soft spoken and honest officer who inspired confidence among his colleagues. The government decided to extend his appointment as CMD of NTPC. When the file for his extension of appointment was in the process, I received a call from the office of the Union Power Minister. It was a strange request. The Minister's office had received complaints against Rajendra Singh, and they wanted these complaints to be inserted in his personal file. One of the Minister's staff came to the PMO with the complaint papers. I advised him that such things could not be done. If there was a complaint against the CMD or any other officer, the complaint would be processed as per the procedure laid down by the CVC. After following all procedures laid down by the CVC, if there was any indictment of the officer, only then that would figure in the personal file. The inclusion of fresh complaints was a mischievous attempt and was bluntly rebuffed. The reputation of officers like Rajendra Singh reach the higher echelons of government very fast and all governments need such officers to perform efficiently.

ROLE OF MoS IN PMO

During my tenure in PMO, there were a couple of Ministers of State (MoS) in the PMO. In the normal processing of files, the files are put up directly by Principal Secretary or Secretary to the PM. As per the Government of India (Allocation of Business) Rules, the main work of the PMO is to provide secretarial assistance to the prime minister. There is no other work allocated to the PMO. I used to wonder about the role of the MoS in PMO. I did not find its need unless the MoS was handling some other work independently in a ministry. Just for answering Parliament questions there need not be a minister in the PMO.

NEW AIRPORT NEAR GREATER NOIDA

The government of Uttar Pradesh had proposed a new airport about 30 km away from Greater Noida. As per guidelines of the Ministry of Civil Aviation for the location of new airports, it could not be constructed within 150 km of the existing airport. This made the proposal of the UP government unfit for consideration. However, the UP government had exerted tremendous pressure on the PMO that many meetings were held on this issue and the flying aeroplane holding spaces for the proposed airport were also discussed repeatedly. After hectic discussions, a slight relocation of the proposed airport towards Agra addressed the technical objection of Ministry of Civil Aviation satisfactorily.

The real and more important point about the new airport was about its financial viability. This was important as the proposed airport was near the Delhi airport. But to our surprise, the UP-government officials produced data about cargo and traffic which made the new airport perfectly viable. During one of the meetings, when we asked about the authenticity of the data about so much cargo and traffic, we were told that this would be supplied to the PMO. The PMO after considering the viability of the new airport approved the proposal. We, in the PMO, were pretty sure that if the new airport was viable, private investment would flow, and the airport would be built. We were also sure that before investing, the investors would do due diligence about the cargo and traffic data, cost and other performance parameters given by the UP government in their brief feasibility report.

Surprisingly, the new airport never took off the ground. It seemed the UP-government data about the cargo and traffic was exaggerated and the private investors were not fully satisfied with the data used for establishing the viability of the airport. The officers who used to frequent the PMO quite often never gave any feedback to the PMO about the responses from the private investors. It seemed the senior officers who used to present rosy picture to the PMO about the cargo and traffic data had realised that they would not be able to justify these data or answer the queries of investors as the due diligence would be a detailed scrutiny.

CONTRADICTIONS IN NHRC

The Chairperson of National Human Rights Commission (NHRC) of India is a retired Chief Justice of India. As such, the choice for appointment of the chairperson is very limited and the government has to select among the one or two available persons. In the PMO, I used to process matters relating to approvals of the tour programmes of the Chairperson of NHRC for going abroad. While processing the tour programmes, I found that the spouse of the Chairperson was also allowed to travel at government expense. All other entitlements given to the Chairperson were also given to the spouse. I found this quite strange as I had not seen such practice anywhere else in the government. When I enquired from the NHRC officials about the rules under which such claims had been proposed, I was told that as the Chairperson was a retired Chief Justice of India, he was entitled to the same privileges as his last post where the privileges of his post were extended to his spouse too. I returned the proposal a couple of times and asked clarifications about the travel rules applicable for the Chairperson of NHRC but did not get a proper answer. Even the PM wondered why such facilities were extended to family members.

JUSTICE DEPARTMENT

The Home Secretary was the Secretary of the Justice Department, which processed and sent proposals for appointment of judges to PMO. After approval of the PMO, these proposals were sent to the President of India. There is a well-laid-out procedure and the Collegium of Supreme Court used to initiate proposals and make recommendations. The recommendations of the Collegium are binding on the government and hence, there was not much examination of these proposals in PMO. These were routine cases going up to the President through PMO. There were, and still are, guidelines for the eligibility of persons who were to be recommended from the Bar for appointment as judges of the High Court or Supreme Court. One of the eligibility conditions is that the person so recommended should be 45 years or more at the time of appointment.

A proposal from the Department of Justice recommended a candidate below the eligibility age. Naturally, the PMO raised an objection and referred it back to the department. The department again strongly recommended the case by overruling the minimum age criteria. Against much hesitation I processed the proposal which was approved by the PM and sent to the President. In my entire eight years in the PMO, this was the only case where the minimum age criterion was violated.

A LAST-MINUTE RUSH OF PROPOSALS

The Ministry of Disinvestment was a new ministry. The Central government had decided to go for disinvestment of selected PSUs and organisations. The disinvestment of PSUs was itself a tricky and sensitive subject. The valuation criteria and the prices estimated for disinvestment were easily challengeable. The valuations done by different agencies were based on their appraisal techniques, and there was a chance of some subjectivity, even though the persons appraising might be honest and objective. The notes prepared by the Ministry of Disinvestment for Cabinet used to reach us in the PMO at the last minute, just before the Cabinet meetings.

Generally, the notes prepared by the Ministry of Disinvestment to be placed before the Cabinet used to be long, with numerous assumptions and complicated criteria followed for the valuations. It used to be difficult for me and my junior colleagues to go through these notes and prepare briefs for the PM. We used to have a tough time processing these notes and proposals. Due to non-availability of time at our disposal we used to get worried about possible mistakes. We could have done a much better job if the Ministry of Disinvestment had sent these notes to PMO a few days before the scheduled meetings of the Cabinet.

LACK OF TENDERS IN MINERALS PROSPECTING

I handled the matters relating to the Ministry of Mines for some time in the PMO. A few times, when proposals were received from the ministry, the matter was raised about the need for floating bids for awarding mineral prospecting rights similar to the award of rights for oil explorations. Some chief ministers too desired that mineral exploration rights should be given after floating of open tenders. From the PMO too, this proposal was moved. I found that a number of people were not in favour of grant of prospecting rights based on open tenders due to various reasons. We, in the PMO, had thought that open tender based award of mineral prospecting rights could bring in better technology in prospecting, and hence commercial scale exploration of minerals in the country. This could have also attracted more investment in prospecting and hence minerals exploration. This did not happen due to strong resistance from some unseen group/groups.

30

VAJPAYEE YEARS: TWO COMMENDABLE CONTRIBUTIONS

KISHANGANGA HYDROELECTRIC PROJECT

In 2002-03, the National Hydroelectric Power Corporation Limited (NHPC) planned a 330 MW power project on Kishanganga, a tributary of Jhelum river, in the northern most part of the country. The Kishanganga Hydroelectric Power Project of 330 MW was planned as a run of the river hydroelectric scheme that would divert water from the Kishanganga river to a power plant in the Jhelum river basin. It was to be located 5 km north of Bandipore in Jammu and Kashmir.

The project proposal was in the planning stage. Yogendra Prasad, the CMD of NHPC, was interested in starting work on the Kishanganga Project as soon as possible, and the delay in starting the work concerned him. His worry was that even if the Ministry of Power started the process of sanctioning the project, it would take years to get environmental and forest clearances as well as financial sanctions. Such long delays would give Pakistan adequate time to approach the World Bank or the Permanent Court of Arbitration to prohibit India from starting work on the project on the grounds that it violates the Indus Water Treaty.

Pakistan was planning the construction of the Neelum-Jhelum Hydropower Plant downstream of Kishanganga Project. It was their fear that when the Kishanganga project would become operational, the water available to the Neelum–Jhelum Hydropower Plant would get reduced and marginally affect the Pakistan power project.

Yogendra Prasad met me several times in the PMO to explain his concerns about this delay. He frequently approached the Ministry of Power too, to give ad hoc approval so that he could start work at least on the barrage at Kishanganga. In those days, the understanding was that if India started work even on the river barrage, it would be difficult for Pakistan to get a stay either from the World Bank or the Permanent Court of Arbitration. Thus, starting of work on the barrage was a critical factor to lay claim on the use of Kishanganga water for power generation.

Yogendra Prasad was focussed on this, and I have seen very few like him in the government who have the national interest in their heart. On his persuasion, I explained the Kishanganga Project and its significance to the Principal Secretary, and the need to start the work early. I shared Prasad's suggestion that initially Rs 20 crore could be released to NHPC to begin work on the barrage on an ad hoc basis, without waiting for the Public Investment Board (PIB) approval and other financial sanctions. He agreed to the suggestion immediately.

I quickly sent an approval note and NHPC was asked to start work on Kishanganga Project Barrage. NHPC started some preliminary work on the barrage quickly. Pakistan approached the World Bank and the Permanent Court of Arbitration to prohibit India from taking up any work on Kishanganga Project. Eventually, the work was not stopped by the international bodies. In fact, in August 2017, the World Bank allowed India to continue the work, subject to its obligations under the Indus Water Treaty. In June 2018, PM Narendra Modi inaugurated the Kishanganga Project. At the time of inauguration of the project, I am sure people in NHPC must have forgotten Yogendra Prashad and his efforts to get the project off the ground. I would say that the credit for Kishanganga Hydroelectric Project goes to Yogendra Prasad alone, and nobody else. He had the courage of conviction and perseverance to follow the matter at all platforms in national interest.

'LOKAPRIYA' GOPINATH BORDOLOI

Gopinath Bordoloi was the Prime Minister of Assam before Independence, and later the Chief Minister of the state. A follower of the Gandhian principle of non-violence as a political tool, his unselfish dedication towards Assam and its people led the then Governor of Assam, Jayram Das Doulatram, to confer on him the title 'Lokapriya' or 'loved by all'.

After India's Independence, he worked closely with Sardar Vallabhbhai Patel to secure the sovereignty of Assam against China on one hand, and Pakistan on the other. He had organised the rehabilitation of millions of Hindu refugees who fled East Pakistan to escape widespread violence and intimidation in the aftermath of the Partition of India. He played a major role in securing the future of Assam when he did not allow the plan to incorporate Assam in East Pakistan to happen. This was the best contribution by any political leader for the country at that time. It was surprising to see that a person of such unparalleled contribution for the country was not given the Bharat Ratna.

According to the guidelines formulated by the Padma Award Review Committee headed by Vice President K.R. Narayanan, the conferring of Bharat Ratna is left broadly to the wisdom of the Prime Minister. When Ashok Saikia came into the PMO, the importance of Assam and north-eastern states increased. During one meeting in PMO, it was felt that Gopinath Bordoloi, the person who was responsible for the association of all Indian states beyond the Chicken's Neck with India had not been conferred Bharat Ratna. It seemed strange that the people of India had forgotten and belittled the contributions of Bordoloi who, perhaps, was responsible for saving more than 8 per cent territory of the country. Ashok Saikia took the initiative and prepared a note for conferring Bharat Ratna on Lokapriya Gopinath Bordoloi and sent it to the PM. PM Vajpayee knew of the contributions of this great son of India. The President of India approved the proposal and Bharat Ratna was conferred on Lokapriya Gopinath Bordoloi in 1999, 49 years after his death. This was a tribute to the statesmanship of PM Vajpayee and the initiative of Ashok Saikia.

31

INDIA SHINING AND AN ELECTION LOST

The Vajpayee-led NDA government had done outstanding work from April 1998 onwards, particularly in the areas of infrastructure development and opening of economy to competition. The important initiatives taken up by the NDA government made a tremendous impact in expediting economic growth of the country, and included development of highways, rural roads, opening up of the telecommunications, aviation and electricity sectors, upgradation of railway infrastructure and construction of airports and opening of Petroleum and Natural Gas sectors in exploration, refining and marketing and that of new institutes in health and technical education.

The economic growth rate of India in 2003-04 was at 8.5 per cent. The domestic savings rate in 2003-04 was 28.1 per cent against a rate of 26.1 per cent in 2002-03. The per capita income at current prices was estimated at Rs 20,989 in 2003-04 against Rs 19,040 for the previous year, which showed a growth of 10.2 per cent. There was widespread optimism in the country about the better days ahead and sustaining the economic growth. The government had initiated all possible reforms and was moving at good speed in that direction. The economy had shown steady growth in the last few months of the government and the disinvestment of government-owned production units, a continuation of India's liberalisation policies initiated by the Narasimha Rao government, was on track too. The Foreign Exchange Reserves of India stood at more than US$100 billion which at that time was the seventh largest in the world, and a record for India. The service sector led by Information Technology (IT) had also generated a lot of jobs among the young. The NDA government was apparently riding on a wave of the so-called 'feel good' factor among the people of India. The economy was very strong and most of the economic and fiscal parameters were in favour of NDA.

On an average, about 11 km of four-lane expressways were being built daily. Despite failed attempts to improve relations with Pakistan, India had gained prominence in international relations. The BJP and NDA leaders were very optimistic of winning the coming Lok Sabha General Elections. Besides excellent achievements on the economic, foreign policy and domestic fronts, the image of PM Vajpayee as a statesman and the tallest figure of that period was acceptable to all across the political spectrum. The young politicians in BJP were quite high on the possible win of BJP in the coming elections and suddenly, a majority of BJP leaders suggested pushing forward the elections to May 2004.

The BJP coined the 'India Shining' slogan for the upcoming elections. The Union Cabinet recommended the dissolution of Lok Sabha and holding of elections in April-May 2004. Accordingly, after the approval of the President of India, a Presidential Proclamation was issued dissolving the 13th Lok Sabha on the 6 February 2004. In terms of the constitutional provisions, a new Lok Sabha was required to be constituted before 6 August 2004.

The elections were held in four phases between 20 April and 10 May 2004 and counting of votes on 13 May 2004. Prime Minister Vajpayee led the election campaign for the BJP and other allies in NDA. He led with a positive campaign. As is the case with some BJP leaders, I had never seen him criticise any political leader, even in private, though he differed with many on some issues. Perhaps, it was this trait of his that made him command respect of all leaders. He projected the achievements of his government and the future plans of the BJP and NDA.

All public opinion predicted a comfortable win for the NDA. Most analysts believed it would win the elections and this assessment was supported by almost all opinion polls. In the past, BJP has been seen as a hard line Hindu party having close ties with Hindu organisations such as Rashtriya Swayamsevak Sangh (RSS), Bajrang Dal and Vishwa Hindu Parishad (VHP). Over the years, the party had distanced itself from its Hindutva policies. In the last few elections, the party had realised that its voter base had reached a ceiling and had concentrated on pre-poll rather than post-poll alliances. The foreign origin of Sonia Gandhi was made as one of the campaign points by some leaders of NDA during the elections. The PM and most of the important leaders of NDA though emphasised the economic gains during the NDA government as their main election campaign slogans.

Most of the opinion polls, including *NDTV*, *The Indian Express* and A. C. Nielsen, forecast that the NDA would win the Lok Sabha elections and storm into power again. It was expected to bag 287 to 307 seats against the Congress-led alliance, which was expected to secure around 143 to 163 seats. The poll forecast survey claimed to be the largest ever opinion poll and covered a sample of 45,000 people in 207 constituencies, which included 80 per cent from rural areas. The opinion polls made the BJP top brass very enthusiastic for the election results.

In those days Arun Nehru, the former Minister of State (Power) used to write columns and predict possible seats of NDA and UPA in the elections after each phase of polling. I read his columns carefully, as his poll forecast was supported with well-reasoned arguments. In his concluding column, he too predicted a comfortable majority for the NDA.

The counting of votes was taken up on 13 May 2004. By afternoon it became clear that the BJP and NDA were going to lose the elections. When all the votes were counted, the election results announced the Indian National Congress-led UPA had stormed to power. The Congress and its alliance partners won 275 seats, the BJP and its alliance partners won 180, the Left parties won 60, other parties had 80 seats and three Independents. After the results were out, the ruling NDA conceded defeat. The INC, which had governed India for all but five years from Independence until 1996, and then was out of office for eight years including the Vajpayee tenure had come back to power. It was able to put together a comfortable majority of more than 335 members out of 543 with the help of its allies and Left parties. The 335 members included both, the Congress-led UPA, the governing coalition formed after the election, as well as external support from other parties.

The BJP leaders were stunned by the result. There was one general refrain in BJP circles that the 'India Shining' slogan had done the maximum damage to the BJP and NDA election campaign. Some even blamed the young BJP leaders who were over enthusiastic to come to power again without realising the pulse of the people. The INC was largely backed by poor, rural, lower-caste and minority voters who did not participate in the economic boom of the previous years that created a large wealthy middle class and thus, achieved its overwhelming victory.

Another reason not mentioned much was that the BJP supporters were working class people, and the poll surveys that predicted the BJP win did not reach the ballot. On the other hand, the Congress support base—the weaker sections of the society—does not miss voting and voted with enthusiasm. There were varied other reasons, including NDA's focus on national issues rather than local issues such as drought and agriculture, effect of Gujarat riots of 2002, less interest shown by RSS workers, anti-incumbency against BJP and its allies. These perhaps were reasons for different pre-poll surveys predicting a comfortable majority for the NDA.

A STATESMAN BIDS ADIEU

After the election results were out, we met the Prime Minister. He did not exhibit any sign of defeat. He hosted a tea party for his staff. Some staff members were given letters by him expressing his gratitude for working sincerely for him and helping him in implementing the NDA government's programmes. I was touched by the PM's letter to me. What touched me the most were his words of appreciation for my family who tolerated my long absence due to office work in the PMO.

प्रधान मंत्री
Prime Minister

New Delhi
May 18, 2004

Dear Shri Jarnail Singh,

I take this opportunity to convey to you my deep sense of appreciation for your commitment, hard work and contribution to the efficient functioning of the Prime Minister's Office. Your disciplined and enthusiastic application to the areas assigned to you strengthened my hands in carrying out my responsibilities as Prime Minister.

I have no doubt that your dedication and inputs have contributed immensely, not only towards enhancing the prestige of this office but also in our mission of implementing and monitoring the plans and projects of the Government.

I would also like to thank all the members of your family who would have missed you for long hours and on holidays because of the extraordinary demands of this office.

I wish you a very happy and successful future.

Yours sincerely,

(A.B. Vajpayee)

Shri Jarnail Singh
Joint Secretary
Prime Minister's Office
New Delhi

32

UNFINISHED INITIATIVES

In 2003, two important initiatives—Provision of Urban Amenities in Rural Areas (PURA) and interlinking of rivers in India—were started by the PM. I felt that these could be game changers if implemented with right earnest. I processed these initiatives but had to slow down at a preliminary stage when general elections to the Lok Sabha were announced in February 2004. With the Model Code of Conduct in place, it was not possible to expedite the implementation of these initiatives.

PROVISION OF URBAN AMENITIES IN RURAL AREAS

Provision of Urban amenities in Rural Areas (PURA) was envisaged to reduce the differences in the economic development in urban and rural areas. It was Dr A. P. J. Kalam who had suggested this on the eve of India's 54th Republic Day in 2003. It was a wonderful concept where four main economic development parameters, which divide urban and rural areas, were identified. These were the lack of physical (road) connectivity, electronic connectivity consisting of telephones and internet, knowledge connectivity (lack of higher and professional education facilities), and economic connectivity (integration of rural economy with urban market centres). Each of the four was to have a number of components. The PMO got the concept paper for this and started working on it. In fact, in his Independence Day speech on 15 August 2003, PM Vajpayee announced that the Government of India would start the implementation of the PURA scheme. Even though it was a wonderful programme, its implementation in the vast rural areas required development of a specific plan for each rural cluster.

This was the beginning of a scheme, which could have been a game changer in the economic development of India. Under PURA, it was proposed that urban infrastructure and services be provided in rural hubs to create economic opportunities outside cities. Physical connectivity by providing roads, electronic connectivity by providing communication network, and knowledge connectivity by establishing professional and technical institutions would have to be done in an integrated way.

I was given the concept papers and asked to follow up with the Planning Commission, and prepare the implementable schemes in consultation with them and the Ministry of Rural Development. The Principal Adviser at the Planning Commission started working on this exercise and prepared a list of all clusters to be taken as units under PURA. When I looked at different components to be covered under PURA, most of them were the same components of Basic Minimum Services (BMSs) started by PM Deve Gowda in 1996-97. The difference between PURA and BMSs was that all schemes under BMSs were clubbed, and proposed to be implemented in a cluster, so that chances of their successful implementation under PURA increased. Initially, it was decided to start PURA as a pilot project and then expand it quickly to other areas. The important schemes and programmes covered in PURA included roads, drainage and street lighting, water supply and sanitation, electricity, telecommunication systems, agriculture markets, health services, skill development, and sewerage and waste management.

During my discussions in the Planning Commission, two approaches were proposed to identify the clusters for implementation of PURA. First was to adopt the hub and spoke system, where a big village would be taken as a hub, and the surrounding villages would be connected to it as spokes in a wheel. In this approach, the potential of the big village to create and expand the services under PURA to neighbouring villages would be utilised. The second was to adopt the growth centre approach. In India, at crossings of important rural roads, some commercial establishments, agriculture machinery repairing shops, etc. had already come up over the years. These road-crossings attracted people from neighbouring villages and become attractive places for commercial activities. The planners of PURA would have to use a combination of both as per the requirements of specific areas.

PM Vajpayee, in one of the meetings held in the last week of December 2003, pushed for an early implementation of the pilot project so that within two to three years, all villages could be covered. In that meeting, the targets were fixed for the start and completion of different activities related to the Pilot Project on PURA. The important milestones and their timelines for implementation of PURA were as follows: by 31 December 2003, selection of rural clusters, by 10 January 2004, identification of schemes and programmes for each sector or sub-sector in the clusters, by 20 January, the fund flow to each cluster from the Centre and the state to be identified for each scheme and programme, by 30 January, the phasing of expenditure year-wise for each sector, scheme, and programme and identification of nodal officers for each cluster, on 15 February, exposure and training of nodal officers, and by 20 February, the action plan for each cluster would be completed and uploaded on the internet. The PMO informed the Planning Commission to adhere to these timelines for the implementation of PURA.

LOK SABHA ELECTION RESULTS AND END OF PURA

The PURA scheme was approved by the government 'in-principle' in January 2004. Subsequently, the Ministry of Rural Development started its implementation on a pilot basis in seven clusters for a period of three years starting from 2004-05. However, immediately after the 'in principle' approval, General Elections were announced. With the Model Code of

Conduct coming into force there was a lull in initiating quick actions as this was a new scheme. The new government, which would take over in May 2004 post elections, would decide the budget proposals and the financial allocations for all ongoing and new proposals.

The election forecasts overwhelmingly predicted the incumbent government back in power. The general opinion in the country, as was reflected in various opinion polls, was that immediately after the elections were over and the new government took power, the PURA scheme could be taken up with full gusto. We did not expect Vajpayee government to lose the election. A UPA government led by Dr Manmohan Singh came to power in May 2004. PURA was forgotten as the new government had their own priorities.

INTERLINKING OF INDIAN RIVERS

Another important initiative that remained unimplemented was the interlinking of Indian rivers. PM Vajpayee had chaired a number of meetings of the chief ministers regarding the sharing of river waters, since it was a bone of contention among many Indian states. The prominent disputes included, Cauvery river water sharing between Tamil Nadu and Karnataka, and the sharing of Sutlej, Beas and Ravi waters between Punjab, Haryana, and Rajasthan. There was the issue about Farakka Barrage meant for preservation and maintenance of Kolkata Port by improving the regime and navigability of the Bhagirathi-Hooghly river system. While water from Brahmaputra river was flooding Assam and flowing into sea, some engineers suggested diverting the water to Farakka Barrage from Brahmaputra. Most issues came up for repeated discussion before the PM, but no permanent solution could be found for sharing and better use of river waters.

Most parties to the river water disputes took a rigid and non-negotiable positions making the meetings with the PM of not much use. In most cases, temporary solutions were found and enforced for a short term. In the India, there are areas that can be cultivated, and food crops grown, if sufficient irrigation is available. At the same time surplus water from some rivers flow into the sea, which would have been enough to help cultivate lakhs of hectares of land in the country. It was a very peculiar situation with floods in some parts of the country and drought in others. The country needed better water management of river waters to reduce flooding and drought, increase food grain potential substantially, and increase inland river navigability. Some solution has to be found and implemented for optimal use of river waters.

From time to time, tribunals were set up to resolve the river basin disputes. However, varying cropping patterns and strong political and farmers' interests meant neither governments, nor the tribunals could provide permanent solution for any of the disputes. Often the disputes would peak into conflicts between states at the time of crop cultivation and then cool down during rainy season. Many times PM Vajpayee asked for permanent solutions to end these continuing conflicts between the states. In almost all the cases, the Central government could not take any one position because of varying political views of their partners.

Competitive politics led each chief minister and political leader, whether in power or in Opposition, to make unreasonable demands. In this political environment, the ad hoc system of water allocation continued, despite the PM's desire for a permanent solution that could be in the national interest.

The Ministry of Water Resources had been working on interlinking of rivers for quite some time and had prepared some piecemeal proposals for implementation. The Ministry was advised by the PMO to prepare a blueprint of the interlinking so that diversions could be made from one basin to another for optimal use of the water. By end of 2003, a blueprint of the project on interlinking of various rivers was updated and ready.

The blueprint included the proposal for bringing Brahmaputra river water through either the Chicken's Neck or an alternate way to West Bengal and Farakka Barrage, and further onwards to Krishna river, and to Cauvery river into southern India. I looked at this part of the proposal carefully. Though it appeared costly, yet if implemented, this would take care of the water requirements of Bengal, Odisha, Karnataka and Tamil Nadu. This project would help Bangladesh, too, as it would also get water where it needed the most in the lean season. For bringing water to the Chicken's Neck from eastern Assam and Brahmaputra, two options were suggested—one was to lift water by energy, and the second by gravity flows.

Another river link was from Yamuna, and other rivers from the north of Delhi going all the way through Haryana to Rajasthan and Gujarat. This would have taken care of water requirements of Haryana, MP, Rajasthan and Gujarat. The feasibility report for each link was required so that it was the best and cost effective for the country.

The estimated cost of the total project was indicated at about Rs 5 00,000 crore but the benefits were expected to outweigh the cost many times. The Ministry was expecting to take up these links one by one. Such tremendous investments in irrigation and agriculture sector could have made India a superpower in agriculture. Of course, while implementing projects of such mega scales, there would have been tremendous problems of environment and forest clearances, which could have slowed down the work and even dampened the initiatives of engineers. Since irrigation is a concurrent subject, the concurrence of states would also be required for constructing these river links.

Since, the river interlinks would have benefited all states, it would have been possible to bring on board all stakeholders and put in place a system for quick approvals and clearances. I was quite excited. This was a project of gigantic scale, which might have permanently helped in resolving the problems of floods and droughts, increased agriculture potential, created large employment opportunities, and improved inland water transport systems. In addition to all the economic benefits, this would have strengthened the integrity of the country.

In January 2004, with the Lok Sabha elections, the project was put on a backburner. Under the UPA government, one link between UP and MP, connecting Ken and Betwa rivers to transfer surplus water from Ken basin to water deficit Betwa basin, was initiated. Maybe the UPA government did not feel strong enough to convince the regional satraps, which was necessary to implement the complete project. Nothing has been heard of the interlinking of Indian rivers project in the recent years.

PRIME MINISTER DR MANMOHAN SINGH

(MAY 2004 – AUGUST 2004)

Author's Take

"

Dr Manmohan Singh is a soft-spoken, humble, sensitive and hardworking gentleman. His approach to work is like an officer and not a politician. A man of details, Dr Singh was keen to know the facts of any issue brought up for discussion before him. He meticulously noted down details of important issues on a notepad, something I had not seen any other PM do during my eight years in the PMO. Always courteous to all who came to meet him, he would escort visitors to the door of his office after each meeting. Even though a political lightweight, he commanded respect among politicians across party lines for his sound knowledge of the Indian economy and contribution to the economic development of the country.

"

33

DR MANMOHAN SINGH TAKES OVER AS PRIME MINISTER

The electorate had decisively rejected the Vajpayee-led NDA and voted in a Congress-led coalition spearheaded by Sonia Gandhi. In the elections, the Congress alliance also achieved massive victories for Legislative Assemblies of Tamil Nadu and Andhra Pradesh. Vajpayee resigned as Prime Minister. The general mood within the Congress was overwhelmingly in favour of Sonia Gandhi becoming the Prime Minister of India. The NDA leaders who had made 'foreign origin' as the election issue during their campaigns had to eat a humble pie. It seemed the voters did not buy their arguments of foreign origin.

After the elections, there was widespread expectation that Sonia Gandhi would be elected as the leader of the Congress Parliamentary Party. Even Left Front parties indicated their approval of Sonia Gandhi as Prime Minister. In the Central Hall of the Parliament, where the meetings of the newly elected MPs were held, all leaders supported and exhorted Mrs Gandhi to take charge as Prime Minister. Along with Dr Manmohan Singh, Mrs Gandhi met the President of India to stake claim to form a Congress-led government at the Centre.

APPREHENSIONS AT THE PMO

In the PMO, there were some officers who were considered close to PM Vajpayee. Ashok Tandon and Sudheendra Kulkarni had joined PMO for speech writing, media management, etc. They were not from the organised services of the Government of India. Then there were retired people like Brajesh Mishra who was Principal Secretary to PM. It became obvious that all these people would go with the PM.

A majority of the officers in PMO were from the organised civil services such as IAS, IFS and other Central services, who had been selected by some process and were working for quite some time. I had already spent seven years and nine months as Joint Secretary in the PMO. Even after working for a record number of years, I had not tried for deputation for a foreign posting and was keen to revert to my parent cadre state Manipur after my tenure. I felt that working in my cadre state would be more interesting and satisfying than working in an Indian Embassy. I had heard from a few colleagues that though the post of Minister (Economic) appeared very tempting, yet in real terms, it was mostly meant for liaison work as well as for receiving and seeing off persons dealing with economic ministries in India.

Most officers in PMO were uneasy and not sure about their future in the PMO. As and when a new PM took over, a new set of officers or favourites would enter the PMO. Whether the exit of old officers is abrupt or gradual depended on the new PM and the incoming Principal Secretary to the PM. The general feeling among officers in PMO was that with Mrs Gandhi as PM, the exit of officers from the PMO could be abrupt. There was no reason or argument to back that feeling though. It was equally possible that if Sonia Gandhi became the Prime Minister, she might be very pleasant to work with and the PMO officials might be happy working with her.

SONIA NOMINATES DR MANMOHAN SINGH AS PM

Defying the requests of her MPs, Congress party workers and political observers, Sonia Gandhi surprised all by declining to become the Prime

Minister. Though there was no provision in the Constitution of India which could have stopped her from becoming the PM, she proposed Dr Manmohan Singh as the new PM.

Dr Manmohan Singh has been one of the architects of India's first economic liberalisation plan in 1992-96, and had staved off an impending national economic and monetary crisis during the Congress government of Prime Minister Narasimha Rao. Even though he had never won a Lok Sabha seat, he had considerable goodwill among all Indian political leaders. The UPA allies and the Left Front, supported Dr Manmohan Singh. Dr Singh's nomination by Mrs Gandhi surprised all political pundits and won a lot of praise for her. This appeared to be the biggest sacrifice by any political leader in Indian history. Nobody in the past had declined to become PM; rather politicians have tried to score over each other to become the PM.

I was happy that Dr Manmohan Singh had become the PM. I had known him from his days as Deputy Chairman of the Planning Commission in 1987. A colleague, U. Sarat Chandran IAS, was his private secretary. The size of the annual plans of all states used to be finalised in the meetings between the Chief Minister concerned, and the Deputy Chairman of the Planning Commission. So was the case of Manipur. The finalisation of the annual plan size for the state was discussed in a meeting between Dr Singh and Rishang Keishing, the Chief Minister of Manipur. In that meeting, Dr Singh specially mentioned the good efforts made by the Manipur Electricity Department in reducing power losses. Since during 1986-88, I was Secretary Power in the government of Manipur, it was my effort that was recognised by him. In fact, at the end of the meeting, he came forward and patted me on my back and asked me to improve further. Surprisingly, in those days he used to address me as 'Karnail Singh' and not Jarnail Singh, and I wondered why? I had met him again when he was the Leader of Opposition in the Rajya Sabha. He had at that time led a delegation of Congress party to meet PM Vajpayee to request deployment of Central Paramilitary Forces in Nagaland Assembly elections, to keep the NSCN (IM) cadres away from influencing elections and intimidating voters.

DR MANMOHAN SINGH TAKES OVER

Dr Manmohan Singh took the oath as the Prime Minister of India on 22 May 2004. There were expectations that some new officers would join the PMO. A few names mentioned in corridors of PMO were Pulok Chatterjee IAS of the UP Cadre, Rahul Khullar IAS and B. V. R. Subrahmanyam IAS of Chhattisgarh cadre. While Pulok Chatterjee had been with Sonia Gandhi for the last many years, Rahul Khullar had earlier worked with Dr Singh.

Immediately after taking over, the personal staff of the PM sent a message that Dr Singh would meet all PMO officials in the meeting room of the South Block PM Office. It was also mentioned that those officers appointed by the previous PM on contract appointments or not from organised services should not attend the meeting. This was an indication that only serving deputy secretaries, directors and joint secretaries on tenure postings were to attend the meeting. Speech writers, Media Adviser and Economic Advisor to PM were asked not to attend the meeting. This was a message that they stood removed from the PMO.

Dr Singh met the PMO officers in the committee room of the South Block. We introduced ourselves and briefed him of our areas of responsibility. He patiently listened to us and advised us to work with dedication and without any fear. We were asked to continue in our positions till completion of our tenures. He once again referred to me as 'Karnail Singh' in that meeting.

Ashok Saikia left the PMO and was expected to join Asian Development Bank. He was a very dignified officer who did not want to be told by the new dispensation to leave the PMO. He knew that the new PM would like to bring his person to handle ACC matters in PMO.

A few days later, T.K.A. Nair took over as OSD to PM, though his work was that of Principal Secretary to PM. The convention is that the Principal Secretary is the senior most official in the PMO. However, there was no clarity regarding T.K.A. Nair's post. He was appointed as OSD but performed all duties and work of the Principal Secretary and sat in the same room. He was Secretary to PM during the tenures of I.K.

Gujral and A.B. Vajpayee. I had good working relations with him. After a few days he was appointed as Principal Secretary to PM.

Pulok Chatterjee was my batch mate from UP cadre and he joined as Joint Secretary in charge of ACC matters. In fact, except for the initial years, he had been mostly away from his cadre. His closeness to Sonia Gandhi made him one of the most influential persons in the PMO and bureaucratic hierarchy. I found him very polite and considerate and never saw him exhibit arrogance. J. N. Dixit, former Foreign Secretary also joined the PMO as National Security Adviser. All other officers, who had been in the PMO before Dr Singh took over, continued to handle all matters and cases as we were handling earlier, except that the work of Ashok Saikia was now handled by Pulok Chatterjee.

In the PMO, an officer who handles ACC is taken as powerful by the bureaucracy. He is the person who is approached and consulted in matters relating to appointments, transfers or promotions. In that sense Pulok Chatterjee took over the position of most powerful bureaucrat in the PMO. As Mr Chatterjee had neither worked enough in his cadre nor handled departments or ministries in his state cadre and in the Central government, he lacked skills in project management and economic policy. He compensated this by hard work, sincerity and dedication. Sanjay Baru joined as Media Adviser to PM. With these changes, the new PM got his team to assist him in his work in the PMO.

34

DR MANMOHAN SINGH: A MAN OF DETAILS

Dr Singh goes into details of all issues placed before him or discussed with him. His approach is like an officer and not a politician. He will take a writing pad and note down the details, which I have never seen any PM do during my eight years in the PMO. Since PMs have many important issues before them, they are not expected to micromanage but macro manage. In that sense I found Dr Singh different from other PMs.

I remember B.N. Yugandhar's advice to K. Padmanabhaiah during PM Deve Gowda's tenure regarding the briefing of PM to be covered in 15 minutes or it would not be possible to keep his attention on the issue for more than half an hour. This in nutshell summarised the importance of time of the PM. With Dr Singh the method of working was different. He wanted to understand the pros and cons of all matters fully before coming to any decision. Maybe, only if one goes into detail does one come to know the strength and weakness of each argument. I found Yugandhar's advice did not hold in Dr Singh's case.

P. Chidambaram was the Finance Minister in the UPA government.

The Finance Ministry had prepared budget proposals for the year 2004-05. Due to the General Elections, the main budget was to be presented later. The PM wanted to know details of 2004-05 budget proposals. He had two long meetings with the Finance Minister and his officials, and each meeting lasted for nearly three hours and without any break. Dr Singh went into the minutest detail of each proposal. I remember him instructing that there should be no taxes on toothbrush and other items being used by the poor. I had never seen a person get into so many details. He was very particular about the burden of taxes on the poor. He discussed all tax proposals one by one with Finance Minister in detail and showed a lot of patience and perseverance during discussions. Maybe, after the detailed discussions on the budget proposals, the budget for the year was more or less ready and could be approved in the Cabinet without much discussion.

MINISTER GOES MISSING!

Shibu Soren, Coal minister in the Manmohan Singh government and Jharkhand Mukti Morcha chief, had an arrest warrant issued against him in July 2004 by a court in Jharkhand. It was in connection with a 1975 case of rioting and murder of 11 persons in Chirudih, Jharkhand. Soren was accused of inciting the mob to kill the *Dikus* (outsiders). As soon as a police team from Jharkhand came to Delhi to execute the arrest warrant against him, the minister went underground. There was speculation that he had gone to West Bengal or Jharkhand and taken shelter in some unknown location to avoid arrest. It was a big embarrassment for the government.

While the Coal Minister was missing, the public opinion was that since the minister had taken oath of office he should also uphold the Law and the Constitution. Many opinied that he should present himself before the police or the court. Here was a case where a minister was missing and the police was searching for him. Even his personal staff could not give any information about his whereabouts. Dr Singh was embarrassed as the TV channels repeatedly aired the news. During one of these tense days, Dr Singh was taking a meeting on another subject at his official residence. I was sitting on the left side of the PM and most of the other persons attending the meeting were sitting in front of PM. There was a television fixed in the wall on the right side of PM which was on but with low volume. The TV was tuned to a Hindi channel and unfortunately, the news about missing Shibu Soren was appearing again and again on the TV. As if to taunt the government and also to dramatize the news as well as to emphasize the significance of the event, after a gap of a few minutes, the TV channel was showing the photo of Shibu Soren and then suddenly the photo used to disappear. Then the TV news used to say 'Minister La-Pata' (Minister Missing) and the TV screen used to become blank. This kept on repeating. I noticed that as and when this news flash used to appear on the screen, the PM would look towards the TV seriously. This happened several times and it seemed to me that the PM was feeling very embarrassed that one of his ministers was absconding from the law and avoiding service of arrest warrant. Also, it was a distraction for a PM who otherwise was so much attentive to his work. So I asked the PM's office staff to switch off the TV.

The government wanted Shibu Soren to obey the court orders and follow the due process of law. Later on, under intense government pressure, Shibu Soren surrendered and faced trial for the murder of his former personal secretary Shashinath Jha. In December 2006, he was convicted and was given life sentence. In August 2007, Shibu Soren was acquitted by the Delhi High Court, which ruled that 'The trial court's analysis is far from convincing and not sustainable'.

OBSERVING COURTESIES: DR SINGH SHOWS THE WAY

Dr Singh is very humble and polite. When visitors would leave after a meeting, he would get up and see them off up to his office door. During the first few days, when I saw him get up and walk up to his office chamber door, I thought the people were specially known to him. However, as time passed, I saw him see off all his visitors. This gesture of the PM won the hearts of all who visited him, irrespective of the fact whether he agreed to their proposals or not. He has genuine respect for the people who come and meet him. I had not seen any other PM do this even though all of them were courteous to their visitors. Leave aside PMs, I had not seen either any Minister or senior bureaucrat show so much courtesy to visitors as was shown by Dr Singh.

SAHAJDHARI AND SGPC ELECTIONS

A delegation from the Sikh Gurdwara Parbandhak Committee (SGPC) was coming to call on PM to resolve the issue of voting by Sahajdhari Sikhs in SGPC elections. The background of the matter was that in 2001, SGPC had adopted a resolution to debar Sahajdharis from voting in the SGPC elections. The NDA government under PM Vajpayee accepted the SGPC resolution in 2003. However, the Sahajdhari Sikhs Federation challenged the government decision in Punjab and Haryana courts. The SGPC delegation wanted Dr Singh's government to resolve this and debar the Sahajdharis from participating in the elections. Before the meeting with SGPC and other Sikhs, MHA officials briefed the PM, and I was present at the briefing.

This was a sensitive matter and nothing could be resolved in such meetings. After listening to MHA officials, PM was not clear about what to say or not say to the delegation. While going to the meeting at 7 RCR office, PM asked me about my views. I was also not clear as the matter was still sub-judice. I suggested that he listen to the suggestions from the delegation and not say anything substantial as the matter was in the High Court. In such matters, it was always safe not to take any view without proper examination of issues at bureaucratic and political level. This was the only meeting I found the PM go into the conference room just to listen and not to say anything.

MATHEMATICS AND SCIENCE EDUCATION

The PM had a meeting with the chief ministers of all the north-eastern states. Since he had been representing Assam as a member of the Rajya

Sabha he knew the problems and issues of those of the North-East. Moreover, he had been Deputy Chairman of the Planning Commission for about four years and Finance Minister during the Narasimha Rao government from 1992-96 and had a good understanding about the weakness and strength of each state in the North-East. In his meeting, I was happy and surprised to hear Dr Singh stress repeatedly about the need for improvement of science and mathematics education. He also drew the attention of the chief ministers to developing a scientific temperament and rational thinking in society.

During my service in Manipur I had seen that in the hills of the Manipur, teaching of science and mathematics was very poor. The PM's emphasis on science and mathematics was the need of the hour. Moreover, the teaching of these subjects would increase the technical strength of the tribal societies where local people were dependent on simple technicians from outside even for setting up small industries such as rice husking mills etc. The improved teaching of science and mathematics would help in producing more technicians, engineers, and doctors.

MANORAMA MURDER: HIGH-LEVEL MEET AT PMO

In the last week of July 2004, the law and order in Manipur was spiralling out of control. Public anger against the security forces, particularly Assam Rifles, was pouring out on to the streets of the state after the brutal killing of Th. Manorama Devi, a 'suspected' PLA cadre. She was arrested by Assam Rifles personnel from her home in the wee hours of 11 July 2004 and killed while in their custody. Her bullet-ridden body was found in a nearby field in the morning. Manorama's horrific death sparked off massive protests in the state with people demanding repeal of Armed Forces (Special Powers) Act, 1958. Twelve elderly women of *Meira Paibi*—Mothers of Manipur—stripped naked and stood outside the western gate of the historic Kangla Gate, where Assam Rifles was stationed, holding placards that read 'Indian Army Rape Us'. This protest, covered by *BBC News*, reflected the deep hurt in the Manipuri society after the brutal killing that shocked the nation.

The public demand for punishment of the security force personnel involved in the killing was not being properly addressed. The national level television channels showed property being damaged and burnt daily in the streets of Manipur. Panic had gripped the streets of Greater Imphal area. During the agitation, the security forces remained mostly confined to the barracks. The killing of Th. Manorama Devi had serious implications on the law and order in the state. The counter insurgency operations by security forces virtually stopped. A high-level meeting was held in first week of August 2004 in the PMO wherein Home Minister, Defence Minister, Senior Civil and Army Officers were present. Incidentally, the Congress President Sonia Gandhi also attended the meeting. The agenda of the meeting was—'How to restore normalcy in Manipur?'

During the course of meeting, it was noted that though the situation in Manipur was grave, the Governor and the Chief Secretary were in Delhi. It was also learnt that the Governor was pursuing the extension of his gubernatorial tenure. I was present in this meeting as I was looking after the affairs of the north-eastern states in the PMO. The meeting took a serious note of the absence of senior level functionaries from the state in the time of such crisis. After discussion, it was decided that there was an immediate need to change the senior functionaries particularly the Governor and the Chief Secretary of the state. Immediately, Dr S. S. Sidhu, an experienced administrator and retired Secretary to Government of India was appointed as Governor of Manipur.

Since my deputation tenure in the Government of India was also coming to an end, I was advised to go back to Manipur quickly and take over as Chief Secretary. I informed the establishment wing of the PMO that my services can be placed back at the disposal of the Manipur government, which was my parent cadre. To appoint a person as Chief Secretary or in any other position in the state government is the state government's call, and the PMO had no direct role in that. The Home Minister Shivraj Patil talked to the Chief Minister of Manipur for my appointment as Chief Secretary Manipur. The following news appeared in the *Times of India* on 5th August 2004:

'JARNAIL SENT TO ASSIST GOVERNOR'

Mahendra Ved | TNN | August 5, 2004 11.30 PM IST

NEW DELHI: Amid growing doubts about the firefighting skills of the just-appointed Manipur Governor, the Centre on Thursday despatched a seasoned north-east hand in PMO, Jarnail Singh, as State's new Chief Secretary.

Singh has been asked to take charge immediately. Meanwhile, the Home Ministry sources said that there was no change in Centre's stand on the question of withdrawal of the Armed Forces Special Powers Act, especially since a political consensus had been arrived at among the major political parties...

NO TIME FOR GOODBYES

It was a Friday evening, and I quickly packed my personal papers. I had no time to prepare and hand over the charge. J.N. Dixit, the then National Security Adviser, came to my room and presented a bouquet to me as a sign of farewell. He requested me to leave for Manipur that very evening if possible. I told him that Manipur did not have night landing facilities, so he asked me to leave the next day. I left the Prime Minister's Office on 6 August 2004 at 4 p.m. without any farewell even though I had served as Joint Secretary to four prime ministers for about eight years, a record in itself.

Late in the evening, I got two calls, one from the PS to the PM and one from the PM himself. The Prime Minister asked me to go early and handle the situation in Manipur carefully. He expressed his concern at the situation. He also informed me that whatever assistance would be required by the state government, for economic development or law and order related issues etc. the Government of India would provide it. He advised me that I could always contact T.K.A. Nair for any assistance the state government needed. I could sense that Manipur situation had caused a lot of anxiety for the Prime Minister.

35

MY REFLECTIONS OF WORKING IN THE PMO

A posting in the PMO depends either on your luck, or the proximity to the PM or personally knowing the Principal Secretary to the PM. The vacancies here are not circulated as such but the PMO may ask the EO of the Department of Personnel to send names of suitable persons for specific posts. For higher positions such as Joint Secretaries, Additional Secretaries, etc. it is the personal knowledge about the officers which matters much more than anything else. After a person joins the PMO, he feels a slight elevation in status due to his posting here.

Common people, too, perceive those working in the PMO to be of a higher status. For some, the PMO name itself creates an aura of awe and eminence. I have seen people begin their introduction with 'Working in the PMO...'. This is common in a society, which is status conscious and where people feel proud of being linked with the high and the prominent. I never felt that way. I enjoyed working in the PMO by keeping a low profile and it had its own charm.

Some officers use their PMO posting as a stepping stone for postings in World Bank, ADB or in Indian embassies in Europe or in the USA.

During my PMO tenure, I saw many officers here getting foreign postings simply because of where they worked. I am sure that if they were working in some other ministry, department, or with the state government it would have been difficult to get these prized foreign postings. If you are in the PMO and information about a plum post is known, the approval of the PM could be obtained on an internal note. Of course, this can happen only if the Principal Secretary supports the proposal. The PM's approval is then sent to the DoPT where the government orders are formally issued. Since, the PM is the final authority to decide such appointments and is the ACC Chairman, his approval of a proposal is not challenged by any ministry. This is not a correct system, but it had happened in many cases. Just as the officers of ministries or departments of the Government of India are in a better position to get foreign postings vis-à-vis their counterparts in the states, similarly, those working in PMO are at a much better position vis-à-vis their counterparts in the other ministries or departments of the Government of India.

I had heard that even though the posts in our embassies abroad sound tempting yet, in real terms, the work did not appear worthwhile as far as job satisfaction was concerned. Yes, these postings were good if one wanted to stay abroad with the family and earn more salary. Somehow, I did not have any strong fascination for a foreign posting. Maybe because of my two-year stay in the USA during the Edward S Mason Program in 1988-89, and later on in 1992-93 at Cambridge in Massachusetts, I did not feel much charm for a foreign posting. I found work in the PMO much more challenging, interesting and satisfying. It was possible for me to contribute better in policy making and expediting projects and schemes of the government. I was able to push through many projects and proposals, particularly, those relating to the infrastructural development and the North-East, which I am sure might have been difficult otherwise.

Another important lesson I learnt over the years was that the knowledge of the rules such as the *Government of India (Allocation of Business) Rules, the Government of India (Transaction of Business) Rules, General Financial Rules* and the latest instructions issued by the government helps in quick decision-making as well smooth functioning.

This is very important for a person who is working in the Government of India, more so in a high office such as the PMO. The *Government of India (Allocation of Business) Rules* and *the Government of India (Transaction of Business) Rules* lay down the bounds within which a bureaucrat and the ministries and departments have to work and conduct the government business. These also lay down the levels at which different decisions are to be taken. If a person working in the government does not have an updated knowledge of these Rules, he or she could make mistakes, adopt incorrect channels for processing files or papers while taking decisions. Small mistakes committed in the PMO get magnified many times over in the media and in the government system and reflects poorly on the functioning of the government of the day.

FOUR FINE MEN

H. D. DEVE GOWDA

I was appointed Joint Secretary in the PMO when H.D. Deve Gowda was the Prime Minister. He took several initiatives relating to rural areas and farmers. He initiated a set of new programmes called the Basic Minimum Services for rural areas, which included provision of drinking water, sanitation, electricity, nutrition, etc. He was the first PM to have toured the north-eastern states for six days at a stretch and announced, 'New Initiatives for North Eastern Region'. Later, these initiatives became a mantra for development of the North-East during the tenures of successive governments. It also increased the fund flow to the North-East and led to the creation of the Non-Lapsable Central Pool of Resources as well as a separate Ministry of Development of North Eastern Region during the tenure of PM Vajpayee.

Many of the projects and schemes initiated or expedited in his time are now giving benefits to the people of the North-East. These projects included North Eastern Indira Gandhi Regional Institute of Health and Medical Sciences [NEIGRIHMS], upgradation of airports, Tuirial

Hydroelectric Project, Numaligarh Refinery, extension of railway lines, completion of Jogighopa Bridge, etc. His push for development was well supported by able bureaucrats such as B. N. Yugandhar, Secretary to the PM and G. K. Pillai, Joint Secretary (NE) in MHA at that time.

INDER KUMAR GUJRAL

I.K. Gujral not only continued with the projects initiated by PM Deve Gowda but also focused on external affairs issues and improving relations with Pakistan. It was during his time that ceasefire agreement with NSCN (IM) was signed. Also, increased autonomy for CBI and Jain Commission Report were the highpoints of this period. The Gujral government lasted for about 11 months (three out of which were after the announcement of elections). Hence, there was not much time to initiate new projects except continue with the ongoing projects/ programmes.

ATAL BIHARI VAJPAYEE

A. B. Vajpayee was PM for about six years. He was politically strong, liberal and a quick decision taker. I enjoyed working in PMO under him. His tenure could be termed as the period during which major economic decisions were taken and when important sectors of the economy were opened. It would not be incorrect to say that the Vajpayee period from March 1998 to May 2004 was the 'Golden Era' for infrastructure development in India. Major initiatives were taken in all sectors of the economy, particularly, in the infrastructure sectors. Petroleum and Natural Gas sector saw major initiatives taken to provide energy security to the country. The administered price mechanism (APM) was dismantled and a New Exploration Licensing Policy was announced to provide a level platform to both public and private players in oil and gas exploration.

Important initiatives during his period transformed surface transport in the country with the construction of National Highways, East-West and North-South Expressways, Pradhan Mantri Gram Sadak Yojna and Delhi Metro. It started a safety fund for the railways, the railway line to Baramulla with the tunnel at Qazigund, an approval for tunnel below Rohtang Pass, etc. It opened the telecommunications sector and also converted the Department of Telecommunications into BSNL and MTNL. Aviation received a huge push with private airports in Hyderabad and Bangalore and the entry of private airlines in India. The power sector saw a new Indian Electricity Act 2003, bringing private sector in power transmission, privatisation of electricity in Delhi, starting of Mega Thermal Power Stations. With the NLCPR and Ministry of Development of North Eastern Region, PM Deve Gowda's initiatives were brought to its logical conclusion during this period. Most importantly, India's race to Moon began with Chandrayaan I.

PM Vajpayee did not want his officers, particularly below the level of Secretary to be exposed to media. He knew very well the complications of middle-level PMO officers getting exposed to media.

DR MANMOHAN SINGH

I worked under Dr Manmohan Singh for about three months, from May to August 2004. Dr Singh gave special emphasis on rural development and employment generation. During his period, maximum funds flowed into the north-eastern states. A new scheme, initially called the Reconstruction Plan, and later changed to Special Plan Assistance (SPA), was launched to complete important schemes particularly relating to infrastructure in the North-East. Top priority was given to complete the ongoing irrigation projects. I had excellent working relations with him. Dr Singh was always very polite and went into the details of any issue brought up before him. Immediately after taking over, his focus was on budget formation, scrutinising it to its smallest detail with a pro-poor thrust. One felt comfortable and at ease while working with him.

GREAT LISTENERS

One thing which I noticed while working with all four PMs was that they were very good listeners. Be it meetings or conferences, they listened very carefully without any interruptions. Not once in my eight years did I see any PM interrupt or undercut a speaker. They had great respect for the views of those whom they met. I have heard that listening is an art. Indeed, it is. Those who do not have the patience to listen to others cannot appreciate perspectives and hence cannot give balanced arguments. That is why to be a statesman, one must learn to have patience, listen to others and appreciate their views. I found all four PMs excelled in this.

LOW PROFILE AND LONGER TENURES

The aura of the high office of PMO is such that many who join this office feel exalted and elevated in status as compared to their colleagues who work in other ministries and departments. This is not to take away from the many others who keep a low profile and attend to their work with dedication. My experience is that the offices such as the PMO need people who are known to keep low profiles and mind their own business. They bring dignity to the office, maintain secrecy and improve the efficiency of its functioning. I have seen a number of such people who have contributed tremendously to the functioning of the PMO. In general, they are accepted by governments of all political parties, and tend to have longer tenures in such high offices.

A VALUABLE TAKEAWAY

While working in the PMO, I was shielded from ministerial and political pressures. People outside the PMO do not know the procedures followed in PMO for taking decisions as well as the reasons advanced in the PMO files for or against different proposals. The only tension in the PMO was that everything is time bound and I was responsible to deliver on time. When I left the PMO after eight years, it was as if time just flew by. As I got ready to join back my cadre state Manipur in August 2004, I felt as if it was just a few days back that I had joined the PMO. The excellent working environment in the PMO gave me an opportunity to give my best, and I did just that.

INDEX

7 Race Course Road (7 RCR) 102, 123, 180, 221, 223, 227, 271
1962 Sino-Indian War 75

Accountant General (AG) 191
Additional Development Charges (ADCs) 229
Administered Price Mechanism (APM) xxi, 109–11, 119, 278
Agra Summit 194
Agriculture 33–34, 40, 46–47, 50, 78, 125, 138, 252, 255–56, 259
Air connectivity 33, 37, 40
Airport Authority of India (AAI) 157–58
Airports xx, 35–37, 40, 43–44, 67, 151, 157–58, 163, 168–69, 176, 229–30, 240–41, 249, 277, 279
  private xx, 279
  upgradation of xx, 157, 277
Air Vice Marshal Case 62
All India Anna Dravida Munnetra Kazhagam (AIADMK) 93
All India Institute of Medical Sciences (AIIMS) 164
Annual Confidential Reports (ACRs) 4
Anti-incumbency 252
Appointments Committee of the Cabinet (ACC) xix, 21–23, 80, 239, 266–67, 276
Arunachal Pradesh 12, 40–41, 76, 85, 88, 148–49, 155, 166, 169, 188
Arunachal Pradesh–Goa–Mizoram–Union Territories (AGMUT) 76
Assam 12, 35–37, 47, 66, 78, 84–86, 107, 110, 148–49, 155–56, 159, 176, 182, 184–85, 197, 221, 232, 236–37, 247, 257, 259, 271–72
  agitation 236
  violence in 184
  Assam Gas Cracker Project 36, 159
  Assam Oil 110
  Atomic Energy Commission (AEC) 15
  Attorney General 59, 60

Bahujan Samaj Party (BSP) 93
Bajrang Dal 251
Bangladesh 26–27, 36, 43, 86, 115, 159, 184, 232, 237, 258
Banking 33
Basic Minimum Services (BMSs) xix, 2, 50, 255
Bharatiya Janata Party (BJP) xxi, 68, 72–76, 79, 81, 86, 93, 95–97, 101–02, 192, 216–17, 230, 236, 250–52
Bharat Petroleum Corporation Limited (BPCL) 110, 118–20, 123
Bharat Sanchar Nigam Limited (BSNL) xx, 151, 222, 279
Bodoland Territorial Autonomous Districts (BTAD) 155

Bodo Liberation Tigers (BLT) 184
Bodo Territorial Council (BTC) 115, 184–85
Bogibeel Rail-cum-Road Bridge 159
Border Area Development Programme (BRDP) 37, 46, 203
Border Roads Organisation (BRO) 106, 163
Brahmaputra Board Act 1980 154

Cabinet Committee on Economic Affairs (CCEA) 214–15
Cabinet meetings xix, 10, 11, 214, 243
Ceasefire xx, 60–61, 177–78, 180, 278
  agreement xx, 60–61, 177–78, 180, 278
  extension of 180
  monitoring group 178
Central Bureau of Investigation (CBI) xx, 25–26, 56–57, 59–60, 168, 217, 220–21, 278
Central Electricity Authority (CEA) 135–36
Central Road Fund (CRF) 100
Central Vigilance Commission (CVC) 60, 240
Central Water Commission (CWC) 156
Centre for Science and Environment (CSE) 235
Chakma refugees 85
Chandrayaan I xxi, 92, 234, 279
Chief Secretary xxiii, 6–7, 18, 83, 89, 176, 189, 199, 219, 238, 273, 274
Civil aviation 45, 92
Civil Services Board (CSB) 4, 5
Coal
  challenges 171
  industry 172, 175
  mining 171–73
  problems of transportation 173
  regulator 173
  reserves 63, 171
  sampling 174
Coal India Limited (CIL) 28–29, 171–75
Coal Nationalization Act 98
Common Minimum Programme (CMP) 80
Communist Party of India (CPI) 94
Communist Party of India-Marxist (CPI-M) 24, 36, 94
Community Information Centre (CIC) 148–49
Comptroller and Auditor General of India (CAG) 191–92
Connectivity 33, 37, 40, 99–100, 140, 157, 159, 163, 254–55
  air 157
  inter-state 100
Counter Insurgency (CI) operations 88
Crude oil 64, 108–10, 113, 115–17, 121–22, 158
  cost-plus formula 110
  ex-refinery price 109
  production of 109–10, 121, 158

Dabhol Power Project 28–29, 126–27
Delhi Electricity Supply Undertaking (DESU) 141
Delhi Metro xxi, 278
Department of Economic Affairs (DEA) 199
Department of Jammu and Kashmir Affairs 204
Department of Personnel and Training (DoPT) xvii, 3–4, 6–7, 25, 276
Department of Telecommunications xx, 279
Desai, Morarji, Prime Minister 61, 152, 179
Detailed Project Reports (DPRs) 154
Deve Gowda, H. D., Prime Minister xviii–xx, 1–2, 12, 22–26, 29–30, 33, 35, 37, 41–42, 45, 47, 50–51, 54–56, 58, 67, 79, 84, 86–88, 114, 145, 147, 152, 159–60, 163–64, 167, 255, 268, 277–79
  Guwahati press conference 88
  loses confidence vote 55
  meetings in
    'New Initiatives for North Eastern Region' xix, 44–45, 48–50, 86–87, 145, 158, 163–64, 168–69, 277
    policy initiatives 2, 45
  visit to
    Arunachal Pradesh 40
    Assam 35
    Manipur 37

Meghalaya 41
Mizoram 37
Nagaland 39, 150
Tripura 36
North-East 32, 44, 86, 147, 159, 164
Dibang Mutlipurpose Project 155
Directorate General of Hydrocarbons (DGH) 121
Dravida Munnetra Kazhagam (DMK) 58, 68
Drug addiction 46

East/Eastern Nagaland 181–82
East-West Expressway 107, 278
Economic
development xviii, xxiii, 2, 16, 33–34, 36, 41, 47, 78–79, 84–86, 92, 105, 112, 117, 145–46, 160–61, 181, 190, 204, 254–55, 262, 274
growth 96, 109, 112, 125, 149–50, 249
Economy xviii, xx–xxi, 46, 72–73, 92, 96, 98, 101–02, 108–09, 112, 115, 249–50, 255, 262, 278
rural 98, 102, 255
Education xix, 2, 33, 50, 84, 92, 145, 148–49, 161, 182, 207, 249, 254, 271–72
Mathematics And Science 271
Election Commission of India (ECI) xvii, 6, 73, 95, 97
Electricity xix, xxi, 2, 28, 74, 125–26, 138–42, 144–45, 198, 230, 249, 255, 277, 279
Electricity Act xx, 138–40, 279
Electricity distribution, privatisation of 139, 141, 144
Electricity Regulatory Commissions Act 1998 138–39
Electricity Supply Act 1948 139
Employment xxi, 34, 36, 45–46, 48, 74, 136, 149–50, 153, 167, 194, 204, 259, 279
creation of opportunities 36, 48, 74, 149–50, 153, 167, 194, 259
Employment Assurance Scheme 46, 48
Energy consumption 108–09
Engineering Procurement and Construction (EPC) 28–30, 132–34
External affairs xx, 54, 76, 79, 205, 210, 278

Finance 92, 100, 112, 123, 127, 189, 212
Five Year Plan, Ninth Plan 50, 159, 169
Food Corporation of India (FCI) 223, 228
Foreign Direct Investment (FDI) 122
Foreigners Act 1946 236
Foreign exchange crisis 132–33
Foreign Exchange Management Act 98
Foreign postings xviii, 230, 276
Fuel Supply Agreements (FSAs) 28–29

Gandhi, Indira, Prime Minister xx, 14, 35, 42, 152, 277
Gandhi, Mahatma 153
Gandhi, Rajiv, former Prime Minister xx, 41, 57–59, 68, 74, 152
assassination of xx, 57–58, 68
Gandhi, Sonia xxii, 74, 81, 96, 106, 251, 263–64, 266–67, 273
Ganga water 130
General Financial Rules (GFR) 166–67
Golden Era xxi, 92, 278
Government of India
BJP-led NDA 74–75, 79, 95–98, 135, 142, 226, 231, 249–51, 271
Deve Gowda 30, 84, 86, 164
development agenda of 81
Dr Manmohan Singh 269, 271
formation 56
Indian National Congress-led UPA xviii, 106, 117, 159, 189, 251–52, 257, 259, 263, 265, 268
initiatives of 98
Narasimha Rao 30, 80, 96, 125, 177, 250, 272
objectives of 110
policy 20, 44–45, 112–13, 121, 250
Vajpayee 80, 83, 93–95, 99, 101, 114, 116, 160, 193, 226, 257
Government of India (Allocation of Business) Rules xviii, xxii, 12, 17, 124, 134, 209–10, 212, 240, 276–77
Government of India (Transaction of Business) Rules xix, xxii, 17, 124, 134,

209–10, 276–77
Gross Domestic Product (GDP) 109
Gujral, Inder Kumar, Prime Minister xviii–xx, 54–58, 61–62, 66, 68–69, 73, 76, 79, 177, 267, 278
  ceasefire with NSCN (IM) 60, 178
  downfall of the government xx
  Manipur boycotts visit 66
  takes over as prime minister 56
  visit to J&K 65

Hanumantha Rao Committee (HRC) 128
Health care system 33, 84, 92, 145, 161, 169, 228, 249, 255
High Speed Diesel (HSD) 64, 99–100, 110
Highways xx, 33, 45, 98–100, 153, 231, 249
Hindustan Petroleum Corporation Limited (HPCL) 110, 118–20, 123
Horticulture 33–34, 40, 46, 203
Hospital Services Consultancy Corporation Limited of India (HSCCL) 164–65
Hydroelectric/hydro electric projects xx– xxi, 49, 127, 129–31, 136–38, 142–43, 167–68, 198–99, 245–47

Illegal migrants 237
Illegal Migrants (Determination by Tribunal) (IMDT) Act 36, 86, 88, 236–37
Independent Power Producers (IPPs) 28–30, 125–27
  projects 28–29
India Electricity Act 1910 138
India Hydrocarbon Vision 2025 98, 112
Indian economy xviii, xx, 96, 108, 262
Indian Electricity Act 1910 139
Indian Electricity Act 2003 138–40, 279
Indian National Congress (Indira) (INC (I)) 55–58, 68, 73–75, 96–97, 252, 264–65
Indian Oil Company Limited (IOCL) 110, 118–19, 121, 123
Indian Strategic Petroleum Reserves Limited (ISPRL) 116
India Shining 250, 252
Indo-Bangladesh political equations 26
Information Technology Hub 228
Infrastructure xxi, xxiii, 2, 33, 36, 39–42, 45, 47, 49, 58, 84, 87–88, 92, 98–100, 120, 137, 145, 157–58, 162, 172, 185, 194, 204, 222, 249, 255, 278–79
  development xxi, xxiii, 2, 45, 84, 145, 185, 194, 249, 278
Integrated Tourism Development Plan 46–48
Intelligence Bureau (IB) 18, 82, 177–78, 193, 219–20
Interlinking of Indian rivers 257, 259
International Financial Institutions (IFIs) 28
Inter Village Roads (IVRs) 101
Iran-India Gas Pipeline 20, 114
Irrigation xxi, 50, 127, 129, 143, 155, 257, 259, 279

Jain Commission Report xx, 57, 68, 278
Jammu and Kashmir (J&K) xviii, 12, 56, 65–66, 83, 96, 98, 104, 137–38, 149–50, 193–208, 245
  development and security issues 193, 208
Jammu-Baramulla Railway Line 104, 106, 200, 202
Jogighopa Rail-cum-Road Bridge 86–88, 278
Joint Parliamentary Committee (JPC) 236
Justice Department 242

Kalam, A. P. J., President 239, 254
Kargil Martyrs' families, allocation delay for 212
Kargil War 81–83, 96, 105, 153, 194, 206, 212
Kashmiri Pandits 65–66, 195–97, 205
Kashmir issue 83, 208
Konkan railways 104

Lahore Bus Diplomacy 83
Lahore Declaration 83, 194
Lal Bahadur Shastri National Academy of Administration (LBSNAA), Mussoorie 8

Land compensation and rehabilitation 172
Law and order xxii, 33, 161, 176, 190, 194, 272–74
Line of Control (LoC) 104, 195, 201
Liquefied Petroleum Gas (LPG) 110–11, 197
Lok Sabha elections 95, 101, 251, 256, 259
Look East Policy 84
LTTE 68

Mahanagar Telephone Nigam Limited (MTNL) xx, 222, 279
Mangalore Power Company (MPC) 28, 126
Manipur xvii, xxii–xxiii, 3, 5–8, 12, 37–39, 42, 49, 66–67, 83, 85, 148–49, 157, 161–63, 169, 177, 179–80, 190–91, 230–31, 264–65, 272–74, 280
Manipur State Congress Party (MSCP) 230–31
Marketing 2, 49, 109–11, 123, 213, 249
Mega Thermal Power Stations xxi, 279
Meghalaya 12, 41, 43, 78, 85, 148–49, 218, 219, 220
Memorandum of Settlement (MOS) 184
Memorandum of Understanding (MoU) 28–30, 126, 132–33
Mialand Issue 232–33
Micro Finance Institution (MFI) 47
Minimum Support Price (MSP) 223
Ministry of Civil Aviation 229, 240–41
Ministry of Coal 171–73, 175
Ministry of Commerce 4, 227–28
Ministry of Defence 62, 79, 149
Ministry of Development of North Eastern Region (MDoNER) xx–xxi, 41, 160–62, 169, 185, 277, 279
Ministry of Disinvestment 243
Ministry of Energy 3, 135
Ministry of Environment and Forest 216
Ministry of External Affairs (MEA) 19–20, 58, 76, 79, 114, 141, 210–11
Ministry of Finance 28–29, 98, 112, 119, 124, 126, 133, 159, 198, 203, 214, 269
Ministry of Health and Family Welfare 49, 164–65
Ministry of Home Affairs (MHA) xx, 12, 25, 32–33, 35, 48, 58–59, 61, 67, 79, 85, 87, 146–47, 149, 161, 168, 178–79, 181–83, 187–92, 210, 218–21, 237, 271, 278
Ministry of Information and Broadcasting (I&B) 58
Ministry of Mines 243
Ministry of Petroleum and Natural Gas 10, 64, 109, 113–15, 119, 123, 158, 212, 238
Ministry of Power 130–34, 139, 143, 156, 245–46
Ministry of Railways 159, 200, 214–15
Ministry of Rural Development 100–102, 103, 255–56
Ministry of Textiles xvii, 4
Ministry of the Road Transport and Highways 107
Ministry of Tourism 48
Ministry of Water Resources 154, 156, 258
Mizo National Front (MNF) 178
Mizoram 12, 37, 76, 85, 148–49, 167–68, 178, 182–83, 218
Mizoram Accord 178
Myanmar 26–27, 86, 107, 115

Nagaland xx, 12, 39–41, 49, 85, 148–53, 169–70, 177–82, 191–92, 232–33, 265
Naga National Council (NNC) 177
Narasimha Rao, P. V., Prime Minister 28, 30, 42, 47, 61, 80, 96, 125, 146, 177–79, 265, 272
Narayanan, K.R., Indian President 68, 73, 247
Narayan, Loknayak Jayaprakash 153
Narco-trafficking 46
National Association of Software and Services Companies (NASSCOM) 229
National Bank for Agriculture and Rural Development (NABARD) 46, 48
National Conference 93
National Democratic Alliance (NDA) xviii, xxi, 74–75, 79–81, 92, 95–98, 116, 135, 142, 226, 231, 249–52, 263,

271
National Democratic Front of Bodoland (NDFB) 184
National Highways Authority of India (NHAI) 99
National Highways Development Programme (NHDP) 100
National Human Rights Commission (NHRC) 81, 241–42
National Hydroelectric Power Corporation Limited (NHPC) 136, 155–56, 245–47
National Institute for Smart Government (NISG) 228–29
National Security Advisor (NSA) 78
National Socialist Council of Nagaland (Isak-Muivah) [NSCN (IM)] xx, 60–61, 67, 88, 150, 177–82, 265, 278
ceasefire with 60, 177–78
National Socialist Council of Nagaland (NSCN) 177
National Thermal Power Corporation Limited (NTPC) 135, 239–40
Nepal, hydroelectric projects in 142–43
New Exploration Licensing Policy (NELP) xxi, 109, 121–22, 278
NGOs 39–40, 42, 47, 67, 146, 182–83, 195
NITI Aayog 161
Non-Lapsable Central Pool of Resources (NLCPR) xix–xxi, 2, 41, 49–50, 87–88, 92, 148, 160–62, 277, 279
Non-Performing Asset (NPA) 34
Non-Utility Generator (NUG) 28
North Eastern Council (NEC) 157, 161–62, 166
North Eastern Development Finance Corporation Ltd (NEDFi) 47–48, 155
North Eastern Electric Power Corporation Limited (NEEPCO) 39, 155–56, 161, 167–68
North Eastern Indira Gandhi Regional Institute of Health and Medical Sciences (NEIGRIHMS) xx, 42, 164–65, 277
North-eastern (NE) regions/states xviii–xxi, 2, 12, 32–35, 37, 41–42, 44–51, 56, 61, 65–66, 78, 83–87, 98, 107, 145–52, 154–55, 157–61, 164, 167, 176–78, 180, 182, 187, 203, 218, 247, 271–73, 276–79
economic and infrastructure development push for 2, 41
new initiatives 44
reconstruction plan xxi, 279
North-South Expressway 278
NSCN (K) 177
Numaligarh Refinery 46, 158, 278

Odisha 116, 119, 121, 142, 258
power reforms in 142
Officer on Special Duty (OSD) 58–59, 77, 123, 227, 234, 266
Official Secrets Act xxii
Oil and natural gas xxi, 109, 113–15, 121, 278
explorations xxi, 26, 121, 243, 278
Oil and Natural Gas Commission (ONGC) 110, 114–15, 121, 239
Oil India Limited (OIL) 64, 110, 113, 115–16, 121
Oil Industry Development Board (OIDB) 158
Oil Marketing Companies (OMCs) 111
ONGC Videsh Limited (OVL) 114–15
Opinion polls 251, 257

Padma Awards 30–31, 218–19
recommendations for 218
selection of nominees for 30
Padma Awards Review Committee 31, 247
Pakistan xx, 20, 72, 82–83, 105, 114–15, 137, 193–94, 199, 201–06, 208, 246–47, 250, 278
Neelum-Jhelum Hydropower Plant 246
relations with xx, 72, 193–94, 250, 278
Pakistan Occupied Kashmir (PoK) 201, 204
Parliamentary Committee on Energy 133
People's Democratic Party (PDP) 206
Pesticides in soft drinks 235
Petroleum and natural gas xviii, xxi, 10, 12, 26–27, 33, 45, 63–64, 92, 98, 100, 108–10, 112–16, 118–19, 121, 123–24, 158, 212–13, 238–39, 249, 278

Planning Commission 20, 50, 87–88, 96–98, 113, 117, 128, 139, 156, 160, 189, 214, 239, 255–56, 265, 272
Pokhran Nuclear tests 72, 83
Power
 challenges to initiatives 135
 generation 28–29, 108, 125, 137, 142, 155–56, 174, 246
 producers 28, 125
 projects 132, 141, 174
 sector 21, 29, 125, 135, 138, 239–40, 279
 tariff 29, 126–27, 130, 133, 138, 140–41
 transmission xxi, 140, 279
Power Finance Corporation Limited (PFC) 199
Power Purchase Agreements (PPAs) 28
Pradhan Mantri Gram Sadak Yojna (PMGSY) xx, 100–102, 278
President's Police Medal 220–21
Press conference of PM 41–44, 67, 77, 88, 150
Prevention of Corruption Act 217
Prime Minister's Office (PMO)
 apprehensions at 264
 decision-making in 75, 79–80, 92
 functioning of 79
 high-level meetings in 272
 monitoring in 89
 officers in 18, 75, 264
 postings in 8
 role of MoS in 240
 work and working environment xviii, xix, xxii, 12–14, 16–18, 74, 77, 92, 240, 253, 267, 275–76, 280
Privatisation xxi, 141–42, 144, 175, 279
Provision of Urban Amenities in Rural Areas (PURA) 254–57
Public Accounts Committee (PAC) 191–92
Public administration xxi, 218
Public Enterprises Selection Board (PESB) 76
Public Interest Litigation (PIL) 57, 59, 168
Public Investment Board (PIB) 77, 246
Public Sector Undertakings (PSUs) 5, 16, 110–11, 123, 154, 243
Public Works Department (PWD) 101, 161
Purulia Arms drop case 210
Putin, Vladimir, Russian President, visited India 210

Railway Board 103–05, 203, 215
Railway(s) xx–xxi, 29, 33, 36, 40, 43, 45, 50, 84, 87, 99–100, 104, 173, 175, 200, 202–03, 205, 214, 249, 278
Rashtrapati Bhavan 13, 238
Rashtriya Swayamsevak Sangh (RSS) 75, 79–80, 251–52
Refineries 109–10, 118–20, 123, 158
 bid evaluations 101, 122–23
 foreign partners and lenders 120
 land acquisition and environmental clearances 120
 objections from state bureaucracy 119
 private sector 123
Relief and Rehabilitation (R&R) 127–29, 172, 247
Research and Analysis Wing (RAW) 82–83, 193
Rohtang Pass tunnel 105–06, 202–03, 279
Royal Bhutanese Army (RBA) 184
Rural development xxi, 2, 98, 148–49, 279
Rural Infrastructure Development Fund (RIDF) 46, 48

Sadar Hills Autonomous District 231
Security Related Expenditure (SRE) 85
Shillong Accord 177
Shukla Commission Report 50, 85
Sikh Gurdwara Parbandhak Committee (SGPC) 271
Sikkim 12, 35, 148, 154
Singh, Dr Manmohan xviii–xix, xxi–xxii, 47, 96–97, 111, 157, 159, 257, 262–72, 279
 a man of details xxi, 268
 Sonia nominates as PM 264
Singh, Jarnail
 appointment as Joint Secretary to the PM 9
 as Chief Secretary of Manipur xxiii, 83
 as Joint Secretary in the PMO xix, 14,

187, 264, 277
as Joint Secretary (PWD) in Manipur 161
as the officer-in-charge of Jammu and Kashmir 194–95
Brochure on Public Policy Analysis Techniques 8
deputation in the Department of Power 3
eight years stay in PMO 15
first meeting with PM Deve Gowda 11
initial days at PMO 16
joined the PMO xviii, 8, 12, 18
learning on the job 17
low profile and longer tenures 280
working with governors 186
Society for Social Action (SOSA) 168
Special Plan Assistance (SPA) xxi, 279
Special Protection Group (SPG) 15, 180, 217–18
Standard Operating Procedure (SOP) 217–18
State Human Rights Commissions 186
State Public Service Commissions 186
Steel Authority of India Limited (SAIL) 171–72
Strategic Petroleum Reserves (SPR) 116
Surface transport 45, 92, 99, 101, 157, 278
Surrendered United Liberation Front of Assam (SULFA) 85

Techno-Economic Development Fund (TEDF) 47
Technology Mission on Horticulture 49
Tehelka Expose 216
Tehri Dam 127, 129–31
Tehri Hydro Development Corporation India Limited (THDCIL) 127, 129, 131
Telecommunication services xx, 33, 84, 87, 92, 98, 145, 148–51, 222–23, 249, 279
Telecom Regulatory Authority of India (TRAI) 98
Track II diplomacy 205, 208
Tripura xvii, 12, 36, 66, 148–49, 162, 182–83

ULFA 184
Union Public Service Commission (UPSC) 86
United Front xviii–xx, 24, 35, 55–58, 68, 73–75, 85, 96
United Nations 76, 230
US sanctions 210

Vajpayee, Atal Bihari, Prime Minister xviii–xxi, 30, 41, 50, 72, 74–76, 79–81, 83, 86–88, 92–97, 99, 101–03, 106, 112, 114, 116, 136, 142, 145, 152, 157, 159–60, 175–76, 181, 193–95, 198, 200, 202, 205–06, 208, 219, 223, 226, 230, 238–39, 248–50, 252, 255–58, 263–65, 267, 271, 277–79
a democrat at heart 102
announcement at Manali 225
fall of government 93
initiatives 112
meets Kashmiri Pandits 195
no to tobacco cultivation 227
qualities of 96
quick decision-maker 106
visit to
areas near the Line of Control (LoC) 201
Assam 84, 176
Kashmir 205
Lahore 194
Manipur 157
working of 81
Village Development Committees (VDCs) 203
Vineet Narain case xx, 57, 59
Visakhapatnam Thermal Power project 28, , 126, 132-134
Vishwa Hindu Parishad (VHP) 130–31, 251

Wandhama Massacre 65
Water supply schemes 2, 162, 185, 188–89, 255
World Bank 77, 142, 230, 246, 275
World Energy Conference 9, 20